Praise

"Liberia was a cou[ntry ...civil] war left our country scared and devastated. So many were left homeless, existing without jobs, education, and adequate medical care. Ganta United Methodist Hospital's 24,000 patients every year endured operations by flashlights and without anesthesia. Power From The SON came to give these patients hope. This is the story of that quest."

— BISHOP BENNIE WARNER
FORMER VICE PRESIDENT OF THE REPUBLIC OF LIBERIA

"Steve Vincent's book is a testament to faith and caring, an inspiration based on perseverance. His story is an examine that in a world too often divided by politics and selfishness, the light of truth and love can lead us to a better world."

— DR. RABBI PETER TARLOW
CHAIRMAN OF THE TEXAS HOLOCAUST AND GENOCIDE COMMISSION

"Steve Vincent is a man of deep faith whose personal journey connected his spiritual commitment with his professional and technical expertise to make an enormous difference in the world. This book is the story of how he combined his engineering knowledge, his business acumen, and his sense of Christian mission to launch the transformative project that delivered gifts of healing to tens of thousands of people. While it is a story of a journey from Texas to Liberia, it is also the story of Christian faithfulness becoming a mission of service in the name of Jesus Christ."

— WILLIAM B. LAWRENCE
FORMER DEAN OF PERKINS SCHOOL OF THEOLOGY AT SOUTHERN METHODIST UNIVERSITY

"*When Faith Lights the Way* chronicles the story of an engineer who, inspired by his faith and guided by core values he learned from his time at Texas A&M, designed and constructed a modern electrical system to serve a hospital complex in a war-ravaged area of Liberia. This incredibly complicated initiative saved thousands of lives in an area of desperate need, and this story is an example of what a strong faith and sound values can accomplish."

— ERLE NYE
FORMER CHIEF EXECUTIVE OFFICER OF TXU CORP

"Stephen Vincent has a good heart. When he heard about the devasting Liberian Civil War and how it destroyed lives and the electrical power of Ganta United Methodist Hospital in Nimba, Northern Liberia, he immediately recruited a team of dedicated men and led them to Liberia to help restore electricity at the hospital. From this humanitarian gesture, hundreds of lives were saved. In other words, the doctors, nurses, and staff returned to work and gave hope back to the thousands of people who were about e to face death. This is faith in action! The faith of Steve and his men deserves to be told. And exactly this is what this book is about. I congratulate Steve and his people for touching and saving lives people in Liberia during a time of great need. I am a witness to their faith. May God bless them throughout their lives."

— JOHN INNIS
FORMER BISHOP OF THE LIBERIA AREA OF THE UNITED METHODIST CHURCH,
EDUCATOR, AND AUTHOR

"The story of Texas A&M and our commitment to service above self is embodied in our graduates like Steve Vincent. I have known and admired him for fifty years."

— JOHN SHARP,
CHANCELLOR OF THE TEXAS A&M UNIVERSITY SYSTEM

When Faith Lights the Way

The Quest to Restore Electricity to a War-Ravaged African Hospital

Stephen H. Vincent

STEPHEN H. VINCENT

Copyright © 2018 Stephen H. Vincent.

All rights reserved. No part of this publication may be reproduced, distributed, or transmitted in any form or by any means, including photocopying, recording, or other electronic or mechanical methods, without the prior written permission of the publisher, except in the case of brief quotations embodied in critical reviews and certain other noncommercial uses permitted by copyright law. For permission requests, write to the publisher at the address below.

Fedd Books
P.O. Box 341973
Austin, TX 78734
www.thefeddagency.com

Published in association with The Fedd Agency, Inc., a literary agency.

ISBN: 978-1-949784-02-2
eISBN: 978-1-949784-03-9

Table of Contents

Foreword vii
Introduction xi
Prologue xiii

Section One: Saying Yes xvii
Chapter 1: Who Outsold Whom? 1
Chapter 2: The Journey Begins with Yes 5
Chapter 3: Life at the Cleaver's 11
Chapter 4: Scholarly and Other Pursuits 17
Chapter 5: Why Am I Here? 27
Chapter 6: This Ain't Texas 35
Chapter 7: What We Came to Do 39
Chapter 8: Cultural Lessons 47

Section Two: Mapping Your Course 59
Chapter 9: Finding My Purpose 61
Chapter 10: A Study Abroad 67
Chapter 11: A Plan in Motion 75
Chapter 12: Good, Better, or Best? 83
Chapter 13: Uncertain Times 89
Chapter 14: No Turning Back 103
Chapter 15: Loose Ends 107
Chapter 16: Into the Stormy Seas! 113

Section Three: Leading by Faith 119
Chapter 17: I Don't Think We're in Kansas or Texas 121
Chapter 18: It's Different Here 129
Chapter 19: Radio Stars 137
Chapter 20: On to Ganta! 149

Chapter 21: Plan B 161
Chapter 22: Where Is the Cavalry? 167
Chapter 23: Time Is Wasting 175
Chapter 24: I Can't Believe My Eyes! 181
Chapter 25: We Make Progress 187
Chapter 26: Life in Ganta 193
Chapter 27: Military Precision 199
Chapter 28: Is It All Worth It? 205
Chapter 29: Life Goes On 209
Chapter 30: There Will Be Hiccups 213
Chapter 31: The Big Event 219
Chapter 32: Last Chance 225
Chapter 33: Hard to Say Goodbye 231

Epilogue 243
Appendix 251

Foreword

Andrew S. Natsios

When Faith Lights the Way reads both as a travel book and a faith-journey memoir, but is also a case study on international development. It is at times entertaining and sad, but it is always an informative account of his work trying to build an electrical system for a Methodist hospital in Liberia. His book is also a candid narrative of the difficulties and challenges of trying to do good in a poor country—one which had been devastated and destroyed by a horrific civil war that lasted a decade, killed 250,000 people, displaced 500,000, destroyed its limited infrastructure, and where crimes against humanity were committed on a grand scale. His account describes the heat, the dust, and the dirt roads filled with the potholes big enough to consume the trucks that the Power From The SON team were riding. It describes the frustrations and disappointments of working in a post-conflict society that is recovering from deep wounds and terrible scars.

Steve's journey embodies the challenges of a Christian believer struggling to define what is "good" in a fallen world and therefore challenges readers' own motives for trying to do good. He observes that international development in poor countries carried out in a Christian context requires

When Faith Lights the Way

respect by the giver for the receiver where the help is not a one-way transaction. As the work progresses, the respective roles of the giver and receiver often become blurred, where the giver can be transformed in the process. Development, all development, is about the process of change which ultimately entails building institutions that have integrity, meet real needs, and can be sustained over long time horizons. While technology—whether electric utilities, cell phones, or new seed varieties—can transform societies, without institutions to set the rules of the game, the technology will fail and the transformation will short-circuit.

As with all good travel writers, Steve Vincent has an eye for detail of what he sees and experiences. He explains the local cuisine and the dietary habits of Liberians. He remarks on the appearance of the countryside that is so different from his native Texas land. He describes the difficulties of accomplishing even the simplest tasks, such as getting their electrical equipment out of Liberian customs that made impossibly complicated by the destruction of the infrastructure of the country during the civil war and by the ever-present problem of corruption that he neither ignores nor minimizes, but faces head-on in his story. Vincent observes the absence of the rule of law and of common bribery requests from public officials who can quickly shut down the project if they choose. He describes the "harsh landscape and unpredictable environment" which he must deal with on a daily and even hourly basis. The book honors the Bangladeshi UN Peacekeeping troops and their commanding officers who worked with Vincent's team to move large transformers to the hospital site in a remarkably quick and successful fashion. He honors the Liberians as well, who labored so hard on the project and made it their own.

The Americans working on the electrification team all faced health problems as they were exposed to disease outbreaks that their bodies were unaccustomed to defending against. Sanitation and water systems are not the same in United States and Liberia, and precautions had to be taken by the American visitors who did not have the natural immunity that Liberians had to common ailments.

Foreword

Steve Vincent has learned the basic principles of international development work the hard way: by doing and failing and then trying again. He understands the importance of building for Liberians who will have to maintain the electrical system once it is installed. He repeatedly acknowledges the centrality of the ownership principle where Liberians must be involved at each step of the process, so the electrification project is not an American effort, but a Liberian one. He recognized early on that the Liberians will be the ones that constantly guard and protect it after the Americans have long gone home. The book describes the looting of electrical power lines during the civil war, where warlords stole cables hoping to harvest the copper which was selling for a premium. This problem can only be addressed through accountability systems in the project to ensure the funding goes for its intended purpose. Vincent emphasizes the importance of sound economics, so the system produces and delivers electricity at an affordable rate and can be maintained by the operators well into the future. He sees the hospital electrification effort as a pilot project that could be scaled up for a broader effort that might be extended to other institutions and regions of the country.

Steve Vincent has written a memoir of his own faith-journey out of the safe and predictable world in which he spent his earlier life in the United States, to one different in so many ways but similar in their Christian faith. His faith drove him to leap out of the American "bubble" into Liberia with the mission of saving lives and improving the human condition.

Introduction

I am in my boat navigating an uncharted river. This river is my life. Sometimes, fellow travelers are with me, but no one journeys the entire length of my river. My river constantly changes direction. At times, my river is unpredictable, changing from calm, smooth waters to raging rapids, and I fear my boat will capsize. Sometimes I lose my paddle and am at the mercy of my river. When there are forks in the river, I choose which direction to go. Experience and education largely influence my choices. Sometimes, my choices are influenced by family, teachers, and great friends. For the most part, I have stayed well inside my boat and relied on it to keep me safe and secure. But there have been times when I felt called to step out of my boat, causing me to feel less safe, more insecure, and out of my element. It is counterintuitive, but so many of those times when I left my secure boat were when I also experienced deep feelings of calm, safety, satisfaction, and joy. In those blessed moments, I felt I understood and was true to my life's purpose: to make an impact in my community and the world.

You are also navigating your own river, and you never know what's around the bend. Life does not stand still. Decisions you make and actions you take lead you down one fork or another. Some of the forks in your river offer unique adventures and opportunities—adventures that

When Faith Lights the Way

require leaps of faith, and opportunities to trust God to lead you. I hope that in learning about my journey, you might be encouraged to venture off course and step out of your safe, comfortable boat.

What do I mean by "stepping out of the boat?" In school, I learned that Christopher Columbus would look out to sea and watch ships as they approached the harbor. When he spotted a vessel on the horizon, all he could see was the top of its mast. As it moved closer to port, more and more of the boat became visible until, finally, he could see all the way to the ship's waterline. He reasoned that the earth must be curved—even round—for this to be so. He *trusted this reasoning* when he sailed west, and you know how the story ends. Columbus *stepped out of the boat.*

In another example, about two thousand years ago some guys were crossing a large body of water in a boat when a storm suddenly enveloped them, buffeting their boat with high winds. They were terrified. One of the men, Peter, saw his teacher, Jesus, on the water in the distance, encouraging the frightened sailor to come to him. Peter got out and walked across the water! That's *unquestioning faith*. It's faith that says, "I may not trust myself when I'm outside of this boat, but I trust that *you* will see me through." Great things can happen when people are compelled to get out of their boats.

As you read vignettes of my river journey, traversing several decades and periods of my life, it is my hope that you will understand *why* I chose to step out of my boat and see the beautiful consequences of doing so. The episodes you read are only snapshots of my life—they do not portray the whole me. I am and always have been average. More often than I would like to admit, I say, do, and believe things that I later regret. I feel things deeply, even though I don't express them. I'm a flawed person. Yet I have had opportunities that led to some pretty unique experiences. I don't share these experiences to toot my horn or gain recognition. I share them because I want to encourage you to take a walk of faith.

"Why, and for what purpose?" you might be asking. Read about my journeys across the globe—from Haiti to China to Liberia and more—to see why finding and living your purpose matters.

Prologue

Ganta, Liberia, West Africa. 2007.

The morning started at a cool seventy-five degrees Fahrenheit, but the temperature had risen to about eighty-five before the rainstorm passed through. During the storm, the temperature dropped back to a chilly seventy-three. But the benefit of the brief, cooling rain did not last long. Now, the sun was totally in control again and had driven the temperature back up to almost ninety in both operating rooms. It was so sticky the scrubs of the dedicated operating crew were soaked, and streams of sweat were running down their eyeglasses.

One operating room was becoming bearable because a nurse had started the small portable gasoline generator that powered the air-conditioning. For those working in the other operating room, there was no such luck; there was no second generator. The surgeons had been halfway through a difficult childbirth when the storm blew in. The electrical system went out as the storm knocked loose a wire nailed to a palm tree. These storms were an everyday occurrence, dumping an inch or more of rain then leaving the sun to bake out all the moisture. That's just the way it was in Ganta, Liberia, at the start of the six-month-long rainy season.

When Faith Lights the Way

Ganta is in Sub-Saharan Africa, five hundred miles from the equator and two hundred miles inland from the Atlantic Ocean.

In the operating room where the childbirth was taking place, the team broke out battery-powered flashlights and held them in their mouths—the most effective way to see where one was working and have both hands free. The heat grew unbearable. "Raise the windows. We have got to have a breeze in here, or one of us, the mother, or the baby won't make it," a surgeon said.

Both operations finished about the same time. Dr. Willicor had been working on one case after another since the early morning. A Liberian and a dedicated, gifted surgeon, Dr. Willicor had been the chief medical officer at Ganta United Methodist Hospital since the facility reopened in 2004, after the war. "Meet me at seven-thirty tonight," he told his administrative staff as he walked down the hall past the line of patients.

After the storm passed, one of the men from the hospital's electric department climbed a ladder twelve feet up, to where palm fronds emerged, and nailed the wire back onto the trunk.

As Dr. Willicor addressed the group that night at the meeting, the anemic electricity allowed only a brownish white glow to emanate from the few lights in the room. "As you all know," he began, "this is the only hospital serving the 450,000 people in Nimba County. This hospital was a magnificent gift to the people until thirteen years of civil war virtually destroyed it. We've been open three years now since the war ended, and we have to keep improving. We work around the clock and see about twenty-four thousand patients a year. We don't have air-conditioning. Some days it's so hot that we have to raise the windows, and that introduces contamination. We don't have enough light to see what we are doing. Again, electricity. We don't have a method to ensure our instruments are sterilized because we don't have adequate electricity.

"I walk by patients involved in horrible accidents, people with internal injuries, patients with diseases. Some could be helped by modern medi-

Prologue

cine; we can only make them comfortable. We don't even have an x-ray machine, and it wouldn't work if we did. Not with this meager electricity.

"We can't use machines to administer adequate general anesthesia. All we have are techniques that the medical community moved on from at the turn of the twentieth century. The drugs we have available are commonly used to anesthetize animals, and they present unacceptable and unsafe side effects in people. Except in rare instances, it isn't prudent to work on patients unless a spinal anesthetic will suffice. I understand a team is coming from Texas next year that includes an anesthesiologist, Dr. Stegall. He is bringing a portable anesthesia machine used by veterinarians on small animals that we can use while he is here. That will be a big improvement, but it's temporary. We need modern anesthesia machines to help more patients, but the machines require quality electricity to operate.

"We have so many problems, but dependable electricity would save so many lives. We need to talk to the bishop and see what can be done."

SECTION ONE

Saying Yes

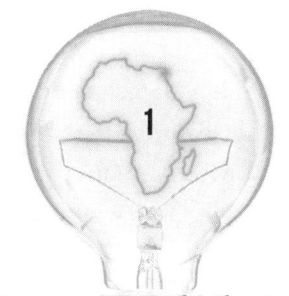

Who Outsold Whom?

Spring 2008.

The series of events that changed the course of my life started with an e-mail exchange. It was in February 2008 that I began writing to Samuel Williams Dixon, Jr., the then-Deputy General Secretary of the United Methodist Committee on Relief (UMCOR), the humanitarian and relief arm of the United Methodist Church. I had a plan for providing solar lighting to villages in the developing world and needed his support on the project. I was optimistic that my plan was aligned with the purpose of UMCOR.

During our e-mail exchanges, Sam began to tell me about a hospital in Liberia. The hospital was part of the Ganta United Methodist Mission Station, established in 1926 by two American Methodist missionaries, Dr. George Way Harley and his wife, Winifred. The Mission catered to the health, spiritual, and educational needs of impoverished, rural people in northeastern Liberia. Besides the hospital, Ganta Mission Station encompassed a church and an elementary school with girls' and boys' dormitories. Dr. Harley kept the hospital up and running despite great challenges through the years until he died in 1965.

When Faith Lights the Way

Ganta Mission remained open and operational for nearly four decades after Dr. Harley's death. But the hospital eventually fell into disrepair after two civil wars, and it had to close in 2003. It had been severely damaged and thoroughly looted during the wars. The electric system that supported the entire Ganta Mission Station had been destroyed. Fortunately, the hospital reopened in 2004 with makeshift electric support to serve the suffering people of Nimba County. In 2009, Ganta was the only hospital serving the county's more than 450,000 residents, despite being too small and operating under severe financial difficulties.[1]

The system that distributed electricity around the hospital and the mission desperately needed repair. Apparently, the situation was so bad that Sue Porter, the dean of the School of Nursing at Ganta Hospital, made it her mission to get the system working again. Dean Porter had also been e-mailing Sam Dixon, and he passed along her e-mails to me. It was clear I wasn't the only one with a project that needed support.

I had requested to meet with Sam Dixon in person at the next General Conference of the United Methodist Church. It would convene in April 2008 in Fort Worth, minutes away from where I lived in Arlington, Texas. Reverend Guy Ames, to whom I had been introduced some months prior, arranged a luncheon for us, my wife, Linda, Pastor Tim Bias of Peoria First UMC, and the Dean of Africa University. My goal for the meeting was to persuade UMCOR to provide organizational support and aid our village-lighting efforts.

Over lunch, I talked at great length and detail about my thirty years of experience selling (and sometimes installing) utility electric power systems in the United States. I talked about my plan for providing solar village lighting by adapting the model created by Barefoot Power, whose founders I'd recently had the chance to meet. Barefoot Power had been doing this kind work in underdeveloped countries and seeing great results.

I explained all the benefits of our proposed lighting system using solar panels and solar-powered LED desk lamps. Families could lease-to-own a solar desk lamp, battery, and solar panel developed by Barefoot

Who Outsold Whom?

Power for a few dollars a week—about the amount they were spending on kerosene for their lamps or sticks dipped in paraffin. This lighting system would provide about seven times the light of the kerosene lamps, and it was much safer and didn't cause pollution. Of course, being able to read after dark provided a huge educational benefit. But the biggest benefit of all was that this lighting system created a business income within the community. This, coupled with mentoring to set up sewing and other small business opportunities, would result in more disposable income for the community.

"Suppose we were dealing with a fishing village," I explained. "Our system could support enough solar panels to power a refrigerator. Without refrigeration, villagers must go to the market daily, or at least every other day. With refrigeration, market visits would be reduced to once a week. That gives you an extra day to fish, to make 20 percent more money. As the village becomes more prosperous, more solar panels could be added and wires run between houses. This establishes a minigrid, which reduces the cost of electricity per household. Each of these steps helps the village learn to move toward self-sufficiency. There are villages in China making one color and one size of one type of garment, such as men's belts. In Bangladesh, it's shirts. Why not do the same thing in Africa?" I asked.

We had long-term vision and had thought it all out. I felt that I had argued my case exceptionally well.

Sam Dixon was a distinguished gentleman with a closely cropped gray hair and a perfectly manicured beard to match. If his hair and beard were any longer, he would have passed for Santa Claus. He was very eloquent. His smooth, deep voice was gentle and kind. After listening to my proposal, he replied, "We would love to help with your project, if you can help us with the Hospital in Ganta, Liberia."

I was so pumped to have his support for our plan and flattered to be asked to electrify Ganta Hospital that I said yes without a second thought.

I asked tons of questions about the current electrical system to get a sense of what we would be working with. But to be honest, I wanted to

When Faith Lights the Way

show off my knowledge and fully convince them I was the right man for the job. Despite being an executive at my company with thirty years of experience, I still felt I needed to prove myself.

The group asked me if I had been to Africa, and I hadn't at that time. However, being a salesman, I related my experiences in Haiti. I assumed people living in similar conditions had similar lifestyles. I described the women carrying baskets on their heads, the people crammed into buses, the size of the houses. I explained how happy the Haitians were, despite how little they had.

I can only guess they were convinced that I could do the job, because they told me about some unused emergency funds at UMCOR, earmarked for war assistance, that could help defray the cost of the project. There's also the possibility that I was the only person naïve enough to take on this project with so little information and no idea what it would cost. Whatever the reason, they enthusiastically asked me to electrify Ganta hospital. I could always light villages after this job was finished.

I'd gone to UMCOR hoping to get support for a plan to provide lighting to villages around the world. Instead, I was now going to electrify a hospital in Africa. I was elated. I had stepped out of my boat, ready to walk on water.

It would be months before I realized what I'd agreed to.

2

The Journey Begins with a Yes

One Step at a Time

The day after my meeting with UMCOR, I began researching power systems in Liberia. This was going to be a huge undertaking, from planning and material supply to logistics and staffing.

My career focus had been material logistics for electric utility companies, so my first thoughts concerned the material we would need. I scoured the web for resources and articles that could offer insight into what I might be facing. I came across a blog written by a gentleman who was either building or rewiring a house in Liberia. (I haven't been able to find the article again, but I can recall the key details that influenced my early planning.)

▷ Quality materials that met international specifications were likely not available in Liberia; for example, conduit would be labeled 1½ inches but was actually about 1/16 of an inch smaller.

▷ At first glance, labels on parts gave the impression that the parts were manufactured by reliable brand names, but the items were actually knockoffs; for example, a "General Electric" label, upon closer inspection, might be "Genreal Electric."

▷ Material sourced locally supported 220 volts, whereas our material would have to supply electricity at 7,200 volts.

▷ There was no local store or supplier where we could buy anything we forgot to bring.

It was clear that materials would have to be purchased in the United States and shipped to Liberia. Before I could think about purchasing materials, I needed a design that would be adaptable to almost any situation we might encounter. But how do you think of all the possible problems and potential scenarios if you've never done a build of this size in a place like Liberia? This would certainly be a challenge, but I didn't have any worries.

I thought to myself, *we can do this.*

A Primer on Electricity

To provide electricity to Ganta Hospital and Mission we would need to establish an electric utility system like those we have in the United States to distribute the electricity produced by their existing onsite generators. In rural Liberia. Before I get too far ahead in describing the project, perhaps a short explanation of how electricity gets to homes and businesses might be helpful.

Electricity can be thought of like water in a hose. When a faucet is opened and a hose is attached, pressure is applied to the walls of the hose, even if there's no water flowing. On the new "shrinking" water hoses, if you turn on the faucet at the house and turn off the sprayer on the end of the hose, you'll see the hose fill up and become rigid. The rigid hose shows there is water pressure when the hose is full of water. No more water is moving from the faucet into the hose, because the hose is full and is designed to withstand city water pressure. If the city installs a more powerful water pump, the increased pressure from the city pipes

The Journey Begins with a Yes

puts more water in the hose and increases pressure. If the new pump puts more pressure on the hose than the hose is designed to withstand, the hose will burst. But ideally, when the sprayer is opened and the water shoots out five feet, it does so because of water pressure. This pressure in electricity can be thought of as *voltage*.

When a person opens the sprayer, water shoots out. There are water molecules that are moving past the end of the sprayer and onto the grass. In electricity, electrons in the atoms move their energy in the wire like water moves through the hose. This electric flow of electrons is called *current*. As the water flows down the hose, some of the water scrapes along the side of the hose and is slowed down by this scraping. These sloweddown water molecules, which are crowded in with other water molecules, slow down the flow. This is called *resistance*. In electricity, the electrons are also subject to this slowing process, another form of resistance.

There are two important types of materials when it comes to electricity: *insulators* and *conductors*. To understand insulators, think of how the water hose moves the water from the faucet on the house to the location where you want to use the water. If there were no hose, the water would pour out onto the ground below the faucet, and it couldn't be used to water grass several feet away. An insulator serves the same purpose as the hose for electricity. It keeps the electrons in the wire contained so they can be used where needed. As with a water hose, the type of material and the thickness of the hose determines how much pressure or voltage can be applied.

One thing that doesn't work in this water comparison is the conductor. But imagine a freeway of electrons moving in the same direction, like cars along a roadway. The roadway is the conductor. Conductors normally consist of aluminum, copper, or a combination of aluminum and steel.

When you buy a light bulb, hair dryer, microwave, or any electric equipment, the amount of electricity it uses to do its job is measured in watts, which is the way we measure electric power, or work, represented

When Faith Lights the Way

by the symbol "w." The "K" in front of the w (watt) means 1,000. One of the generators at the at Ganta Hospital and Mission was a 312Kw machine. That means it could produce 312,000 watts of electricity for several hours at a time. Another example, closer to home: your microwave might be a 1,500w microwave. That means there's a generator somewhere that is producing at least 1,500 watts.

Electric utilities generate electricity and build and maintain the big transmission towers, substations, and overhead or underground lines. The generated electricity is ultimately delivered to the meter on houses and businesses.

To Do the Best, Go with the Best

The Ganta hospital deal was a completely different project than my idea of lighting villages with LED desk lamps and solar panels. But we were going to be providing electricity to people who desperately needed it, and it was at least in line with the utility projects I'd overseen in my professional career with Priester Supply, an employee-owned electrical material manufacturer and distributor. I had designed and helped build some electrical systems for several electric cooperatives, from hospitals to shopping centers to residential subdivisions. Those projects all had electric generation available, so there was no need to concern myself with generating electricity, but they did require installing equipment to distribute electricity.

With my job at Priester, I assembled and supervised teams of skilled professionals for various sized projects, so I felt confident I could assemble and lead a team for this Ganta project. I would form a not-for-profit organization, act as president, and recruit the volunteer specialists needed for the administration, design, and construction work. I can't say that I followed that order.

I first set out to recruit volunteers from the people I knew and had worked with. Utility people are self-sacrificing, so I didn't expect to have any trouble. They worked in the scorching heat, freezing rain, sleet, and

The Journey Begins with a Yes

dark nights to get the lights back on after storms or natural disasters. They would work until the job was finished. I would need people like that for this Ganta project. I had worked with some of the best, so I contacted them.

Steve Hawrylak and Mark Abbe were already involved; they were my partners and sounding boards. Both worked in the electric utility industry—Steve as a colleague at Priester Supply and Mark Abbe with TXU and a material supply company. We had brainstormed the idea of using solar devices to light villages, so we just shifted direction and began to plan how to construct a utility system in Africa. The three of us could handle the acquisition of material, logistics, and transportation of the material and workers to Liberia. But we needed a generation expert to make sure we understood all that was involved with interfacing our distribution system with Ganta's generators, a professional design engineer experienced in designing utility distribution systems, and a team to construct the system that would get electricity where it needed to go.

Even though Ganta had generators in place, several didn't operate or were sitting unused. I contacted Ron Seidel to get his expertise and input on the mechanics of generators and to eventually enlist his involvement. Ron is the former President of Texas Independent Energy, a former Senior Vice President of Fossil Generation, and former President of Energy Trading at TXU Energy. In other words, he was highly qualified. One of the best. It was a bonus that Ron had been a family friend for many years. He and his wife Janice were in the same Lamplighters Sunday school class at First United Methodist Arlington as my wife, Linda, and I.

Some engineers are practical and have a lot of experience in making things work or fixing things that don't work. Other engineers are better at looking at a problem and understanding and applying all the laws of electricity. They love numbers and details. One might call them "design geeks."

Frank Daniel is a design geek. He has engineered and overseen the installation of many cutting-edge projects as an engineer with Oncor,

When Faith Lights the Way

one of the largest electric utilities in the United States. One of his stellar accomplishments is having engineered the protective scheme for AT&T Stadium, better known as Cowboys Stadium. Frank was responsible for designing the protective scheme that detects when something isn't working correctly in the electrical system, activates equipment that isolates the problem, and keeps the electric service operating without blinking the lights in the stadium. It's an astounding job when one considers how much electricity the stadium uses, how much damage can be done by that much power when something goes wrong, and the impact a "lights out" situation would have during an event at AT&T Stadium. Frank and I worked together on several projects when I was with Priester Supply. He was also a member of First United Methodist Church Arlington.

I met with Frank about a week after the Sam Dixon meeting and asked if he would like to be part of our little group. He was enthusiastic. We were a good match; he is a design guy, and I had more hands-on experience in the construction of a basic underground system. Frank would make the first stab at designing the ideal system for the hospital, and together we would craft it into a workable solution.

Jay Ryan joined our group to help us with communications. Jay and I had met through Lamplighters and been friends for several years. He owns VisionQueste, a communication, strategic planning, and marketing firm. He built a collaborative web tool for us to post our bios, create a project schedule, and record our progress. He also maintained our blog.

I had assembled a core team of experts for the early planning phase. We would recruit people to help us with the construction phase once we knew what we were building. For now, what we needed was a name.

Steve, Mark, Jay, and I decided on "Power From the SON." The name combined the type of work we were going to do, electric power, and the word "Son," which was play on "solar power" and the "Son of God." On April 30, 2008, we launched our website, www.powerfromtheson.com, to raise awareness and funds for our projects.

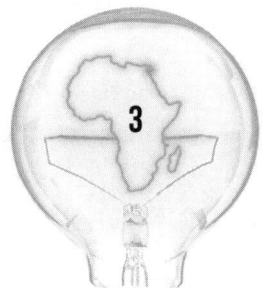

Life at the Cleaver's

The Adolescent Years

Nothing in my early years suggested that my journey would lead me to serve in the mission field. My parents weren't missionaries. I didn't go on summer mission trips during my youth. I don't recall doing much community service or volunteer work either, outside of my Cub Scouts service projects. But upon further reflection of my upbringing, I can recognize the lessons learned and the challenges faced that helped develop my character. I realize that the sum of my life experiences had prepared me for this fork in my river and given me the experience to see it through to a good ending. My journey to Liberia would surely take me down a long river full of unexpected turns, much like my life had been.

Let me start at the beginning. My dad, Hollis Vincent, moved from Reno, Oklahoma, to Bonham, Texas, as a kid. He and my mother, Martha Kathleen "Kitty" Hatley, graduated from Bonham High School in 1942. Dad played football there and was the team captain, despite only being five-foot-five. Somehow, he received an offer to play football for a college in Denton, Texas. However, WWII had just begun, and he enlisted in the Army Air Force right after high school graduation, pursuing his dream of being a pilot. He and Mom were married during pilot's

When Faith Lights the Way

training, and he became a B-24 bomber pilot, serving in Panama and the Pacific during the war. He flew in over thirty combat missions. Mom stayed in Bonham and worked throughout the war at Texas Power and Light (TP&L) the largest electric utility in the northeast part of Texas. (Maybe it's in my blood.)

After the war, Dad came back to Texas and looked for a job. Mom had heard that TP&L needed meter readers to staff a traveling work team that would test electric meters on the system. Dad was hired, Mom quit her job, and for some time, they bounced around North and East Texas, moving every month or so to a different town.

Dad was always an overachiever, did exemplary work in several jobs in his TP&L career, and eventually retired as the assistant manager of purchasing in 1982.

My family could easily have been the model for the Cleavers on the *Leave it to Beaver* television show, except it was just Dad, Mom, and me. The year after I was born in 1951, my parents purchased a house in the Oak Cliff area of Dallas—not in the upscale part of Oak Cliff, but in the more spartan Dallas Park area. The small homes there were constructed during World War II to provide housing for workers at the North American factory, which built B-24 bombers like the ones my dad flew. My mother was a full-time mom until I reached junior high, when she took a job in circuit-board assembly. A year later she became the Court Clerk for the City of Cockrell Hill, Texas.

My early life was filled with school, scouting, football, baseball, and lots of boy stuff. Scouting was big part of my childhood and my character development. I worked diligently to uphold the twelve values taught to us through the Scout Law: trustworthy, loyal, helpful, friendly, courteous, kind, obedient, cheerful, thrifty, brave, clean, and reverent. I acquired many arrow points and achieved Eagle Scout level, the God and Country award, and the Order of the Arrow award, granted to scouts who best lived the Scout Oath and Laws.

Life at the Cleaver's

Compared to my father's, my football career really isn't worth mentioning except in the ways it shaped my character. I started playing in the fifth grade as a running back, and it wasn't until the eighth grade that it occurred to me I was probably too small to be playing. But I wasn't going to let my size stop me. Given a chance, I knew I could be a good player. I got that chance one day in practice. When it was my turn to run the ball, I gave it all I had. Coach yelled, "That's what I want!" I did it over and over again. The result was that I got to start in that week's game, and it was the only game we didn't lose that year. All I needed was a chance. I did earn two high school varsity letters in football, but my lack of size for a football player always hindered me in athletics. My football career instilled an attitude of "never give up despite the odds" and a strong belief in myself.

Church or religion was not a big part of my family's life in my early childhood. We sporadically visited churches but did not attend regularly until our Cub Scout Pack parents invited us to Irwindell United Methodist Church in Dallas. Irwindell UMC was a small, warm church family that became our church home. I played on the church softball team and sang in the youth choir. Irwindell UMC parents looked after all the kids, not just their own, and at times they disciplined all of us, too.

My personal growth and choices in life probably have more to do with the influence of Irwindell UMC than I realize. I learned the traditional Southern values of love of God and country and the importance of glorifying God. The Bible talks quite a bit about bringing glory to God. As a child, I wondered why *I* didn't get any glory, and what I would get out of bringing him glory. Over time I understood that God's love for me is the same type of love I received from my parents. My mother and father would have sacrificed everything for me, and they did whenever called. There aren't adequate words to describe how I cherish them. I honor them and glorify their names and memory. It's about the same with glorifying God.

God doesn't force his will on me; I have to ask him for what I need, then if it is good for me or part of God's plan, I will receive what I

When Faith Lights the Way

need. I ask God to be with me, to watch over me, to provide for me, to protect me, and to love me, although not as often as I should. But I am most content when I do ask and open myself up to accept God's love. Receiving that love, that closeness, is why I am compelled to glorify God, and not myself. I actively try to practice this in my day-to-day living by sharing the love that I am so generously given.

My parents were both handy, and I learned to be, too. We did all the upkeep of our modest eight-hundred—eventually expanded to eleven-hundred—square-foot house. There was always a project that kept me pretty busy at home. My dad and I, with help from the neighbors, put on a new roof after a hail storm. We painted our house inside and out several times. Our house didn't have a concrete driveway, so my family poured one. We installed "swamp coolers" to cool the house, but later changed them out for wall-mounted air conditioners. I learned quite a lot from working with my dad and mom all those years.

With my extracurricular activities and home projects, we didn't have the time or money to be world travelers. But we did like to explore the scenic treasures and historical landmarks closer to home. Travel in our family consisted of loading up the car and driving to exciting places around Texas, like the beach in Galveston, Garner State Park in Uvalde, the Battleship Texas in Houston, and the Alamo. Once we ventured out of state to Broken Arrow, Oklahoma.

When I turned sixteen I got a part-time job with the City of Cockrell Hill, where my mother worked. Cockrell Hill is a small town, only one square mile, surrounded by Dallas. That summer was filled with new, exciting adventures. David Thompson, a friend and fellow Cub Scout, got a job there, too, so it was a lot of fun. Our work crew was three full-time and three summer employees who were black, Hispanic and white. I read water meters, learned to drive and operate a tractor with a front-end loader and a backhoe, operated a jackhammer, picked up garbage, and

Life at the Cleaver's

drove the six-gear, manual-transmission dump truck. I spread asphalt and tar for road repair jobs.

The city employees were so resourceful and innovative, and they could reason out solutions that were not taught in school. They worked hard in all kinds of weather situations. They were humble and proud of the job they did. They were always there for each other—a band of brothers. My experience working and bonding with those guys would influence my attitude toward people. We are all children of God. No one is superior or inferior. Education level, money, color, or sex don't matter. Heart matters.

During my senior year in high school, a friend and fellow Scout, Delman Alsabrook, was injured in a car accident when he was thrown from a car. He was in a coma for weeks. David Thompson and I wanted to help his family any way that we could. We came up with the idea to coordinate a team of friends to be on hand to take care of any chore the family needed done. Within the first week, we had over three hundred volunteers.

Perhaps that was the moment when service to others became a part of the person I was growing into. These kinds of actions and decisions are defining moments, or "fork in the river" moments. I had no way to know that the decision to serve and uplift Delman's family in such a meaningful way would be repeated a few times in my lifetime, and at an even greater scale.

Scholarly and Other Pursuits

University Years

In high school, I was not the most popular kid, not the really smart kid, and obviously not the star athlete. I didn't have a passion to attend any particular university. But many of the people who attend Texas A&M University, in College Station, Texas, in the early 1970s had the same values as I. I had gone to the "Maroon and White" A&M spring football game one year and had liked the school's Corps of Cadets, who contributed to the excitement of the game. I applied and was accepted into the 1969 freshman class.

I entered Texas A&M as a microbiology major. But after a series of eye-opening, bizarre classroom experiences, I switched to engineering technology. I would recognize later in life that changing my major was a "fork in the river" decision.

Starting my freshman year, I worked summers at Watson Electric Supply Co. Watson was an electrical supply house to the electrical, industrial, and building contractors in North Texas, as well as a major supplier

When Faith Lights the Way

to Texas Power and Light. They had a huge warehouse and headquarters on the east side of downtown Dallas at the time.

My first summer was spent working in the warehouse. There were about ten guys—all college kids—on the summer crew. We organized and restocked material on the shelves, received the material, and filled orders. I loved it! I was fascinated by the material and wanted to know how it was used. I excelled quickly and was made foreman. I assigned the crew work and taught them how do the jobs. Some of the guys on the crew were sons of TP&L vice presidents, some were sons of key personnel at Watson, and one was the owner's son. At times, I've wondered if it was my superior skills that nabbed me the foreman's position or my eagerness and naivete. Could it be the operations manager and warehouse manager felt my strongest contribution to the company was keeping them from getting into hot water? After all, it was me doing all the ordering around of these well-connected summer employees, not them. I even had to fire the company accountant's son. They didn't have to make some of these important sons and their fathers mad. I did it for them. Either way, it was great experience that served me well in my career.

My last summer at Watson, I worked for Vernon Humphries, the inside salesman assigned to TP&L. I was allowed to take phone orders from the purchasing department and go to the TP&L storerooms to fulfill them. I even took a phone order from my dad. That was certainly a highlight! I was enjoying my work so much that I knew I wanted to continue along this path for the rest of my career. I really liked electrical work, and I understood electricity. I could "see it." I understood how it reacted. Providing material to electrical utility linemen after a storm was fulfilling to me. I felt like I was helping in my own small way. I admired those men and women for their selflessness and sacrifice. People's lives depended on them doing their job, and the linemen depended on us to get them the material they needed. I wanted to be part of that world.

During my years at Texas A&M, I changed from someone standing on the back row to someone who tried to inspire and lead others. I was elected president of Milner Hall my junior year. (My strategy of

Scholarly and Other Pursuits

putting together a team of the most electable students in the dorm and running as a ticket paid off.) I ran for a campus-wide office going into my senior year and lost, but I was selected to be election-board chairman. The Student Senate of Texas A&M had just installed a new student government constitution, so, as the first election board chairman, I led our committee, comprised of William Hartsfield, the author of the new student government constitution, and my roommate Jack Barlow, as we set the precedents for all campus-wide elections at Texas A&M. It was an important undertaking that I was entrusted to lead. That role helped me to hone my political skills and to overcome my insecurities toward people in positions of authority. Those lessons would also serve me well in life.

Settling into Working Life

Upon graduation in 1973, I became a Sales Engineer for Allis-Chalmers Corp. I spent four months in Houston, Texas; five in Pittsburg, Pennsylvania; and one month in Gadsden, Alabama. I worked for Allis-Chalmers for only ten months before I got the call for a job I'd wanted since my junior year in college.

Priester Supply was a manufacturers' representative and distributor that supplied the material electric utilities used to construct electric lines. The president, John Sandlin, was a graduate of Texas A&M and was active in the university. During my junior year in my role as dorm president, I'd contacted Mr. Sandlin for help with some campus issues. I remained in contact with him until my graduation. It was John who recommended I take my first job with one of four companies in the electrical manufacturing business, as they had the best training programs. He told me that after I had experience, Priester might have a place for me in about five years. I took his advice. And in twist of good fortune for me, one of Priester's key employees left in less than a year, and I was offered my dream job with Priester Supply.

I remember sitting in my parents' kitchen talking to my Aunt Louise and my mother after accepting the job. We were talking about my job,

When Faith Lights the Way

my future, and the potential I had at Priester Supply. The company had been around since 1932, and it was an employee-owned company. When you retired, you sold your stock back into the company. A strong point for me was that all the key personnel were at least twenty years older than me. The company had a great reputation for strong values and ethics. I remember saying to Aunt Louise and Mom, "This is an unbelievable opportunity. I feel blessed to be given this opportunity because I feel I'm supposed to do something to make a difference." I had no idea at the time what that something might be, but accepting this opportunity was a life-changing decision that started me on a very exciting journey.

When I went to work at Priester Supply, I left Alabama and temporarily moved back in with my parents in Dallas. After three months, I bought a townhouse in Arlington, Texas, near Priester's home office. For my first training period, I worked in the warehouse learning the Priester Supply way and doing some of the same jobs I had done at Watson Electric. Supplying electric utilities' material needs was tough work that required strength and skill. The wooden boxes of galvanized hardware weighed up to sixty pounds, and wire and cable on wooden reels could weigh up to two thousand pounds. Stacking the reels of wire five-high required a skill that few forklift operators possessed.

The warehouse was fifty thousand square feet—huge for that era. Priester had moved into the cavernous space two years before I joined and hadn't had the time or manpower to organize the warehouse. The material only occupied about half of the space but was spread out on the floor, and there were no shelves to properly store the material. I was given the task of shelving the material and arranging the warehouse. I had two high-school boys, Jim Tarpley and Sam Roberts, to do the heavy lifting.

After three months, I moved from the warehouse into the office to learn the "business," a catch-all term that referred to everything necessary to keep a distributorship and manufacturer's representative prof-

Scholarly and Other Pursuits

itable. This was in the days before computers and fax machines, so everything was done with typewriters, file cabinets, first-generation copy machines, telephones with cords, and Kardexes. A Kardex was a metal or wooden cabinet with about twenty drawers, each drawer filled with approximately fifty plastic card holders that each contained a paper inventory card. There was one card for each product we supplied. Each card had the item's description, cost, and order number. On each card, we tracked inventory, status, and transactions in pencil. From this information, we decided when to reorder the material. I learned to calculate, mostly in my head, how long it took to get that material from a supplier and how many we were selling over periods of time.

On the inside sales side, we made quotes, took customer orders, generated billing invoices, and handled shipping and delivery. We went to the post office every day to pick up the paper orders—and hopefully the checks—that customers had mailed. On top of that, we also took care of human resources issues and payroll tasks. The business procedure was not unique to Priester, but back then, we had to do a lot of work in our heads—the basics of the business were not performed by a computer. The personal computer hadn't yet evolved to support the business management systems we have today.

After six months of training, I became the salesman in charge of selling materials to utilities in West Texas and about thirty other electric cooperatives and municipalities located west of Fort Worth, north of Austin, east of Pecos, south of Childress, and along the Texas border with Oklahoma. Three weeks a month, I was on the road from Tuesday to Friday, traveling about a thousand miles each trip.

A salesman needs a "hook" to get customers to buy from him rather than buying from the competition. My hook was to try to convince them that I knew what I was doing. After all, I had an engineering degree. This was the same tactic I used with UMCOR that landed me the Ganta project, if you recall.

When Faith Lights the Way

My first big sale was to Comanche County Electric Cooperative, located about a hundred miles southwest of Fort Worth. Mr. Parker, Comanche's co-op manager, was planning a new subdivision of about twenty homes at Lake Proctor. The homes were to have underground electric service, and Comanche County had no underground system at that time. During a sales call with Mr. Parker, he asked me the most economical way for the co-op to get the subdivision wired underground.

Mr. Parker had just "called my number," and I quickly told him, "I'll be glad to help you with this project. I can do the engineering. I will lay out the placement of the trenches, specify the size and type of equipment needed, and supervise and participate in the installation. All I ask is that you buy all the material from me." He bought my proposal.

I never mentioned that I hadn't done these tasks before. (Sound familiar?) Engineering school teaches one how to evaluate and think. It does not, however, teach one to do specific things. One learns that on the job from his or her employer and the people one works with. I didn't have any experience in designing underground subdivisions, much less installing them and scheduling the work to make it happen. I reasoned I could look at other utilities' design specifications for similar installations, size the material, and pick out all the parts that were needed. How hard could it be to install fittings on cable that was to carry 7,200 volts? All the fittings came with instructions. I could read.

I spent two weeks helping Comanche County install the system alongside Mac Bradshaw, the line superintendent. Mac, a rough-hewn man of about fifty-five with a sixth-grade education, had worked on the crews at the co-op all his life. He was responsible for all the construction and maintenance of the approximately three thousand miles of line. When the project was over, the system worked perfectly. And Mac and I had become close friends.

Looking back, this was a step-out-of-the-boat experience that would influence future decisions to approach work in developing countries with

Scholarly and Other Pursuits

a similar mind-set. From this job, I learned not to reject the opportunity to try something I had never done.

She Said Yes!

It was a season of taking chances. I was always a romantic, and I wanted things to be perfect, but I was shy with girls, reluctant to express my feelings or interest, and only willing to ask a girl for date if I was certain the answer would be yes. My approach of using engineering sales techniques, to the point and factual, may not have been the best way to find the perfect relationship.

In 1978, five years after I graduated from A&M, I was going to the Texas A&M vs University of Texas football game and would be sitting with one of my customers and his wife. I thought it would be a good idea to have a date with me, and I invited a flight attendant I had been casually dating, whom I knew from high school. "Come to the game with me," I said to her. "If you can't, then find me a date." (Not my most romantic request for a date.) She did have to fly on game day, so she suggested I call Linda Beiland, who had been in the class behind me in high school and graduated from the University of Texas. Linda had been a cute, blond cheerleader with a lot of energy. I thought to myself, *Why not ask?*

I called her and said, "You may not remember me, but I'm Steve Vincent, and I went to Sunset High School and graduated in 1969."

"I think I might," she responded. Hearing that, I became the romantic salesman.

"Joan Cunningham gave me your number and told me you might have an interest in the A&M vs. Texas football game. I'm sitting with a client and his wife at the game, and I need a date. If you're interested, we can go to this game, and we'll never have to go on another date."

"In that case," Linda replied, "I would like to see the game. So yes, I can go."

We agreed to meet for lunch at the Dixie House in Dallas the day before the game so things wouldn't be strained. Over lunch, we learned

When Faith Lights the Way

we knew many of the same people, but we ran in different crowds. Our paths just didn't cross in a school of 1,500 students. After dating for three weeks, we knew this relationship was different. One year later, after returning from our second A&M-Texas game, I proposed marriage. She said yes!

I was now heading down a totally different river in my life. In sweet and playful ways, she cajoled me to expand my world and tried to bring sophistication into my life. While I had spent all but a few months of my life in Texas, Linda had lived for a time in New York City and for a time in Cuba, and she had traveled to England. Her influence in my life was sorely needed. Once, a more polished husband of a friend asked me what my pattern was, and I told him "a post pattern," a type of pass route in football. He just smiled and walked away. How was I to know he meant China pattern? Linda coached me in those and so many other ways, encouraging me to challenge myself.

Growing up, our family vacations were car trips. In fact, my first flight was for a job interview just before graduating from college. After college, I flew for business but never internationally. For vacations, I felt we should see the United States before we worried about the rest of the world. However, in 1981, Linda, my wife by then, heard about a local radio station sponsoring a three-day trip from Dallas to London. Without telling me she booked us tickets, much to my angst when I found out. I thought to myself, *Why would anyone want to spend all that time and effort to go that far?*

Of course, she turned out to be right. The experience was unforgettable. I enjoyed the trip, and by chance we were at Buckingham Palace when Charles and Dianna announced their engagement. I fell in love with England and travel. I doubt that I would have so many cherished memories in my life if it weren't for Linda. She shows me that life happens outside the boat.

Scholarly and Other Pursuits

Life with Linda was and still is, a barrel of monkeys. Linda has a bachelor's degree in Education from the University of Texas, and a master's in Reading Education from Texas Women's University. It didn't take long before her teaching, paired with my business traveling, grew to be too much. Linda retired and spent her time managing our lives, and I tried to bring home the money. She scheduled us ski trips and vacations to the beach. Life was busy.

During our first years of marriage, we both felt the need for church, but we had differing visions of the ideal congregation. Linda grew up in Cliff Temple Baptist in Dallas and wanted to join a large Baptist church. I favored a small Methodist church, similar to Irwindell. We compromised on a five-thousand-member congregation, the First United Methodist Church of Arlington. There we developed a lot of friendships and felt a kindred spirit with the Senior Pastor, Dr. Don Pike, and his wife, Joyce. Joyce and Don remain our most trusted advisors, like older brothers and sisters. Joining First United Methodist Church of Arlington would prove to be another "fork in the river" decision.

Linda and I longed for a family, and we were blessed in 1984 with Shannon Louise Vincent. We had a new house, a great career with a bright future and lots of friends, and now we had our family! I could stay in my boat and lead a dream life. But, as if guided by an invisible hand on my back as a parent guides a child, I again took a fork in my river. Not long after Shannon's birth, I took a trip that would leave a lasting impact on me.

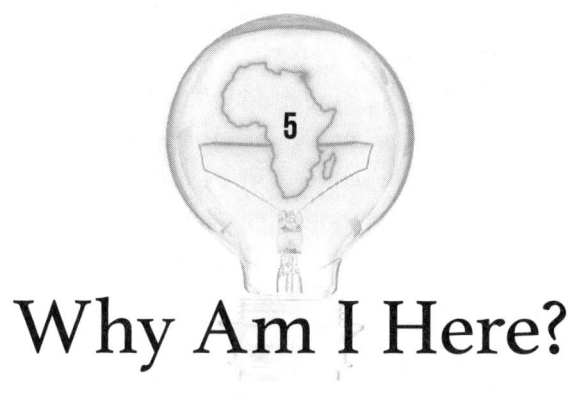

Why Am I Here?

A Half-Hearted Yes

The First United Methodist Church of Arlington, better known as FUMC Arlington, planned a mission trip to Haiti in the summer of 1985. FUMC Arlington was sending a work team to build a church. My wife, Linda, decided it would be good for me to help others and to see a completely different part of the world. I thought, *why does she always want to change me?* Seeing England was good, but why should I go to Haiti? I'd never even heard of Tovar, the small town in the northern part of Haiti, outside Cap Haitien, where the church was to be built.

Here we go again, I thought, *another trip that was not my idea.* I seemed to be in a canoe, traveling leisurely down a river and then losing my paddle. I really had no desire to do this. Besides, my daughter, Shannon, had been born the previous November. I was uncomfortable with the idea of being so far from her when she was still just a baby.

FUMC Arlington joined with New World United Methodist Church of Arlington to supply two teams, each staying two weeks in Haiti. There was no way I could go, I thought. I only had two weeks of vacation at Priester Supply. I built up in my head all the reasons to turn down the trip. I would tell my wife and the church, "Sorry, I would really like to go,

When Faith Lights the Way

but I just can't give up all my yearly vacation on a mission trip. It would be great; hope you guys enjoy yourselves." I had a solid excuse, or so I thought. The next thing I knew, I was part of the work team.

I really don't know who found a workaround to allow me to make the trip, but I suspect it was our senior pastor, Dr. Don Pike, who thought it would be fine if I only went for one week. I could go down with the first group and return by myself after a week. *Something's wrong here*, I thought. I was not in control, and I was a person who liked control. My excuse for not going was a good one, and it should have gotten me out of the trip. But it seemed I was being led down another fork in the river—one I had no plans of taking.

As far as actually building a church, I had a little construction experience, but nothing on this level. Of the eleven of us taking the first trip, only two or three had experience. I didn't have a whole lot of faith that we would even get the foundation finished and the walls up. But here we were—Skip Johnson, Sherri Smith, David Taylor, John Thorburn, Jr., Casey Bowland, C.C. Herter, Jan Houchin, Denzil Huff, Ed Thulin, and Virginia Thulin—headed off on an adventure.[2]

On the day we departed for Haiti, I felt I was leaving my life for the deepest and darkest of the "who-knows-what?" I was very anxious and not clearheaded, and I didn't know what to expect. I was leaving with a bunch of strangers. David Taylor was the only one I sort of knew; we were in the same Sunday School class, but I didn't know him well.

On the flight from Dallas to Miami, I didn't sit by anyone in the group. In Miami, we boarded an Eastern Airlines flight to Port-au-Prince, Haiti. Going to a country like Haiti was not something any of us had done. We were all apprehensive, but the flight crew was fun, so we all started to loosen up and forget about where we were going.

After landing, we exited the plane and stepped down a flight of stairs that the ground crew rolled up to the side of the plane. It was dark, hot, and humid—conditions that left me with an eerie, foreboding sense of unease. We were directed to immigration, and I noticed several Haitian

Why Am I Here?

soldiers with rifles in the shadows of the airport. That surprised me, the novice world traveler. We entered the building, a dimly lit room with no air-conditioning, and were directed to line up under the single sign for visitors. Despite warnings about having our items searched and confiscated, we made it through without incident.

Upon exiting customs, we were met by the Methodist missionaries who were to shepherd us through our time in Haiti. Laurie was a slim young woman in her twenties, and Bill was a man in his late fifties, with a beard and hair that gave him the appearance of a nineteenth-century fur trapper. They were accompanied by Bill's Haitian helper, Eric. We split up into a van and a pickup truck to head to the Methodist guesthouse, located inside the city of Port-au-Prince. There were stop signs, but no one stopped. They just honked their horns to let people know they were coming through. All along the road, an incredible number of people were walking. We had never seen anything like this.

The guesthouse was made of concrete blocks, painted white with jalousie-style windows and four large rooms. There was a swimming pool, which drew most of our attention. After a day of travel, we were all exhausted and sticky from the heat and decided to go for a swim in the warm water, despite it being ten o'clock at night. The grass surrounding the pool was lush green and so fine that I felt like I was walking on velour-covered foam padding. After a short swim, we headed for bed. And we heeded the advice to drink and brush our teeth with only bottled water.

That first night, I hardly slept at all. I was amped up about the trip, plus it was hot and sticky. And noisy. Dogs barked, and trucks went up and down the rocky road near the guesthouse, honking horns. I must have dozed off at some point though, because I was startled awake by five gunshots.

Long Leap of Faith

Despite of the nocturnal gunfire, Haiti in 1985 was a magical place. The landscape was a rainbow, highlighting the deep blues of the clear

When Faith Lights the Way

Caribbean water, the brown sparseness of the arid west side, and the rich greens of the lush tropical forests that covered the hills and mountains of the central region. It was an ideal tropical island with beautiful beaches. The people were extremely happy, friendly, and hardworking. There was, however, a dark parallel universe.

Evil spirits are believed to be everywhere in Haiti. Voodoo is practiced as openly as Catholicism, both being the country's most practiced religions, often intertwined in one's beliefs. The two date back to the French introduction of Catholicism to the colony and to African slaves retaining elements of religious or ceremonial practices from their homeland. Over centuries, the two have formed part of Haiti's rich culture, often serving to sow more fear and harm than faith and healing.

I was in Haiti, almost against my will, but I was committed to making the best of the situation. This was my first experience in an environment that was foreign in every way and where I had no control. My only other trip outside of the United States had been to England, but England wasn't so vastly differently from my life in Texas. Haiti was not Texas.

My first morning in Haiti, I awoke to a beautiful, sunny day. While showering, I remembered the instructions about avoiding water contamination and tightly closed my eyes and mouth and kept water from going in my nose. *I will not be a victim of the dreaded turista,* I thought to myself.

After dressing, I had a pleasant conversation with Laurie about her time in Haiti. I was starving but in no hurry to go downstairs, since Laurie told me that the cooks would ring a bell when breakfast was ready. In time, David Taylor came upstairs and asked if I was going to eat. Food was ready, but there had been no bell.

Rushing downstairs, I found that there was very little food left but made the best of a picked-over buffet. I sat down to eat with associate pastor Skip Johnson and Doug, Laurie's husband. They were discussing martyred Methodist missionaries, a great topic to impress someone who was apprehensive about being there in the first place! *Maybe everyone is plotting against me,* I thought.

Why Am I Here?

After breakfast, we walked four blocks to an English-speaking Christian Church—basically a roof with open sides and benches for pews. It was really a treat, though, because it allowed a cool breeze to blow through, and I could look out on the many beautiful flowers and plants that surrounded the church. Many *blancs*, the Haitian term for whites, and a few Haitians attended the service. Looking around at the people, I decided they sure weren't concerned about fashion. It seemed most of the missionaries had left the United States a long time ago and had given up the distractions of material life. I had respect for these people, who were willing to give up the good life back home to help others. On the other hand, I didn't understand why these people wanted to spend their lives like this. I was so young, had no experience in the world outside my small bubble, and hadn't discovered my own purpose, so I wasn't able relate to that kind of sacrifice and dedication.

After the service, the team prepared to leave for Cap-Haïtien. We quickly pitched our duffel bags on top of our bus, latched them to the luggage rack, and squeezed in. When we stopped for gas, a Haitian approached the van selling fried banana skins. We were wary at first, being in a strange land with people trying to sell us strange food. But we decided to be adventurous and buy a bag. They tasted like a fried potato skin. We were doing okay as world adventurers.

On the way out of town, we passed through Cité Soleil—one of the largest slums in the Western Hemisphere. It was home to thousands of people who lived in concrete dwellings with tin roofs held together with whatever material they could scavenge. There was no potable water, no sanitation system, and no paved streets or roads—just dirt. When it rained, which was almost every day in rainy season, it was just mud. With no jobs, they roamed the streets. I had only seen pictures of places like this, but witnessing the filth and hopelessness firsthand was something else entirely.

The lack of sanitation and open sewage were huge problems all over Haiti. From the top of the mountains, people and their animals used the creeks as restrooms and as their source for drinking water. The creeks ran

When Faith Lights the Way

down to the sea, along with all the contaminates. Erosion added minerals to the streams. The drinking water, the fish, and the animals they ate all came from or partook of the contaminated water. Waterborne diseases and parasites were rampant and infected almost everyone. Now we understood why we were to drink bottled water only.

It was a long drive to Cap-Haïtien, where we would stay during our trip. Port-au-Prince is on the southern side of the island of Hispaniola; Cap-Haïtien is on the northern tip of the island. As no roads cut through the mountainous center part of the island, we traveled along a coast road. At the time, most of the land was forested and covered with tropical vegetation.

All along the way I saw many, many people walking along the road. The women all carried things on their heads. Food, clothing, boxes... everything but their babies. It was amazing how much they could carry. My eyes wandered from these amazing women with their expert balancing abilities to the cars on the road. Many were taxis, called "tap taps" or "quick, quick." These were old, brightly painted trucks or small buses. There might be twenty people inside, riding on top, and hanging on the outside. The roads consisted of two lanes, so when you wanted to pass a person walking or riding a bicycle, donkey, or tap tap, you honked the horn and they moved to the side of the road.

Upon leaving Port-au-Prince, we saw little villages every mile or so. They were spaced just far enough apart so women could carry goods to sell at the market in the morning and return home by dark with the goods they purchased. The houses we passed appeared to have only one room, about twelve feet by twelve feet, and they were made from concrete blocks covered in plaster with two openings for doors. Pencil-cactus fences surrounded the houses, and most yards contained a goat. All the goats had wooden triangles around their necks to keep them from going through the doors into the houses. In the yards stood beautiful, flamboyant trees that had bloomed fiery red or bright yellow flowers in June. Each house was complete with a clothes-washing area: the bar ditch, or drainage ditch, in the front.

Why Am I Here?

We took a much-needed break, stopping at a Methodist mission in a small town. While there we visited a technical school for machinery. They had a good assortment of lathes, drill presses, and saws, but only one was in working order. We also took a quick tour of the mission's clinic. It was constructed of plaster-covered concrete blocks, and none of the rooms—including the delivery and operating rooms—had doors. The meager, inadequate electrical wiring was all exposed.

The first room we entered was about twelve feet by twelve feet in size, with raised concrete slabs arranged in three rows for the students to sit on. Several posters hung on the walls, visualizing the symptoms and treatments for diarrhea. This was not a surprise given the lack of good sanitation facilities and practices.

We passed another room with only a wooden table inside, and a scale for weighing babies. This struck a chord within me, as all I could think about was that, just six months earlier, our first child had been born in far better conditions. The scale in this room was very much like the one used to weigh our daughter, but that was where the similarities ended.

In the operating room was an old, stainless steel operating table with numerous rust spots. The twenty-watt bulb was just enough to keep it from being a darkroom, but the dim light allowed harsh shadows to hide behind everything. A fear arose in me that the shadows were ghosts of people who had endured who-knows-what in this room. My heart hurt, and I turned away and exited the clinic.

The road to Cap-Haïtien took us closer to the ocean, where the water was a beautiful blue-green and every bit as idyllic as the television commercials you see. We passed a few hotels and several huge homes surrounded by large fences. As we continued our journey, the climate became more arid; the houses were few.

We stopped again in the community of Gonaïves for lunch, at what Bill described as the best restaurant in town. We took his word. I remember the place as a Rotary restaurant because on the back wall of this open-air restaurant hung a familiar sign: a golden spoke wheel on a blue

When Faith Lights the Way

background. It was comforting to see the sign—something that reminded me of home. The restaurant only served egg sandwiches. I had never eaten an egg sandwich before, but this seemed like the perfect time to try one, considering I'd barely gotten breakfast.

After eating, we went back to the van and headed on our way. We were now in a more forested area, and the road twisted as we climbed higher. As we passed through several small towns, we were stopped and inspected by soldiers. At one desolate spot, we came upon fifty-gallon barrels placed on the road, where two soldiers with pistols and rifles looked us over and asked for our destination. They were missing teeth, and their uniforms were ragged. We doubted they had much formal police training. We all had a bad feeling about this. If they didn't approve of us, or if they wanted something we weren't willing to give them, we were dead meat—literally.

For whatever miraculous reason, they rolled the barrels out of the way and let us pass. "They are there to let everyone know who's in charge," Bill explained when we asked why they let us go. Bill went on to say that when there are rumors of revolutions or assassinations, soldiers make you get out and they search your luggage. Bill told us that in the late sixties a chairman of the Methodist Church in Haiti had been in front the firing squad, about to be killed, when it was discovered he was a friend of Baby Doc's, the Haitian dictator Jean-Claude Duvalier. That hit too close to home for me. What was I doing here? I had a family that I desperately wanted to get back to. *This could turn into a bad situation*, I thought. I was so far out of my boat that I couldn't see any sign of it in any direction.

This Ain't Texas

We drove into a lush, tropical forest laced with banana and fruit trees. Like all over Haiti, people were walking everywhere. We passed a rice field, where a naked man was plowing a muddy field without an animal helper. Along the side of the road, women were washing clothes in the drainage ditch. Dogs with their ribs showing poked around the small huts for food. The further we went into this trip, the more sobering it became.

As we drove along it began to rain, and the downpour cooled things off. Rain was an everyday occurrence that time of year. A beautiful, clear morning usually gave way by noon to thunderstorms roiling overhead. These storms would dump their loads of water, an inch or more, in the afternoons. Many of the people walking along the road used cut banana leaves as umbrellas. Some of the kids ran behind our van, dropping their banana leaf umbrellas to try to hop on the back bumper to catch a ride. Their antics were just about the only positive things we encountered that day.

We passed several structures with walls and roofs that obviously had been churches. They were now empty inside, having fallen into disrepair, and vegetation was taking over. A shame, I thought. I'm sure initially there had been a lot of enthusiasm to save the souls of the Haitians by building a church. Any number of scenarios could have contributed to the churches being deserted. Maybe the cost was more than the donor was willing to give, maybe donors lost interest and stopped sending funds, maybe there were no funds for upkeep after the construction was completed, or maybe locals had mismanaged or siphoned off the funds for personal use. I began to wonder how one could donate financially and guarantee that the people one wanted to help would truly reap the desired benefits? How do you ensure you have a lasting impact? How do you know that you aren't throwing good money at a problem that money can't solve?

When we entered the outskirts of Cap-Haïtien it was dinnertime, and families were cooking meals outside on small grills, using charcoal for fire. Charcoal is a blessing and a curse for almost all developing countries in tropical climates. Haiti was no exception. The climate produces vegetation that's perfect for making charcoal. Leaves, wood from trees, any vegetation can be used. In fact, a lot of the people make their living on the production of charcoal, gathering vegetation, binding it in a bundle, and placing it beside the road where a truck will pick up the bundles. The material is carried by truck to a charcoal-making factory, and the final product is sold for fuel to cook food.

While charcoal is a cheap, easy fuel for tropical climates, it has catastrophic effects. The burning of charcoal produces a thick haze of pollution, and the thick black smoke can irritate the lungs and eyes. Open cooking fires are risky, especially during the dry season. An accidental fire can spread very quickly to surrounding areas. The most damaging effect, though, takes place over time. Much of Haiti was a tropical forest in 1985. Today, Haiti is 98 percent deforested.[3] Some of the problems resulting from this deforestation are obvious. Alternate cooking fuels are not as available, and jobs working in the charcoal industry are becoming less plentiful. Jobs are hard to find as it is, in one of the poorest countries in the world. But deforestation has created even larger problems. The soil is unprotected from heavy rain, and runoff and erosion take away the topsoil, leaving the barren land where nothing will grow.

This Ain't Texas

Just outside of Cap-Haïtien, we stopped our van inside at yet another gate. A small Haitian boy approached the van and told us the armed soldiers wanted to see our passports. Bill spoke in Creole with the boy and the soldiers, and we were allowed through by giving them a list of our names and where we were staying. I was reminded again that traveling around Haiti was dangerous, nothing at all like Texas.

From the soldier's checkpoint, we rode to our hotel, winding up a road that was about one and a half lanes wide, trying to avoid hitting all the people who were walking on the road. At the top of a steep hill, we came upon Hotel Beck, a one-story inn with a wide porch leading to the doors to the guest rooms and a wide veranda in front of the dining room, which was located in the center. The walls were yellow plaster, and the floors were glazed tile. Beautiful grounds with flowers surrounded the hotel. Herr Beck, the German owner, had come to Haiti before World War II. Our construction team were the hotel's only guests.

After the long, sticky ride, several of us decided to swim in the hotel's large, half-filled pool. We swam for a short while and then dressed casually for dinner. We dined on roast, carrots, brown rice, green beans, and bread that reminded me of a crescent roll. I felt like I was back home. We were served by Mary, a Haitian dressed in a starched black-and-white uniform. The doors to the dining room were kept open, and there were no annoying bugs to spoil the mood as classical music serenaded us during the meal. From the dining room in our mountain retreat, we had a spectacular view of the Caribbean. It all helped me to forget the overwhelming hopelessness and poverty we had seen all day.

There's a film from the 1950s, *On the Beach*, about a nuclear war that destroys civilization. Those living in Australia were the last humans left alive. At dinner, as we ate and laughed, we compared ourselves to the last remaining humans. We watched as the few lights of the city disappeared, the sky darkened, and the stars took their places in the sky. Every night after dinner, we adjourned to the veranda for conversation. Evening in Cap-Haïtien was surreal.

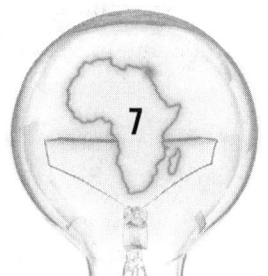

What We Came to Do

The next morning, we woke at six-thirty, eager to get to work. At breakfast, we were served eggs, indescribably delicious bananas, fruit, guava jelly, and really, really, strong black coffee. Doug and Laurie, the married missionary team, arrived in an old Land Rover, and we rode with them past Hotel Beck's white pillar gates down narrow streets, where children dressed in their school colors walked to school. Blue uniforms designated Baptist school students, yellow and brown the Methodists, and the Catholic uniforms were a different shade of blue from the Baptists.

Flying down the rough road in the old Land Rover toward Tovar was an experience. If it had ever had shock absorbers, they no longer worked, and the rusted-out door frame made the door rattle so much that it almost shook off. I looked around at everyone's smiling faces, and it was obvious we all thought the same thing. *Who cares?!* This Haitian adventure could be fun.

We drove out of the city gates, went about ten miles, and turned onto a crushed-rock road. We passed concrete houses, and my nerd senses alerted me that the electric poles were not made of wood. I had never seen these types of poles at that time in the United States. They were solid concrete with reinforced steel rods. There was only one wire on the poles—a very crude way to transport electricity. When there is only one

When Faith Lights the Way

wire, the amount of voltage can wildly fluctuate and damage motors and electrical appliances. This crude attempt at electrification stayed in the back of my mind for many years.

When we arrived in Tovar, we saw that some work had already begun on the church. Most of the foundation had been dug out so the concrete floor could be poured. We were so pumped! This was what we had been waiting for! We could now show the Haitians how it's done! Day one of construction had finally arrived!

We began by moving concrete blocks inside the new church, forming a human chain, much like a bucket brigade. We worked fast and passed blocks to one another like a well-choreographed ballet. Everyone—men, women, children, Haitians, Americans—joked and laughed. We kept this fast and furious show of skill and dexterity going for about ten minutes. Then, our group wore out. It was time for a break, and it was also time to rethink our approach. We needed to calm down and find a more sustainable pace.

Ed Thulin and I had shovels and went to help some men who were leveling the ground for the foundation. A young Haitian man in his early twenties and his girl were helping as well. The guy and his girl stood around with a hoe, talking to each other in Creole and laughing. Ed and I, feeling uncomfortable, wondered if they were laughing at us. We laughed back nervously and kept on shoveling dirt into the wheelbarrow. They were probably laughing because we were paying for the privilege of shoveling dirt, and they were getting paid two dollars a day.

At about ten o'clock, I went behind the shed that stored the used lumber and saw an old man and a young boy sawing up the rough, old splintered boards from the previous church. I decided holding boards while they sawed them was better than shoveling dirt or mixing mortar. They held the saw perpendicular to the board, with the teeth facing away from them. *How weird,* I thought. At home, we're taught to turn the hand saw with the teeth down and angle the blade at about a forty-five-degree angle in relation to the board we're going to saw. Their way seemed to be

What We Came to Do

less work, and they seemed to have better control, allowing them to saw a straight line. I thought that that was pretty cool. I had unexpectedly learned something.

We began to nail the scraggly boards together. Why, I didn't know. There wasn't a translator working with us, so I didn't have a clue what we were doing. I just followed their lead. We worked on the ground and put these scraggly scraps of boards side-by-side, then nailed scrap boards as connectors to the boards lying on the ground until they created a plank about twenty-four inches wide and about ten feet long. It was flat on the side that laid on the ground, except for the numerous holes and cracks in the plank. That is what you get when you use rough, scraggly wood that should have been used to make a fire.

By the time we broke for lunch, we were hot, sticky, and tired, but we all felt really macho. We were becoming a close-knit group. It was eye opening to watch and learn the Haitians construction techniques, which were different from ours. They built up course after course of concrete blocks, leaving a space for a column about twelve inches by twelve inches, every eight feet along the wall. When they had laid blocks to a height of about eight feet along a wall, they covered the opening for the columns with the wood planks we had pieced together. Then, they slipped steel reinforcing rods, also known as rebar, down between the blocks and the wooden forms. Steel wire was used to tie all the rebar and wood forms securely together. Nothing was wasted. The empty concrete sacks were stuffed in the holes and cracks in the old wood to seal the places where the concrete could run out. Finally, concrete was poured into the top of the columns and allowed to dry. After the concrete columns dried, the steel wires holding the wooden forms were cut away from the completed column. It was all new to me, and it was ingenious.

At the end of the day, I was very dissappointed at the quality of my construction skills. I bent nails and had trouble sawing a straight line. I told myself I just needed to get in the groove, but I had to admit that the Haitian workers were better with hand tools than I was. Being a rookie in the missionary field, and having lived in the bubble that is the United

When Faith Lights the Way

States, I thought I would be better than them at everything. I had an education and grew up and lived in the developed world. I was supposed to bring them knowledge that would change their lives. I was beginning to understand I was receiving as much or more than I was giving.

Each day we rose at six-thirty, ate breakfast, and went to the site to work. One day, I was on a scaffold rewiring rebar to the column forms with the steel wire. I reached inside the hole and suddenly felt something go into my forearm. The tying wire was stuck in my arm. It was too deep for me to work my arm around and pull it free. The tying wire was probably about a sixteenth of an inch in diameter. David Taylor came over and managed to get my arm unstuck. I was hot and sweating, but I felt tough. I kept on working with only a Band-Aid, glad I'd gotten a tetanus shot before I left the United States.

While the others on the crew spent their time laying brick, I continued to work at carpentry jobs. We didn't see much of the old man that had been doing carpentry work on the first day, but his young helper acted as my workmate the rest of my time there. The interpreter, Alan, was busy elsewhere, but we didn't need to talk to get our work done. We understood what we were trying to accomplish and how to do it, and we knew each other's moves. We worked well together, but my partner sometimes annoyed me. I said we didn't talk, and, well, that carried over even when I had my back turned. To get my attention, he threw nails at the back of my head. He could have yelled something, anything. Yes, hitting me with nails got my attention. I pantomimed, "Don't do that!" but he didn't stop. I don't know if he was just picking on me or what, but it really aggravated me!

Some of the Haitians on the site could speak a little English. Since we had learned their construction methods, we wanted to explain to them how things were built in America. We told them we used tractors to dig out the space for the foundation, and that our columns were steel or prestressed concrete. We explained that cement was transported to work sites in trucks with huge rotating drums that mixed the concrete, enough to fill a hundred wheelbarrow loads while en route to the job site, and that the concrete was then poured down a chute to the foundations. We described

What We Came to Do

the large, rotating disc used to finish the foundation. The machine basically floated on top of the concrete, and the rotating disc smoothed it out. This was when they began to doubt us. They just couldn't imagine it. We lost them completely when we described nail guns and explained how they increased efficiency. They had never seen anything like it and thought we were making stuff up.

Leaving the job site after the first work day, Bill, the mountain-man missionary, drove the van carrying our team back to the Hotel Beck. Laurie, Doug, and I followed a little later in the Land Rover. A village was located at a turn in the road, and about forty or fifty people were gathered around what appeared to be a well. Our crew's van had stopped nearby, so we pulled in beside it. Haitians were running around shouting excitedly, and some were even laughing. Alan, our twentyish school-educated Haitian interpreter, was told a girl had fallen into the well, about fifteen feet down. We were all horrified. Alan asked if they wanted our help, and they said yes. There was a horse nearby, tethered with a rope. Alan translated our orders to them: untie the horse and bring us the rope! No one responded; they just kept yelling and scrambling around, even the father of the girl in the well. There was another rope, hanging in a tree. We told them to get that rope! No one moved to help. I thought, don't you hear? What is wrong with you? After five minutes, a man brought a ladder; but no one was getting her out. They just yelled and screamed. What was going on?

Doug and Laurie began to feel uneasy and told us all to move back toward the bus, about fifty yards from the well. No problem! We waited to find out what would happen. After about twenty minutes, the Haitians got her out of the well using the ladder and the rope from the tree. From fifty yards away, it was difficult to see all the details, and we didn't understand the language. She appeared to be about twenty. As soon she emerged from the well, her father began to beat her with the rope. Everyone around the well was yelling and screaming, pulling and shoving. Some of the men joined in the beating, and the girl that had emerged from the well was knocked to the ground. Alan tried to intervene but to

When Faith Lights the Way

no avail. He was shoved aside. The girl was dragged into a house, and we could hear screaming. As they dragged her into the house, we noticed a gash on her head, but no bones appeared to be broken. Our hearts were racing, we were in shock! A helpless, helpless feeling. We stayed around as things calmed, and Alan questioned the crowd for an answer. Someone spoke to him, and slowly he turned to us and related the answer. The girl in the well had tried to kill herself by jumping down the well. She had done this because she found out she was pregnant by a man her father and brother didn't like.

We were stunned and confused. What would we have been accomplished if we'd intervened? As Christians, should we have intervened? What was the most effective way to approach the people at the well? This whole episode was so foreign to our experience. We never learned more about the girl in the well, even though we passed by the location each day. The horror and shock began to recede, but the incident was burned into my memory. I still don't know how we should have reacted.

At the end of each long work day, we returned to our own private Shangri-La. We relaxed in the swimming pool before dinner. Every night we had good food within the eerie ambiance of our isolated world. After that we adjourned to the veranda to discuss the day and solve the world's problems. Usually, at ten o'clock, we headed for our rooms. One night, David, Skip, and I walked between two buildings and were startled by a young woman who jumped out of the darkness toward us. "Please," she pleaded and begged, "sex with me! Only one dallar." After we'd recovered, we told her, "No! Go away!" She came closer and pleaded again. Again, we told her to go away. She turned and ran down the hill, and we never saw her again. I wondered to myself, as I saw her running down the hill. What kind of life would cause a woman to approach men for a dollar?

I'd had a year's worth of experiences in the past week, but I had become comfortable with this life. A part of me wanted to see the project through until the end, but my time was up, and my life in Texas was

What We Came to Do

calling me back. I was proud of what we'd accomplished so far, and we were making good progress. The concrete block walls were over eight feet tall, all but a few of the columns had been poured, and some of the rafters had been completed and were ready to install. I was sad to leave my partner, who'd thrown nails at me to get my attention. As I left, I gave him a blue baseball cap with a gold WTU logo on the front. It had been given to me by a customer who worked for West Texas Utilities. I also gave him my gloves. In return, he gave me a big smile and a strong handshake. I wanted to think he would miss me, too.

Cultural Lessons

Adventures at the Citadelle

On Saturday, we took time off for a trip to the Citadelle Laferrière, an enormous fort built between 1805 and 1815 to protect against future French invasions. The fort was erected on the orders of Henri Christophe, an army general who played a role in Haiti's founding revolution against French rule. The fort rests at three thousand feet on top of a mountain, and it is amazing. It was built by twenty thousand laborers using a mixture of quicklime, molasses, and blood from cows and goats. The fort contained over three hundred cannons and had massive food storehouses and large cisterns, making it self-sufficient for a year if attacked.[4] While touring the magnificent structure, we were told three famous Prussian construction engineers had been hired by Christophe to build the fortress, and as the structure was completed, Christophe had them killed and buried inside it. He wanted to make sure the three engineers couldn't tell anyone of the fortress's vulnerabilities.

The Citadelle is a must see. I know how hard it is to build a small church in less-than-ideal conditions. To build a structure of that size, keep the workers supplied with construction material, and to feed and house that many workers would have been an amazing undertaking.

When Faith Lights the Way

Surrounding the Citadelle were as many street sellers and children as there were tourists—probably more. Everywhere we went in Haiti, children and young people crowded around us and emphatically cried, "Gimme a dallar!" These kids were so cute, they would melt your heart. However, the missionaries explained to us that it doesn't help them to receive something and not give something in return. Their advice made sense where adults were concerned, but these were little children. Surely it wouldn't hurt to give them a dollar. If we didn't give in, we felt guilty. It's a philosophy that I struggled with for some time. It was many years before I fully understood the lesson.

Bartering is a way of life for the Haitians, as it is in most of the world. We were told that if you don't bargain for what you're buying, people will think you're stupid and not respect you. They love the game and consider it a way of getting to know you, and with a little coaching from Alan, our interpreter, we learned how to play. First, we searched the market to see what was available and to check the pricing from various vendors on items we might want to buy. We only expressed curiosity about something we wanted to buy and never said, "I have to have this!" Second, we narrowed our focus to one vendor. When they gave us a price, we reacted by saying, "No. Too much." They would tell us about the quality, or maybe even lower the price. We would then respond with, "I don't think so, thanks." Subsequently, we were asked, "How much would you pay?" We would respond with a number about half of the original asking price. The vendor would say, "No! Too cheap!" We would respond, "I'm not interested," and start to walk away. At that point, the vendor would quote us a price about 60 percent of the original asking price. A good deal—time to buy. That was normally a fair price for him and us. Sometimes it takes much longer and a lot more conversation.

As we reached our van and were finally away from the throng of people that had been on top of us all day, four or five bright, pretty, teenaged girls approached our group to sell us brightly colored woven baskets for three dollars. We were very tired, and our patience had worn thin with street vendors. We went through a textbook barter with them and tried to buy them for a dollar, pushing too hard. They stuck at two. We said no way, loaded into the van and started driving down the rocky, steep road. The girls ran after us finally shouting, "One dallar!" No one really wanted a basket, so we didn't stop. We were looking out the back window and saw one girl trip, all her baskets flying in the air. She hit hard and rolled down the hill. We were all silent for a long time. Whenever I think back to that moment, I wish we had stopped to buy the baskets. It was only a dollar. How do you choose who to help when everyone around you needs help? The memory and the guilt still overcomes me when I think of her.

We were emotionally drained. For the afternoon, we went to lounge on an idyllic private beach with white sand, fresh air, and beautiful clear water. Some of us read, slept, or walked the beach. Being alone was good. We needed a break from the mental stress of the day, of the trip. It felt strange to be constantly surrounded by needy children always asking for something. Our brains were overloaded with questions and emotions. We wrestled with our feelings and reactions to what we were experiencing.

We reluctantly left our beach utopia and returned to the Hotel Beck for my last meal with the group.

Heading Home

The day after our adventure at the Citadelle and beach, it was time for me to head back to Port-au-Prince for my flight home. I was sad to leave my new family, but I also wanted to get back to the routine of home.

Bill and I left early to beat the heat. The ride gave me an opportunity to ask him some questions. One was about voodoo. Bill seemed to give credence to it, which didn't seem right for a Christian. When I asked him about this, he said, "Most of it is superstition, but if a person has a strong enough belief in something, their mind can affect their body. Like curses and voodoo dolls. For a person that has a strong belief, it can have physical consequences, good or bad. I do believe in some of the powders they use. They get them from fish, I hear. I believe if they give

When Faith Lights the Way

you a powder, you appear to die, and then when you wake up, you are a zombie. I've seen that." I felt a lump in my throat. That certainly didn't improve my comfort.

We were flying along the curvy road when a man jumped out in front of our van waving his arms. "Smile," Bill said. "Follow my lead. Only say good things about Haiti and its leaders." Bill stopped the van. The man was older, missing teeth, and had gray hair that took off every which way and looked like he'd stuck his finger into a light socket. He was wearing some kind of old blue uniform that hadn't seen an iron, and maybe even water, in some time. He opened the door, and in Creole told Bill he needed a ride to Gonaïves. Bill replied in Creole, "Sure, get in!" In English, Bill introduced the local sheriff to me, and told me he was riding with us to Gonaïves, which was about twenty miles away. Bill and I smiled and talked about the beautiful weather, the hard-working people, and what a good government Haiti had. When I looked back in the van seat, the sheriff was leaned back up against the seat, with one leg on the floor and one in the seat, his long gray hair flying in the breeze. Sometimes his eyes were closed, sometimes not. If I looked back and his eyes were open, he flashed me a big toothless smile. I wasn't crazy about turning my back on this officer of the law.

When we reached Gonaïves, we stopped at an intersection, and the sheriff said bye, got out, and melted into the crowd. "What was that all about?" I asked. Just then, music started playing, and Bill told me to get out and stand at attention as he leaped out the driver's door. I had learned in Haiti, do first, ask questions later. It was a beautiful, cloudless day, and the huge crowd at the intersection stood at attention, facing the same direction, all quiet. As the recorded Haitian national anthem played, a flag was slowly raised up a flagpole in front of us. As the flag unfurled at the top of the pole, the music reached a crescendo and stopped. Bill climbed back in the van, I did too. Everyone started moving, and we drove off.

"Okay," I said, "Tell me about the Sheriff." Bill explained as he drove with just the two of us in the van.

Cultural Lessons

"You really have to be careful what you say around here. You never know who is part of the Tonton Macoute (the secret police organization of the government) or who might get a reward for turning in someone that spoke against the government. Any of these guys might be able to understand just enough English to turn you in."

I thought on this and said, "All right. What about the flag raising? Why did we have to get out?"

He nodded his head toward me and said, "Same deal. I wanted us in the open, standing at attention, so everyone could plainly see we were supporting the government. You don't leave the prisons."

Beneath the surface, this place is like a bad dream, I thought.

We made good time returning to Port-au-Prince, and since we had some spare time, Bill took me to the Iron Market to look for souvenirs. The Iron Market, located a few blocks from the sea, looked like something from one of the world's fairs at the turn of the nineteenth century. The market had a clock tower and four minarets. It was packed with nearly a thousand merchants selling art, pigeons, turtles, dried starfish, herbs, potions, perfumes, and produce. The market, also known as Marché Hyppolite, was intended to be a railway station in Cairo. It is not clear why it landed in Haiti in 1891, but the Haitians kept it and assembled it.

We parked the van about a block away and started walking. At the corner, Bill paid a young Haitian boy a dollar to guide me through the market. Bill hung back.

"Aren't you going with me?" I asked.

"Nope," said Bill. "I don't want any of the stores in there thinking I'm partial to one or the other. You go with him. You can handle it."

Great, I thought. *Me all alone.*

I walked in and quickly realized I was the only *blanc* in the place. People were all over me asking me to come over here, look at this, this is better, this is cheaper. I strolled through, looked at a few things, bartered for a few things I really didn't want, but didn't find anything I was willing to buy. But I felt good. I was paddling down my river, calm and comfort-

When Faith Lights the Way

able in a strange land and culture. I stayed about an hour and went back to the corner to meet Bill. He smiled and asked, "How did it go?"

"Okay," I said. "I just didn't find anything I wanted."

He smiled again, and we got in the car. I told him I had hoped to find some things of a higher quality. He looked ahead and kept driving. "When you come back I can show you where you can get some better-quality items."

After a brief stop at the Methodist guesthouse, we headed to the airport.

Thankfully, the flight to Miami was short. I suddenly noticed how beautiful the Miami airport was. Everything seemed so clean and fresh. It was good to be home.

Once I had settled back into home life, I was able to reflect on the lessons I'd learned and to question some old assumptions. I wondered how it was that the poorest people were so happy. It seemed that those with the lowest status and the least material goods were the happiest. When it comes to deep faith, Haitians have equally strong beliefs in Christianity and Voodoo, so was the simple act of having faith—no matter where it stemmed from—a factor in their happiness? What could I learn from them to strengthen my faith?

One question I would return to many times throughout my life: How do you really help someone? I had always heard that, if you give someone something for free, it's worth exactly what they paid for it. Said another way, if you don't work for it, you won't appreciate it. How do you know when to trust your gut and give anyway?

I am blessed with a great life, and I believe in the old adage, "To whom much is given, much is required." I wanted to know, for what purpose was I being groomed? In time, this would be the easiest question to answer.

Cultural Lessons

My week in Haiti, and all that I saw and learned, greatly influenced my thinking throughout my life. The memories and experiences haunted or gave me joy for years afterward. The journey shaped my views on poverty, different cultures, and what's important in life. Of the several lessons I learned in Haiti, the greatest were what I discovered about myself:

▷ I can function in an underdeveloped setting and not feel uncomfortable, but rather thrive on the experience

▷ I can do construction on complicated structures or systems with the help of inexperienced labor

▷ I can be open-minded about adopting methods used in other countries, as our way is not the only way—and sometimes not the best way—to do something

These practical lessons would soon influence in how I approached my future efforts to launch Power from the SON.

In 1957, Me proudly climbing into the cockpit of an airplane built by my father from random scrap materials, including a pickle barrel.

The Vincents in 1962. Kitty, me, and Hollis.

Receiving my Eagle Scout Award standing by my proud parents.

High school senior year 1969.

Texas A&M year book picture 1971.

Graduation day from Texas A&M, May 1973, with my roommate and lifelong friend, Jack Barlow.

Instructing and helping with the installation of an underground transformer at an electric cooperative in west Texas in the late 1970s.

Linda Beiland and me. Our engagement picture, 1979.

Honeymoon with Linda Vincent at Copper Mountain in 1980.

Typical house in Haiti in 1985.

Cité Soleil is an impoverished and densely populated slum located outside Port-au-Prince.

Many curious children were outside as we drove from Port-au-Prince to Cap-Haitian.

Some of the great local help we received in constructing the church in Tovar, Haiti.

The walls and the roof supports are up on Tovar United Methodist Church.

The outside view of Tovar United Methodist Church.

Completed Tovar United Methodist Church in Haiti.

SECTION TWO

Mapping Your Course

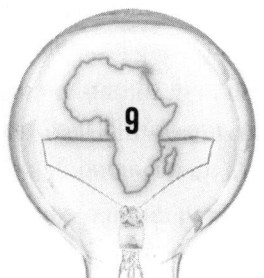

Finding My Purpose

What I said to Aunt Louise and my mom when I first went to work at Priester was always in the back of my mind: "This is an unbelievable opportunity. I feel blessed to be given this opportunity because I feel I'm supposed to do something to make a difference." Thirty-four years later, my life was almost unbelievably blessed. Linda and I had two girls who had left the nest and continued to give us much joy. I had become a key owner and executive in Priester, and we had grown the business to sixteen branches in thirteen states. Two years earlier, we had sold Priester to Stuart C. Irby, and I was an executive with them. At Irby, a couple of the people at work felt they were also blessed, and they also felt a calling to make a difference. To really have an impact, we brainstormed ideas to figure out our strengths. Well, we knew electricity pretty well, and we understood business. How and where could we combine these two areas and make a difference? Nearly everybody in the United States had electricity, but that wasn't the case in other parts of the world. I thought of Haiti—maybe we could use our experience and gifts in the developing world—and a light bulb went off: Christians feed, educate, and heal the needy. But without adequate electricity, it's difficult for people to raise themselves out of poverty.

When Faith Lights the Way

Bringing electricity to the developing world might be my purpose in life, I thought. Many people feel called to convert people to Christianity. I never felt I was called to convert people to my beliefs, but with this plan I could share my faith by action rather than teaching. Maybe someone would ask me why I was helping when I would receive nothing in return, and then I could tell them that my faith requires me to treat others like I would want to be treated, that in fact I was receiving something in return. I might not be good at teaching scripture, but I felt that I could still be a vessel of God's love and mercy.

"'Yes, come,' Jesus said. So Peter went over the side of the boat and walked on the water toward Jesus" (Matthew 14:29).[6]

Why in the world would Peter step out of that boat? I've wondered. It was in no way logical. Something must have overridden his fears and everything he had learned in life. He chose to obey something that compelled him to get out of the boat. And he did. He walked on water! Peter didn't follow what *should* happen but what *could* happen. I believe we all have that same compelling inner guidance available.

Over time the idea began to take shape. So many details needed to be thought through and worked out. Thankfully, I had a network of supportive individuals who wanted to be involved in some capacity. Steve Hawrylak and Mark Abbe worked with me to develop the plan. We knew we would have many obstacles to overcome, as we all were unprepared or unskilled in some way or another for whatever lay ahead. Had we known what we were facing, we logically would have never started, much less persevered.

We wondered if there was someone already doing the kind of work we were planning and began to research. Almost immediately we came upon Barefoot Power, a for-profit social enterprise that provided solar-powered lighting products to rural communities in developing countries. The company was founded and operated by two Australians, Stewart Crane and Harry Andrews. We sent an e-mail introduction to them, with a request for information and offer of partnership.

Finding My Purpose

E-mail to Stewart and Harry, November 1, 2007:

> As an introduction, we are three individuals that have a combined utility experience in the United States of about one hundred years. This experience includes work for TXU (A former owner of an Australian utility) and work with several investor-owned utilities, municipalities, and rural cooperatives through our current employer, Irby (A Sonepar Company), the third-largest electric utility distributor in the States. Our education is in engineering, accounting, and management.
>
> Several days ago, we were all expressing our desire to give something useful to the world with our education & work experience. A Google search turned up your website.
>
> We are very impressed with your approach to improving the lives of others in the world. We applaud your model and the details it includes:
> - ▷ A sound economic offering to a problem
> - ▷ Local participation
> - ▷ A focus on green solutions, but with the foresight to consider and plan for heavier systems that are not offered by current solar technology. To truly develop areas, one must have access to power, not just illumination.
> - ▷ Your willingness to share solutions
>
> Our brainstorming sessions have led us to contact you to see if we can help you and/or learn from you.
> - ▷ We would like to offer similar solutions to developing countries in North America, South America, and the Caribbean. We understand the start would be small.
> - ▷ We think many of the contacts we've made through the years might help with design, construction, or supply of material.

When Faith Lights the Way

▷ We have some contact with nonprofit agencies that work in these developing areas that would guide or assist us in these efforts.

▷ Identify in the Americas suitable manufacturers of needed materials, or it might be feasible for us to secure this material for your efforts.

If we are on the right track, and if we have something to offer, would you please contact us so we can discuss the possibilities?

Thank you for your time.

Mark Abbe
Steve Hawrylak
Stephen Vincent

    Stewart and Harry's response was positive. Basically, they were really brilliant, had experience in developing world electrification, and were more than willing to share information and help out. Their business model was simple and innovative. Villagers in developing countries were buying kerosene lamps, candles, or scraps of wood to create light. As an alternative, Barefoot Power sold a small LED desk lamp that could be charged using a solar panel that measured about eight inches by eight inches. This desk lamp provided seven times more light than the traditional sources, and it wasn't a fire hazard. The cost for this solar lighting system was about twenty dollars, depending on the amount of lighting purchased. The recurring expense of kerosene for lamps, candles, or scraps of wood consumes twenty dollars in no time. And with the solar lighting, those recurring expenses were eliminated. Additionally, Barefoot Power offered training and financial support to villagers who wanted to start a business by selling the solar lights.

    The next step in Barefoot Power's plan was to centralize and increase solar generation by running wire to the houses to provide more light. This would improve people's livelihoods. For example, electricity would allow people to refrigerate their fishing catch or to grind corn. The plan

Finding My Purpose

also included training villagers to produce marketable goods or services. It was a wonderful model for a socially responsible for-profit business.

We did the prudent thing first: Steve, Mark, and I went to a lawyer, an accountant, and a banker for advice on how to proceed with our dream. After heeding their suggestions, we formalized an arrangement and developed a business plan to operate as an extension of the work being done by Stewart and Harry.

My family supported this change in my life's work. For Christmas that year, I received a gift from my oldest daughter, Shannon. She was a graduate student at Northwestern University at the time, working on a master's in Speech Pathology. She had compiled and bound ten papers on solar energy, as well as discussions of how the lack of electricity was hampering the development of African countries. She called it, *Sun Power: Bringing Light to the World*, a scholarly examination of the state of lighting and electricity in the developing world. Some of the best Christmas gifts are those that were gifts of labor.

I got a much-needed boost in seeing our plans validated by some of the foremost experts in the field. These papers confirmed we were on the right track.

Kylie, our youngest, has always demonstrated a genuine interest in what we were trying to accomplish, offering good, solid suggestions. She's a practical thinker. During her junior and senior high years, she embarked on several mission-work trips that gave her a practical perspective of what works and what doesn't. When she agrees with you on a point, you know you're moving in the right direction.

Community service and mission work are core values in Linda's and my families, and we have always encouraged our daughters to help others. A few years earlier, our family had been invited by the United Methodist Committee on Relief (UMCOR) to their headquarters in New York to hear a presentation on all the wonderful services they provide worldwide

When Faith Lights the Way

to help others. Knowing the extent and successes of UMCOR's efforts and their worldwide outreach, I went to my senior pastor at First United Methodist Church Arlington, Dr. David Mosser, to inquire about presenting our lighting concept to UMCOR and ask for support. We needed someone with sandals on the ground to help us do a test and monitor the results.

Dr. Mosser introduced me to Guy Ames, the district superintendent in Ardmore, Oklahoma, who also served as a director of the United Methodist Global Ministries Board. We forwarded him our proposal, and Linda and I met with him for dinner in February. Guy suggested we meet with Sam Dixon, the Deputy General Secretary of UMCOR in New York City. We had to postpone that meeting until April, though, as Linda and I were headed to China.

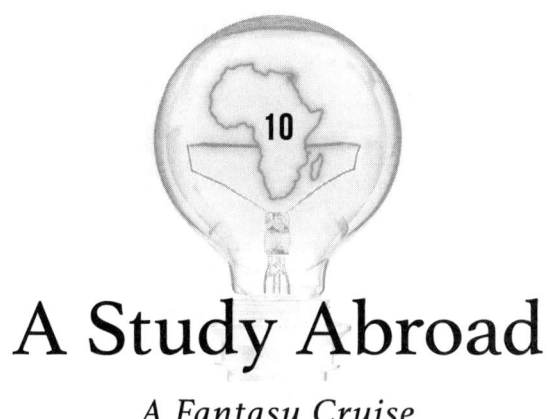

A Study Abroad

A Fantasy Cruise

In 2007, Linda and I began discussing the pros and cons of taking the "trip of a lifetime." The Traveling Aggies, Texas A&M's former-student travel service, was offering a twenty-one-day trip to mainland China, Taiwan, South Korea, and Japan, scheduled for March 2008. Former president George H.W. Bush, former US Secretary of Defense William Perry, and other dignitaries would hold a discussion on world politics, history, and ecology. Bush had been the US Ambassador to China from 1974 to 1975, when the United States and China began efforts to normalize relations between the two countries. The trip, the World Leader Symposium, was very expensive, but how often does one get to learn from people who have changed the world? Besides, our youngest daughter, Kylie, was majoring in International Studies at Texas A&M and was going to study abroad at Shanghai University the following summer. We decided you only live once and signed up.

To be properly prepared for this intellectually stimulating trip, we were given a reading list of books written by distinguished lecturers and authors like Jonathan Spence and Sidney Rittenberg. Jonathan Spence, a popular professor at Yale, was the author of *The Search for Modern*

When Faith Lights the Way

China—a massive tome. Another book, *The Man Who Stayed Behind*, by Sidney Rittenberg, was the story of Mr. Rittenberg's experiences in Communist China during the Mao Zedong years. There were also books on Confucius and Mao. Linda and I were going prepared. Both of us read *The Man Who Stayed Behind*, Linda read on Confucius and Mao, and I read the *Search for Modern China*.

Our trip began in Beijing and ended in Hong Kong. As luck or fortune would have it, Stewart Crane and Harry Andrews of Barefoot Power were living and working just outside Hong Kong in Shenzhen. We corresponded, and Linda and I decided to stay over in Hong Kong for two days after the tour to visit Stewart and Harry at their factory.

In March of 2008, we landed in Beijing and were taken to a five-star establishment, the China World Hotel, for the night. The first meeting the next morning set the tone for my insecurities, which continued for several days. I got the feeling I had outkicked my coverage. In other words, I felt like an imposter and feared that any minute someone would walk up and say, "Mr. Vincent, we've checked, and I am dreadfully sorry, but you shouldn't be here. This tour is for people who have marvelous accomplishments and credentials. You don't qualify."

The tour consisted of about 250 travelers, among them a former US ambassador and chairman of the board for Booz Allen Hamilton, and a former member of the Federal Reserve Board. There were only six of us that booked the trip through the travel program of the Texas A&M Former Students Association, the Traveling Aggies. The majority were graduates of Stanford, Harvard, Yale, and MIT. There was a doctor on this World Leader Symposium whose father had invented the intermodal system and standardized shipping containers.

The first morning began with a welcome speech by the US ambassador to China and President Bush, in the hotel ballroom. While staying in Beijing, we were taken to the Great Wall and given a private tour of the Forbidden City. Things only grew more surreal and intimidating as we

A Study Abroad

moved along. After Beijing, we were driven to the airport and escorted inside the terminal, to fly to Hong Kong to board our cruise ship.

Our group was taken through security, bypassing metal detectors, bag check, and passport check. We lined up in front of the Air China ticket counters and told them our names, and they handed us our boarding pass. We were led out to the plane and took our seats. When we were seated, the airport boarded the first-class passengers, among them Bush 41, his wife, Barbara, and a few other dignitaries. My mouth was agape. I thought to myself, *this is not really happening*. The flight was a pleasant one on a new, fresh-smelling aircraft. The meal included a steamed truffle chicken roll filled with goose liver, a choice of pan-fried beef filet with pesto and brown sauce or steamed flounder with olive paste sauce, and an ice cream dessert. I looked around and shrugged. What did I expect when traveling with a former president?

After landing, we were taken to our cruise ship, *The Silver Whisper*. This was the first cruise for Linda and me, and it was fabulous.

Entry onto the ship was as easy as our checkin at the Beijing airport. Linda and I finished storing our luggage in our stateroom and decided to go on deck to view magnificent Hong Kong. By any standard, Hong Kong's harbor is one of the most vibrant, sophisticated locations in the world. Beautiful, gleaming glass and steel buildings of every shape and color. Some buildings pierced the top of the world, while the balance of the buildings filled all the open space available in no less spectacular a fashion. The harbor was full of faux-Sanpan party boats with red sails, filled with laughing people and loud dance music. There were ferries carrying hundreds of passengers from the urban metropolis of Kowloon in northern Hong Kong to mainland China and returning full of passengers. *The Silver Whisper* headed to sea at sunset, which gave a beautiful glow in a sky filled with wisps of clouds.

Linda and I arrived on deck and went to the rail to take in the view. As we moved around, mesmerized, we ended up leaning on the rail about twenty feet apart. Both of us, out of the corner of our eye, noticed a tall,

When Faith Lights the Way

solitary man fill the space between us. It was President Bush! We both stood frozen for a moment, then simultaneously both slinked back away from the rail and stood against one of the ship's bulkheads. What were we supposed to do? It would have been different if we'd been in a line to meet him, or were expecting him, but there he was by himself, no secret service, just enjoying the view—just like we were trying to do!

As we huddled against the wall, our sanity and courage began to return. President Bush was here because he wanted to be, wasn't he? He's just like anyone else and would be happy to meet new people in a casual setting, wouldn't he? *He probably thinks we are stuck up or something since we just walked away,* I thought. I figured we should say something to him. But what? Suddenly a great idea came to me. Bush is a graduate of Yale University but had adopted Texas A&M University as his academic home. His library is located there, and he goes to all types of sporting events. We had even heard that when he and his wife, Barbara, were staying in their apartment at the Bush Library, Barbara would come out into the public areas and meet and greet people who are there for conferences. I thought of a clever line. We collected our cool and walked over to him.

"Mr. President," I said. "I want to thank you for all you do for Texas A&M University."

"Why thank you!" he replied, greeting me with a firm handshake. "Do you work there?" he asked.

"No, sir. I'm a former student." Texas Aggies are always former students. You're never an ex-Aggie. Once an Aggie, always an Aggie.

He looked at Linda. "Are you a former student?"

"No," replied Linda. "I went to that other school in Austin."

He smiled and laughed. "That's okay. My granddaughters are going to school there. It's a great school!" His smile turned to a frown as he grabbed my hand and pulled me close. "I am worried about our basketball team. They should be doing better!"

A Study Abroad

I don't remember how we closed the conversation because I was too surprised. Bush was as genuine as our friends in Arlington, Texas. He was a real person.

Over the next few days, I grew even more impressed. The former president and his traveling group had rooms in the ship's Owner's Suite. Linda and I discovered our cabin was the closest one to his group of rooms. We like to think we were vetted by the Secret Service and found to be the most mundane, least threating people on the trip. Twice, I opened the door to get the newspaper just as Bush walked by my door. He always showed a big grin and stuck out his hand with a strong, "Good morning!"

At one shore excursion, I remember getting off the tour bus at the same time as the distinguished Jonathan Spence, the popular Yale professor and author of the 916-page *The Search for Modern China*. I wanted to impress him, so I told him I had read every bit of his book in preparation for the trip. He had a big smile and replied, "Really?! I've never met anyone who has read that whole book besides me!" He laughed.

Linda was really impressed with Sidney Rittenberg, an American who'd stayed in China and become part of Mao's inner circle, only to be tortured by him and his regime. She had several onboard conversations with him and remains fascinated by this charming man to this day.

The lectures on history were fantastic. The people who gave us insights into the normalization of US-China relations were the very people who made those decisions. The lectures and discussions described their successes and failures and their good and bad decisions. For me, these events were enthralling. I tried to envision what I would do before they gave their decisions. Unconsciously, I began to realize these people, though brilliant, made decisions the same way we did when we running our businesses. We looked at the facts and tried to find answers or information to fill in the gaps in our puzzles, then we took the actions that appeared to yield the best result. So did they.

When Faith Lights the Way

I began to understand that the world is full of people who are trying to do the right thing. Good people trying to make decisions that will benefit others and themselves.

The Bush party left us when we docked at Shanghai, but the balance of the trip was just as outstanding as the beginning. We visited some storybook places and got to know some fabulous people.

The next leg of our trip was in stark contrast to our World Leaders fantasy cruise. *China by train and bus.* At the end of our Asian cruise, Linda and I left wonderfully vibrant, bright, modern, affluent Hong Kong and headed to Shenzhen, China, by train to meet Stewart Crane of Barefoot Power. When we got off the train, it was like stepping into another world. The smog and air pollution were so thick street lights should have come on, but there weren't any street lights. I could feel a sore throat coming on with every breath. There was an industrial, metallic, toxic smell in the air. So many people were everywhere, all around me, touching me, talking fast. There was no personal space in China.

Stewart and Harry led unusual lives, having met while in Nepal working for the Australian Peace Corps building small electric systems. They were living in a hostel that cost them ten dollars a week.

They both had master's degrees. Stewart's was in Electrical Engineering. They had the most extensive business plan I had ever seen, as well as a number of intensive pro forma, or forecasts, of how they were going to succeed. Both guys were extremely brilliant and had been immersed in their work for so long that it was all they knew to talk about. It was a little difficult for me to carry on a conversation with them.

In a rented van, we drove past street after street of shops the size of one-car garages with roll-up metal doors. Each one looked like the one beside it and the one after it. The only way to tell one shop from another was by looking inside at the work being done. One contained old rusted car frames that were being assembled into usable automobiles—or maybe they were being cut apart for scrap. Inside the open door I saw a man in a chair, welding pieces together or cutting them apart—without

A Study Abroad

eye protection. Another shop looked to be a furniture maker, and another was stacked with mattresses.

Barefoot Power's shop was like all the other garages, except it opened onto a park, a bare stretch of worn, packed dirt dotted with sporadic grass and weeds. Right outside the door sat an old table where two old men played mahjong. Linda tried to take a picture of them, but they shooed her away. Stewart explained that people in the less touristy parts of China felt that having their picture taken could affect their soul.

Once inside the shop, they showed us their inventory of solar panels and desk lamps. They talked about their new circuit board designs for the batteries and their product test plans to reduce the rate of failure. It was all very fascinating. These guys really had a grand plan.

After about an hour of touring the shop, we walked three blocks to a small restaurant that sat about twenty people. If you enjoy spartan ambiance, you would have loved it. The chairs were plastic, and the tables had red and white checkered tablecloths. In the center stood a galvanized pail, so it had the feel of a barbecue restaurant in a small town in South Texas. I wondered what the pail was for. The menu had pictures, so we picked something that looked like cashew chicken. The staff brought us a pot of hot tea, cups, and saucers, and a porcelain bowl-plate. Being conscious of the dreaded turista—traveler's diarrhea—we asked Stewart and Harry if they had gotten sick from eating there. They replied, "We worried about that at first, but the cook showed us what to do. Watch." They took the pot of boiling hot tea, poured some into the bowl-plate, swished it around and poured it into the galvanized pail. "We haven't gotten sick yet." Linda and I did the same. The food smelled great and was delicious! And we didn't have any stomach problems afterward.

Stewart and Harry had to return the rented the van, so they couldn't take us back to the train station, but they offered to take us to a hotel where we could catch a bus. They arranged two seats for us on what resembled a Volkswagen Microbus from the 1960s, although I am sure it was a Chinese product. Every seat was filled. Linda sat in front, and I sat

When Faith Lights the Way

with two guys cramped up against the side of the van on the back row. Beyond the window, we could see bicycles everywhere, loaded down with stuff. And I mean *loaded*, to the point where stuff was stacked at least ten feet high: mattress foam, furniture, car parts, and people.

As the dull sunlight faded and we passed street after street, I began to worry. What if something happened and we had to find our way out of here? There was no way. I didn't have a clue where we were. What if we were kidnapped? No one knew we were here. *Oh, boy, what have I done?*

Thankfully, I had a diversion that helped me forget my concern. The Chinese man crammed in next to me spoke English and was very excited to practice polite conversation. He was a salesman for a factory in Shenzhen that made black dress pants for men. Two days a week he rode this bus, spent the night somewhere near the train station, and the next day, went to Hong Kong to try to sell men's black dress pants to the Hong Kong shops. We discussed politics and other subjects I can't remember, but he made me forget my fears. We boarded the train back to Hong Kong and, once there, dragged ourselves back to our hotel. The next day we returned home to Texas.

Our Asian journey was one of the most life-changing vacations of my life. I learned that stepping out of my boat could open the door to adventure and excitement. Never in my life did I dream I would be in China, conversing with people like President George H.W. Bush or a Chinese stranger on a bus. I had overcome my insecurities, quieted my fears, and found inner strength. I was navigating new waters and growing in confidence as I forged ahead.

A Plan in Motion

Getting a Clear Picture

Linda and I had been contemplating my retirement date since I wanted a change of careers, and we were eyeing December of 2008. After our trip to China and subsequent meeting with Sam Dixon at General Conference in April, I knew we needed to move up the date. My focus had shifted almost exclusively to Ganta Hospital, and the project was going to take a lot of my time. I was committed to pursuing my plan to do electric work in underdeveloped countries. It was not fair to my employer for my heart to be elsewhere. Priester Supply had been purchased by Stuart C. Irby, which was then acquired by Sonepar, an electrical distributor headquartered in France. I felt more changes were coming for Priester/Irby, as the company moved further under the Sonepar umbrella.

I officially submitted my resignation on May 4, 2008, to our president, Mike Wigton, and the utility-group senior VP, Jim Cameron. Both were extremely understanding and supportive of my plans.

I had now stepped completely out of the boat. It is both scary and liberating to walk away from something you've done for more than half your life and that brought you much success. I was nervous, but motivated.

When Faith Lights the Way

Now that I was working only on Power From the SON (PFS), it was time to focus on design engineering, procuring, and constructing an electric power system in Liberia. We needed information on the Ganta Hospital and Mission's current facilities, and on any future additions they were planning. Normally, when a utility designs a system addition for a subdivision or shopping center in the United States, a copy of the site survey from the developer or architect is provided, as is information on how much electricity the customer will initially use and a projection of the usage forty years in the future. That was likely not going to be the case for us.

All electric utilities custom design and build their systems to fit their unique situations. Storms and/or heat have a big effect on design and construction specifications. Lines inside a city might be underground or designed to accommodate high customer growth. Conversely, lines in rural areas must be designed to serve customers at the end of long lines and still give them quality electricity. In every design, the physics and characteristics of electricity are a keystone.

Over the years, utilities have developed strict design specifications. Electric utilities use customized computer design programs that analyze a massive amount of details then create an optimal design to serve each unique customer. These programs also define the type and size of material needed, outline construction specifications to ensure safety, and provide quick and simple installation methods that maximize the life of the systems. Basically, the specifications work to produce electric systems that are safe, reliable, easily installed, and long-lasting.

We had no site survey nor specifications. There was, fortunately, a solution that had been developing behind the scenes for months. The solution was a fortuitous opportunity that's difficult to call a chance happening. It must have been an unseen hand helping us paddle our boat down the river.

Harry Andrews from Barefoot Power was in the process of moving to Ghana, West Africa. He agreed to visit Ganta to map the site and

A Plan in Motion

document the electricity needs of each building. We paid him $7,000 to travel to and spend a week at Ganta and to submit a report of his findings. It was far less expensive than having one us make the trip from Texas. Besides, Harry had experience traveling around Africa, providing power in remote, underdeveloped areas, and he knew just what information was needed; we didn't. Harry arrived in Ganta on May 11, 2008, and began his work. Our haphazard Internet research had certainly paid off.

We turned our attention to figuring out how to acquire the materials we would need. It's not uncommon for a utility to discontinue using materials as safer, quicker, or better products enter the market. This leaves the utility, its distributors, and manufacturers with quality items that now sit on the shelf gathering dust. Most distributors or manufacturers declare these items as obsolete inventory with zero value and will throw away the materials or sell them for scrap. Utilities, on the other hand, tend to hang on to their zero-cost items. It was a gold mine. Our solution for acquiring materials was to ask utilities, distributors, and manufacturers to donate their obsolete material to PFS.

It wouldn't be a win just for us, but also for the companies that helped us. Think of the PR value in donating material to electrify a hospital in Africa, contributing to saving thousands of lives. And a more practical benefit, the companies were creating usable space in their service centers and warehouses. These donations proved mutually beneficial for manufacturers, distributors, utility companies, PFS, and most importantly, for people in the developing world.

Because we were acquiring the material in the United States, it would need to be delivered to Liberia. None of us had ever shipped anything overseas, and we had no knowledge of the business, logistics, or cost of shipping internationally. We discussed the matter with Sam Dixon, and he estimated the cost to ship to Liberia to be $10,000. Feeling optimistic, we planned to buy and acquire the material in June, ship it to Liberia the first of August, and do the work in September. It seemed simple enough. We were quite naive.

When Faith Lights the Way

While we waited for Harry's report, I assessed the different skill sets we needed for the project and considered who we could ask to join the team. Ron Seidel could help us with the generators, Frank Daniels with the engineering, Steve Hawrylak and Mark Abbe with material procurement and transport to Liberia, and I could do a little of it all, including the installation. But we didn't have anyone to direct the installation of a project this size, especially one in remote Africa, on a tight time schedule. I struggled with a problem: *Who do we get to be the general construction manager?* I had no answers. Then one Sunday, as I sat in the balcony at FUMC Arlington, listening to the sermon, a voice in my head said, "Terry Thornhill."

Terry and I met while serving as instructors during the 1980s and 1990s for the National Underground Training School (NUTS), which was sponsored by the Texas A&M Extension Service. It was a weeklong school held once a year at a repurposed World War II airbase. I was on the planning committee and served as one of about twenty instructors who taught students how to install underground electrical systems. In an area about the size of a football field, we instructed students in the right way to install electric power to one house, many houses, and even a shopping center, and how to troubleshoot and fix problems. The instructors were from electric cooperatives, investor-owned utilities, and utility installation contractors; they were some of the most experienced crew foremen in the business. I was the only engineer in the group.

Engineers make fun of linemen and think they have no education. Linemen think engineers can't do anything but sit in an office and come up with designs that the linemen must change to make them work in the real world. I was proud to be accepted by these guys as someone who could build things. I taught a classroom course in how to put fittings on primary underground cable designed to carry electricity from 7,200 volts up to 19,990 volts. Splicing and adding connectors to this type of cable required skilled craftsmen. It was my job to talk in a language the

A Plan in Motion

linemen understood, explaining why it was important to do the work the right way so it would last forty years. I gave hands-on instruction on how to get electricity from the wires from overhead lines on poles to the underground wires.

Terry worked in the electric business until he enlisted in the US Marine Corps, where he served his country for twelve years. He fought in the Vietnam war and was in Saigon during its fall in 1975. After the war, he returned to TLT Construction, as a "grunt"—the lowest level of utility field worker—then worked his way up to vice president. Terry had a quiet confidence and the eye of the tiger, and he knew how to get the job done and how to get men to follow him.

After our stint at NUTS, I rarely saw Terry. I did remember hearing that he had become a strong believer in Christ. In fact, about two years prior, he had asked me to go to a Promise Keepers gathering in Dallas with him. Unfortunately, I had been unable to attend. That was my last contact with Terry.

As soon as church was over, I walked outside and called him. "I need your help," I said. I need you to go with me to Africa to build an underground system for a hospital that has no electricity and serves twenty-four thousand patients a year. It's charity."

To my surprise, he replied, "When do we leave?"

Well, I thought, *we have our installation expert!*

His only stipulation was that he would not eat rice. He said after Vietnam, "I will *never* eat rice again." He meant it.

Doubling Down

The design and construction team was coming together at home. Harry Andrews had made his way to Ganta, Liberia, to document the situation and prepare our report, which arrived in two weeks, on May 26, 2008.

It was exactly what we needed and more! Harry's report provided a clear summation of what we were facing. If we had gone there and

When Faith Lights the Way

stayed two weeks, we wouldn't have brought back nearly as much information as he provided. For months we consulted the report for answers and direction.

The first part was an Excel spreadsheet that listed every building in the mission and everything in those buildings that used electricity: light bulbs, fans, refrigerators, medical equipment, etc. It listed the size of every light bulb and how much electric power each fan used, and for the hospital and woodshop, it told us which items used three-phase power and how much electricity each used. We knew how many hours a week each light bulb or wood saw in the shop was used.

The second part described in detail the diesel generators on the property, providing pictures and diagrams of the generators and how the system was connected to the generators. We learned how many hours a day each operable generator was used and how much fuel each generator consumed. Harry sent pictures of the two generator houses—one by the hospital and one across a paved road, on the mission side.

The third section described all the facilities that were connected to the electric system. Harry had measured the distances between buildings and hand drawn maps of the buildings, plant life, and terrain. There were fifty-two buildings on the site, thirty-three of which were connected to the electrical system. A two-lane, paved main road cut through the site, with the mission facilities on the south side and the hospital on the north. These two facts alone should have alarmed us.

Ganta mission was the size of Central Park in New York City, or 781 football fields! This would be a huge project under any circumstances, but especially in a remote location in Africa. This might have been the perfect time to tell Sam Dixon and UMCOR, "We're sorry, but this is too much, we can't do this."

In truth, UMCOR and Power From the SON had different goals and expectations for this project. UMCOR expected us to go in and fix a few things to make the system work. The system was in such bad shape, though, that our experience told us it had to be completely replaced.

A Plan in Motion

Our attempt to do this project flew in the face of logic. A project of this nature in the United States would require many skilled workers, sophisticated equipment, and a lengthy timeline to complete. And yet, we were so naive as to believe we could accomplish this impossible project with far, far less. It never occurred to us to have doubt. We just kept our minds focused on the mission. We were well outside of our boats and not looking back.

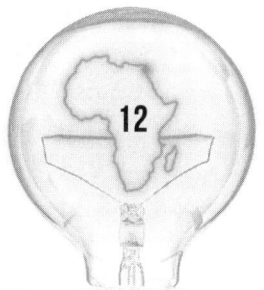

Good, Better, or Best?

With Harry's report as the guide, we moved forward with designing the electrical system for Ganta Hospital and Mission. We had two options: run the electric lines on poles overhead, or bury the wires underground. In the early years of building electric systems, all the lines were run on poles; holes were dug and poles were set by hand. Equipment was installed using ropes and pulleys. Linemen climbed poles with spikes attached to their boots and belts that wrapped around the poles. The methods were primitive, and it was tough and dangerous work.

Today, specialized trucks dig the holes and set the poles in the ground; lineman are safely maneuvered into position by sophisticated rigs with waist-deep, fiberglass, insulated buckets. None of these specialized trucks and equipment were available in the bush of Africa. If we were to build the lines overhead, we would have to go back to the old methods of pole-line construction.

Laying underground lines requires sophisticated equipment, too. It's also quite a bit more expensive, but for what we planned to do, underground construction had more practical advantages. Mainly, there would be no poles for lightning, hurricanes, and windstorms to damage. And logistically, we could substitute machine work for manual labor for a lot of the work that needed to be done. By doing so, we would have the

When Faith Lights the Way

opportunity to work *with* the Liberians and not just build them something and leave. They would get to have some skin in the game.

From a timing perspective, the Ganta Mission could start the project before we arrived by hiring locals to dig the ditches with shovels. Once we arrived with the material, we would place the cable in the ditches. We could put a strong steel pipe through the hole in the middle of reels and rest the pipe on high enough supports so that the bottoms of the reels were a few inches off the ground. Then we could easily pull the cable off the reels and into the ditches. Once in place, the cable would be covered with dirt.

We could move the heavy equipment using similar methods to the ancient Egyptians', pushing the equipment forward, rolling it on heavy steel, six-inch-diameter, four-foot-long steel pipes. As the unit moved forward, a pipe would be uncovered at the back. Then we could pick up that pipe, run it around to the front, and push the equipment onto the newly placed front pipe. Installing underground systems requires a few skilled craftsmen to install the fittings, like splices on the cable, but a lot of the work could be done by unskilled labor with the right training.

One day after receiving Harry's report, we had settled on the direction the project should take. We were going to provide Ganta United Methodist Hospital and Mission with a world-class underground electric system. From Harry's report, we surmised that we had three crucial technical issues to resolve before we could finalize our design. One, we needed to figure out how to practically transform the output of the mission generators to 7,200 volts. Two, we had to calculate the impact of using American-produced 60 Hertz material in Liberia, where 50 Hertz was standard. And three, we needed to combine the mission-side and the hospital-side electrical systems into one.

For context, Ganta's generators produced 240 volts. But to supply electricity to all fifty-two buildings, they needed to distribute the electricity at 7,200 volts and then reduce the voltage back to a useful 240 volts. If we distributed electricity at 240 volts over those long distances of the mission

Good, Better, or Best?

grounds, fans and motors would burn out quickly, and lights would not be as bright. We needed a transformer that would raise the voltage to adequately distribute the electricity throughout the campus and different transformers that would then lower the voltage to levels appropriate for powering small appliances and lighting buildings and houses.

In the United States, electricity completes 60 cycles, or Hertz (Hz), every second. In European and African systems, it completes 50 cycles in one second. When you design a transformer to carry a specific amount of electricity, you must consider the Hertz of the system where it will operate. Without going too deep into the electrical engineering woods and discussing all the problems and considerations, we would use American 60 Hertz transformers on Ganta's 50 Hertz system.

The mission housed its two generators, a 225Kw unit and a 312Kw unit, in one location. The hospital housed its three generators—an 82.5Kw unit, a 27Kw unit, and an 18kw unit—in another. Not all of them were functional or in use. It would be easier and more efficient to house all the units in one facility, so we planned to locate all the generators in the mission's generation house because it had the most room.

The solutions for each of these issues added complexity and expense to an already challenging and costly project.

In a stroke of good fortune, Stuart C. Irby President Mike Wigton had pledged to donate sixteen padmount transformers that had been removed from inventory and were being written off. The cost of these transformers at the time was about $1,300 each, so it equated to a $20,000 donation—a significant gift for PFS.

With our plan solidified, Frank Daniels completed drawings of the system and identified where the transformers were to be located and where the cable was to be run. Steve Hawrylak drafted the list of materials we needed and distributed it to our construction and design team experts for refinement. We would have to purchase some items, but we hoped to

When Faith Lights the Way

secure most through donations. My spirits were high. We had a team of volunteers who were successful in their areas of expertise, and everyone was passionate and eager to contribute and give input. I was not a leader; I was a cat herder, and these giant cats were the best in the business.

Liberia had no standard practices or mandatory guidelines to follow at that time, and we were free to proceed as we best saw fit. In the absence of official rules and regulations, we came up with our own. First, we would specify all the material needed, accepting options when our design had to be modified during construction due to unforeseen issues. Second, the design must be safe to construct and to operate. Third, design and installation must withstand the harsh landscape and unpredictable infrastructure of a developing country. These factors guided our decision making and influenced the type of material we requested for donation.

With our plans finalized and our material list in hand, we set out to contact every friend, acquaintance, colleague, and client we had in the utility industry.

Friends in High Places

Stuart Irby hosted a going away party for me and invited a lot of friends I'd worked with throughout my career. I used the opportunity to give a presentation on Power From the SON and its mission, and some of the manufacturers in attendance pledged to donate material. Mike Wigton offered $60,000 in material, and a vice president of Oncor would give $40,000 worth of wire and cable. It was further affirmation that I should step out of the boat.

In July we sent out a newsletter about the Ganta Hospital and Mission project to our contacts, hoping to encourage material and financial donations. While preparing this newsletter, I noticed the stark difference between the patient-to-doctor ratios of Ganta Hospital and the Harris Methodist Hospital in Fort Worth. According to their website in 2008, Harris Hospital served 33,000 patients per year with over 800 physicians and access to 710 beds. The United Methodist Hospital in Ganta served

Good, Better, or Best?

24,000 patients with three physicians and eighty beds. Staring at these numbers, I knew that whatever happened we could not let this project fail. Too many people depended on us.

In August, a great gift came from Joe and Becky Nusbaum, owners of ACP International. ACP is a sign manufacturer and a distributor of safety products for utility, telecom, pipeline, government, and commercial applications. ACP had a large warehouse in Arlington, Texas, and they offered to let us receive, store, package, and ship the material for our project there. This was very timely, because Irby wanted to ship us the sixteen padmount transformers they had donated ASAP. Each unit weighed a little over 1,100 pounds. The ACP International facility had forklifts that could unload a thousand-plus-pound box of steel, iron, and oil from a truck and move it around with ease.

We had the material logistics solved at home, but how were we going move material to and around the job site in Ganta? Surely we could find a used tractor, something with a front loader and backhoe that could move heavy equipment, dig trenches, and cover them up with the front loader. We began looking for a used unit in a price range practical enough for us to buy and leave in Liberia. As with everything else, we were optimistic and relying wholly on faith.

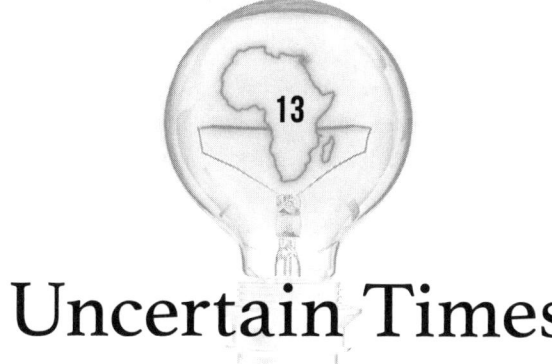

Uncertain Times

There is a cynical, humorous statement along the lines of, "No good deed goes unpunished." Well, it's the truth. 2008 was not the year to leave work and start a charity, especially one that requires the level of funding we needed. Even by 2016, the world had not completely recovered from the financial collapse of 2008. The Dow Jones Industrial Average dropped more than 50 percent between October 2007 and March 2009, and it plummeted to historic lows in October 2008. Housing prices plunged, banks and stock brokerage houses failed and had to merge with stronger banks, companies closed or right-sized their staff to survive the collapse. Those with money in equity markets were hurt the most during this crisis.

Two years earlier, in February 2006, we'd sold Priester Supply to Stuart C. Irby. It was professionally and financially rewarding. I became the vice president of Utility Sales West; I didn't work or travel as much, and my stress lessened. I had stock options, and I didn't spend a lot of my time worrying about money. At the time of the sale, I had run the numbers and felt confident that I could support my family for the rest of our lives living the same way we'd been living. Then, guess who saw a drastic drop in net worth?

I still had two girls in college—one in graduate school at Northwestern and one working on an undergraduate degree at Texas A&M. The

When Faith Lights the Way

first thing I did every morning was see what had happened to us the day before and run more numbers. I was constantly worrying about what would happen the next day. Would we make it? And what about Power From the SON? Companies were cutting back. How would I get material or financial donations? I was panicked, but I reminded myself that I was better off than some of the patients in Ganta hospital. Linda and I discussed our predicament, and we decided we had to keep trying, to keep funding the project.

This was going to be a more involved and longer process than I had planned. There was a lot more to do before we were ready to venture to Africa. We still had to find out what material would be donated, refine our designs based on the material we received, buy and assimilate the material, buy a container, and ship everything to Liberia. We needed to find Liberian workers to help with the installation, learn what shots and visas were required, and book our flights.

It was clear that our goal of installing the electric system in 2008 wasn't feasible as we faced the reality of how much there was to accomplish and how slowly donations were coming in. The team had already discussed moving our construction trip to late April and early May of 2009.

In September, we began the long, rigorous process to establish Power From the SON as a legal charity. Over several months, we worked with our lawyers and accountants to prepare the necessary documents to apply for 501(c)(3) tax-exempt status. We submitted our Form 1023, Application for Recognition of Exemption Under Section 501(c)(3), on December 3, 2008.

While the application process was underway, we didn't see any reason we would not receive nonprofit status, so we continued planning for our trip. In the interim, we had material or funds donated to United Methodist Committee on Relief, a long recognized and respected 501(c)(3), until we received our approval from the Internal Revenue Service.

I wrote to Sam Dixon with an update on our progress. We had about $75,000 worth of equipment donations, and I planned to loan the

Uncertain Times

money needed to complete the project and repay myself after donations came in. I asked for his blessings and support before we started spending money we couldn't get back.

In the meantime, we continued to contact companies and manufacturers all over the country that might have material we could use. Steve Hawrylak and I had dealt with manufacturers, investor-owned utilities, and electric cooperatives all over the United States. We knew the material we needed was in someone's storeroom—we just had to convince them to help us.

We continued to press forward, believing that everything would eventually fall in to place. However, the beginning of 2009 was a frightening period. I was still watching our nest eggs crack while running daily spreadsheets to determine whether Linda and I would have enough to maintain our lifestyle. Maybe the solution was to abandon Power From the SON's effort to electrify the Ganta Hospital and Mission and look for employment. Not many jobs were available, as businesses were in the process of retiring long-term employees to reduce expenses and weather the economic storm. We tried to ignore the economy and focus on our project, but even that didn't always lift our spirits.

I was disappointed that our plan to secure support from the investor-owned utilities had not panned out. Their bureaucracy was formidable, and we never found the right person to open the door. The larger the entity, the more difficult it was to get assistance.

There were some encouraging bright spots with material donations, however. Irby came through with the transformers and some other items, Petroflex donated connection boxes, ACP International gave us tools and personal safety gear, TLT Construction provided more tools, and GVEC Electric Co-op designed and gave us some much-needed equipment. A few individuals also donated personal tools. We received

When Faith Lights the Way

an additional $71,000 in donated material, but this wasn't nearly enough to fund the project.

Retirement was not going the way I had planned. I found my days taken up with chores around the house and way too many hours lying in front of the television. I was bored. I had left a thirty-five-year career where I'd always worked more than ten hours a day and traveled extensively. In my early years, I was given a sales territory and essentially managed it the way I saw fit. Later in my career, I managed several branches throughout the Southwest. Every day at work, there was something new. Every day had a new crisis to solve. There were huge contracts to win or lose. Tornadoes or ice storms ripped down lines and required twenty-four-hour, seven-day-a-week efforts to restore electric service to those without power. I was stimulated. I was important.

Looking around at my life during retirement, I had given all that up. My dream to give electricity to the world was grinding to a halt. It reminded me of a huge train engine, strong and powerful, slowly running out of fuel. It was in this depressed state of mind that I wrote again to Sam Dixon in January 2009. It was followed by an encouraging response, but not the magical salve that I needed.

E-mail to Sam Dixon, January 5, 2009:

> Sam, I need some encouragement or, better still, some help. The end of 2008 means that it is doubtful that I will receive any more material donations for the electrical work on the Ganta Hospital until maybe late next year. At present we have about $75,000 worth of material donated. I think it will take a total of about $200,000 to do the job the way we have designed the project. It may take another $50,000 to do the onsite digging, the shipping of the material, and the transportation of the skilled labor from the United States to Ganta and back.

Uncertain Times

I have sent out e-mails and called everyone I know, but with this economy, I am struggling. I have some avenues left, but they are not my preferred choice.

1. We are in the process of doing alternate designs that will provide overhead lines from the existing facilities to the new hospital. This will reduce material costs. The overhead lines could continue to allow lightning to be a problem.
2. I have applied for 501(c)3 status and should hear back in the next sixty days. This will allow me to take donations and receive grants, but it may take too long.
3. I can loan Power From the SON some of the needed funds, but I can't cover the entire needed amount.

I would really like to do this in April and May before the rainy season starts.

You gave me this project, but I am feeling like I am letting you down. I am willing to visit with anyone you suggest. I just need some help.

Stephen Vincent

E-mail from Sam Dixon, January 7, 2007:

Dear Stephen,

I am very grateful for your continued efforts in seeing this project through to its much-needed successful conclusion. Such projects require an enormous amount of effort. Thank you for all that you are doing. Funding for most of our projects is beginning to become difficult to find. Liberia is also a place that has over the years attracted a lot of contributions. There is definitely some donor fatigue as a visit to Liberia today does not show much in the way of improvements. However, the country is more stable than it has been in decades, and positive improvements to the infrastructure are underway thanks to the leadership of the new president. The church there is also quite

When Faith Lights the Way

strong and is ably served by Bishop John Innis. Bishop Innis and I met yesterday, and he is also quite grateful for your efforts.

Given the need and the local conditions, it is likely best to pursue the overhead lines. While it is not ideal, it will be a definite improvement.

UMCOR has done very little promotion of this project to help find donors. I will ask our director of communications, Michelle Scott, to be in touch with you to develop a story which we can use to help cultivate other donors. Hopefully, it will help close the funding gap.

I have been working in Africa since 1991. The one thing I have learned from that experience is patience. The continent is a challenging place to work.

Raising funds is an even greater challenge. But, let's stay the course, and we can see this through.

I still need to be in Texas in late January or early February. Others keep adding things to my calendar, so it has become a scheduling challenge. Hopefully, when it works out, we will be able to visit face to face.

Best regards,
Sam Dixon

 Strange as it seems, it was a comfort to know what we were attempting was not easy. Evidently, we weren't the first to become discouraged by the reality of trying to raise money for a good cause. We could make it happen. Power From the SON's ability, talent, and experience should be enough to electrify fifty-two buildings in one of the poorest countries in the world. If we gave it our best effort, surely it would be enough to make this project happen. But we needed funds.

 Linda and I did a lot of soul-searching. It was crystal clear that it was going to take a lot more personal money than I had anticipated: about $130,000. We realized that this project was unique, something that had

Uncertain Times

not been done before, and that people were outwardly supportive but inwardly skeptical. We didn't know anyone else in the world who was trying to help the needy in this manner. Many people were drilling water wells or providing clean water, many were educating and helping medically, and many were saving souls. We were trying to provide electricity to the developing world. You can feed people, you can educate them, and you can heal them, but it is difficult to do any of that effectively without electricity. Power From the SON had to prove that it could be done. Linda and I agreed we had to fund this first job. Then hopefully, help would arrive.

A Break in the Clouds

Finally, in February, we were granted a tiny ray of sunshine. Michelle Scott, the executive secretary for communications for UMCOR, sent us an e-mail notifying us that $40,000 was being earmarked for our project! The funds would come from the Liberia Emergency account, which supported "activity or intervention in response to an emergency or crisis situation," and our project qualified as intervention. We quickly submitted the required application and received the funds a few months later.

Up to that point, everything that could go wrong surely had, so with needed funding coming our way we began to feel better about making it all happen. With so much still to do, we still planned to arrive in Ganta on May 15 and return to the United States on May 30, which we communicated to the team in Ganta. We were confident we would have the whole facility up and running in two weeks. Our grand plan was to work with Firestone or Caterpillar to deliver the containers of our material, as we assumed both had a significant presence in Liberia. That was what we planned, but we had yet to contact them. Our heads in the clouds, we weren't going to let details stand in our way; we were going to make it happen. The pieces were falling into place!

In late February, I began to pester Terry Thornhill, our project manager, about some personnel gaps. We had plenty of experts to design

When Faith Lights the Way

and plan the project; what we now needed were skilled people to help us with construction. Some weeks before, Dr. Mosser, the senior pastor at First United Methodist Church Arlington, had encouraged his son, Ry, to join us. Ry was in his twenties and had worked on a farm his whole life. He wasn't afraid of hard work. We were excited to have him.

As usual, Terry came through and found other great additions to the team: Gary Wilson and his son, Wesley. Gary Wilson was a line superintendent for Guadalupe Valley Electric Cooperative (GVEC), overseeing the design, planning, and installation of their regular and contract crews. That's exactly the kind of experience and skill we needed. Gary joined GVEC in 1984 as a warehouseman and moved on to the line crew in a four-year apprenticeship program. He became experienced in both overhead and underground electric distribution construction methods and repair. Gary was promoted to general foreman, responsible for all the construction of underground electric systems within the GVEC service territory. As Terry said, "God is great, not just good!" Wes also had experience working on underground electric systems and was another enthusiastic twentysomething, willing to do more than his share of work.

We had also asked Chris Olson to join PFS in an official capacity as an accountant. Chris was another longtime member of First United Methodist Church and was a certified public accountant. He had a Master's in Accounting from Texas A&M University and extensive experience working with nonprofits. He was instrumental in helping us apply for nonprofit status. Chris would be joining us in Ganta, adding an extra pair of hands.

With spring approaching, we felt trapped between a rock and a hard place. We had to commit to a final material list, which we had revised several times over. But we were anxious about forgetting something or purchasing the wrong thing. Forgotten, missing, or wrong items would not be available in Liberia. We could not make a mistake. This was the "hard place."

Uncertain Times

The "rock" was that we needed to get the material ordered and delivered by a certain—approaching—date. The material needed to be shipped from the United States four to six weeks before we planned to arrive. We needed a week to pack the material, and from experience, we knew some of the material would be delivered late. We were running out of time, and Steve Hawrylak's patience for changes and new requests was running thin. We had reached the point where we had to move forward by faith, to let go of the sides of the boat and walk. By the middle of March, we settled on the material list and placed the final order.

With the balance of the material on order, we still had not solved our most challenging task, to find a transformer that could convert the electrical output of the generators to 7,200 volts. We looked at many different options, including having one specially designed. Utilities have standard designs, and manufacturers build transformers that work with those designs to make replacement easy and to reduce cost. Only a handful of niche manufacturers will build specialty units—they take longer and cost more money, and manufacturing machines must be reprogramed to build the one-off designs. So far, we hadn't found anything prebuilt that suited our budget or design, and it was becoming apparent that we would need a specialty unit.

At the end of March, and a couple of months away from our target travel dates, we still didn't have a transformer.

We began to wonder if our goal to install a modern underground electric system was too advanced. The teams in Ganta were comfortable with stringing small copper wires through trees. We were going so far in the opposite direction that, for them, our plans were beyond imagination.

It was exciting for us, but were we giving them something they didn't need? Was this too much for them to handle? Liberia was many years away from standardizing how the power system for the nation would be built. The choices were to wait decades for standards to be enacted, risking thousands of lives in the delay, or to build the best system we could. We decided to keep pressing forward.

When Faith Lights the Way

By this time, Steve Hawrylak had left Irby and was serving as director of purchasing and operations at Utility Supply & Service, which was part of Texas Electric Cooperatives, or TEC. TEC also owned and operated transformer repair facilities. Sometimes their customers didn't want the units returned, and TEC would keep them for parts, or to make a special unit. Steve approached TEC with our design plan and specifications, and they agreed to build it for us. They built and delivered the unit that would normally be produced in eight to ten weeks in two weeks! We had finally accomplished what seemed impossible. What a thrill when you step out of the boat and out of your comfort zone and moments like this happen.

This transformer is just one of the 211 unique items we purchased for the Ganta project. Most did not require as much engineering or have as short of a delivery requirement as the large transformer. We placed our orders and stored them in the ACP warehouse when they were delivered. Things were going according to plan. That is, until our primary cable supplier called to tell us they didn't have as much cable as their inventory indicated. They were 7,500 feet short, and they discovered the shortage on the day they were to ship the cable to us. *Oh boy,* I thought. We had designed our system around that cable construction, and we had already purchased our cable connectors based on using that type of cable. We put our heads together and looked for an alternative.

We needed a little over 18,500 feet of primary cable (the equivalent of three and a half miles), and we were 7,500 feet short. At $1.42 per foot, this was a big expenditure. Murphy's Law was at work again: Anything that can go wrong, will.

In the end we found a better cable, although a little more expensive. In the United States, strict specifications wouldn't permit the use of different cable construction on the same job. Strict specifications are fine when one has the infrastructure and supply chain to readily provide all the necessary components to get work done. But there are times when one's job—or one's life—does not go as planned. At those times you must ask yourself, what's most important? If I postpone until everything is perfect, does that give the best outcome? Or is it best to forge ahead and

Uncertain Times

do the best I can with what I've been given? It was an easy choice for us, and we've never found fault with our decision.

Now we had to figure out how to get all of our material from Texas to Liberia. None of us had any experience with shipping overseas, much less delivering sixty-five thousand pounds of material to rural Africa. I had hoped to ship the containers through Firestone or Caterpillar, but I hadn't made any inquiries about it. When I finally did, I learned that neither company was providing shipping services for nonprofits to Liberia at the time. We were on our own, but where did were even start?

It was suggested that we use a logistics solution provider, a shipping agent based in New Orleans with experience working on humanitarian projects. The agent would make sure the containers were picked up, taken to the port, and loaded on a ship that would get them to the destination on time. As best we could tell, they were as good as anyone, so we contracted them to move our containers to the Freeport of Monrovia, Liberia's main commercial port facility.

We chose to use the standard forty-foot-long container, which was eight-and-a-half feet tall by eight feet wide. By April, we had a ballpark calculation of how much room all our material would occupy in a container and concluded that we needed two containers. We considered leasing containers, but it wasn't a good solution since leasing required us to ship the empty units back to the United States. We could buy containers for $2,200 each, and it would cost us at least that much to return them. We decided to purchase two containers, and on the advice of our contacts in Liberia, we would leave them for Ganta United Methodist Church to use.

The hospital administrators were experienced in receiving material at the Freeport of Monrovia and worked through an organization called the Christian Health Association of Liberia (CHAL). CHAL would hire trucks to transport our containers from Monrovia to Ganta. The

When Faith Lights the Way

transport fees included getting the material through customs, loading, transportation, and unloading. They advised us to hire a crane or forklift in Monrovia and have it follow the containers to Ganta to help unload and move our material during construction. That idea just wasn't practical. It would cost too much to transport heavy unloading equipment five or six hours from Monrovia, pay for three weeks of use, and then pay transportation back to Monrovia after we completed construction. There had to be equipment we could use in the Ganta area. Sometimes when you're out of the boat and walking on water, you get pretty cocky about your own abilities.

With some of the biggest challenges in the process of being solved, we turned our focus to travel logistics—namely immunizations. Julie Warren was our guide on what to expect in Liberia. Julie attended First United Methodist Church in Mansfield, Texas, a town next to Arlington. At the time, she was serving as a volunteer mission coordinator for the Central Texas Conference, the regional body connecting United Methodist Churches in a portion of the state. She was a nurse, originally from England, and had taken doctors from Mansfield to Ganta. She gave us lists of personal items to take and explained the "tricks of the trade" in Ganta. She coached us on the administration of the Ganta hospital and what challenges we might face. Thanks to Julie, we had a clearer picture of what we were up against.

Toward the end of March, Julie came to FUMC Arlington to talk to us about the immunizations we would need for the trip. She stressed the importance of Malaria prevention. In fact, she strongly advised that if our doctors prescribed anything other Malarone, to insist on Malarone, even though other medications might be less expensive and require fewer doses. The strain of malaria found in Liberia is virulent, and you don't want to take any chances.

Besides malaria, we had to be concerned about potential exposure to other diseases or infections: diarrhea, intestinal parasites, AIDS, hepatitis A, hepatitis B, typhoid, dengue, filariasis, leishmaniasis, onchocerciasis (river blindness), cholera, and trypanosomiasis.

Uncertain Times

The prescribed shots and oral immunizations were required by the US Center for Disease Control for travel to Liberia. We received immunizations for hepatitis A, hepatitis B, polio, and typhoid. It took three trips to get all the hepatitis B shots.

We all received our International Certification of Vaccination or Prophylaxis, as approved by The World Health Organization. This yellow, foldable card is just as valuable as a passport when entering other countries. If the required immunization isn't listed on the yellow card, officials in foreign countries won't let you in.

Although we all were stressing about the project, we could rely on Terry Thornhill to inject a little humor. He sent me an e-mail that displayed true Texas wit:

I am about to pursue the immunizations and malaria prescription.

I guess I will have to find the Wilsons a doctor since his family doc is a veterinarian!

Since You're Going...

As word spread about our upcoming trip and project in Ganta, special requests for additional repairs and courier needs started coming in. We agreed to take on each request, even though it made an already aggressive timeline even tighter. Maybe it was the excitement, or the feeling that we could accomplish anything, that made us say, "Yes, sure!"

The first request was to patch 110 bullet holes in the Ganta water tower that stood about thirty feet above the ground on a lattice steel platform. The water tank was about twelve feet in diameter and eight feet high, with a cone-shaped roof rising about four feet above the rim. Terry guessed the bullet holes were from a fifty-caliber machine gun, destruction from the last civil war.

We then learned that the hospital and mission didn't have running water. Plastic PVC pipes had been installed before the war, but time, wear, and tear had taken their toll on the infrastructure. We bought all the material necessary to rebuild the fresh-water system that was supplied

When Faith Lights the Way

by wells. (We also bought forty-five cases of bottled water—about eighteen bottles per man, per day. It gets hot in Liberia, and we were going to need a lot of water.)

Even though the list of supplies we were shipping to Liberia was extensive, we agreed to transport books and educational materials being donated by First United Methodist of Mansfield to the mission's schools.

In April, we received an e-mail from Mark Schroeder, an anesthesiologist from Madison, Wisconsin, who had just returned from Ganta. He had installed a 220 volt, 50 Hertz anesthesia machine in the hospital's operating room, but the hospital generators didn't support it. Dr. Schroeder asked us to convert the system to one that would accommodate American *and* European equipment. Frank and I put our heads together and found a solution. It required additional equipment, and Dr. Schroeder agreed to wire the funds to cover the expense. Thankfully our suppliers could deliver another rush order!

Then later, just days before our departure, we received a request from James Labala, senior pastor at Miller McAllister UMC in Ganta, to bring brakes for his Subaru Outback. I thought to myself, *What in the world?* I suggested he go online, pick out what he needed, add up the cost, and get back to us, as there was no way for me to know exactly what he needed. I was hoping he would be sluggish in his response, but he responded quickly with the part numbers for the brakes *and* an air filter, for a total of $120.00. He said he would send the money the following day, but I suggested that he pay us when we arrived.

As if that wasn't enough, he asked me to call a friend of his and give her my mailing address so that she could send me a document to bring to him. There seemed to be no end. Terry and I grumbled about this for a while, but Terry bought the brakes and packed them with his luggage. I received the document and packed it with mine.

No Turning Back

It was time. It seemed like we filled out a whole tree's worth of paper forms to get the material shipped. There were bills of lading, duty-free permits, preshipment inspections called "BIVACs" (*bureau veritas*), shipping instructions, marine certifications for the containers, shipper-owned container request forms, cargo movement request forms, and more.

The process was difficult enough, and our shipping agent's confusing communications made it more so. Granted, we were probably too inexperienced to do all the right things, but it didn't help our stress to be told several times that we had missed deadlines we were not aware of, that our containers would not make it aboard the ship, and the material would not arrive on time.

Scared that we might miss our shipping window, the team met at ACP International on May 1 to pack the goods for the trip. Joe and Becky let us use their equipment to pack supplies for the shipment. It took us the entire Friday and Saturday, but we got all the material packaged, palletized, and secured for the long ocean journey.

The following Monday, our two empty containers arrived three hours apart at the ACP warehouse. We loaded all the wire and cable into one container with one large transformer and sent it toward the Houston port. As soon as we accomplished that task, the second empty

When Faith Lights the Way

container arrived, and we filled it with the rest of the transformers and miscellaneous material, secured the doors with a Power From the SON lock, and sent the second container on its way. Later that evening, I sent a long-awaited update to the team.

E-mail to the PFS team, May 4, 2009:

> Two totally full containers left Arlington, Texas, this afternoon for Ganta, Liberia. Everyone has done a marvelous job, and I can't think of a thing we are missing...but we will when we arrive and start construction. The two large transformers, one weighing 3,800# and one at 6,000#, are in the backs of separate containers. We must have a lifting device to remove them from the containers. The total shipment weighs about 65,000#.
>
> This has been an exciting, consuming experience. Thank each of you for your work thus far. The journey has begun. Pray for its completion.
>
> Stephen H Vincent

Our containers were shipped by Safmarine, an international shipping company. We could track the location of our containers online in real time, just like seeing a car's location and progress on a smartphone. Each intermodal shipping container has a unique number, and using that number and the shipping line, we could follow our container using marine tracking websites. These websites posted the planned route and dates of our shipment. The sites showed the ship's speed, direction, destination, and scheduled arrival, and we could watch the ship maneuver around all the ships in its vicinity.

On May 8, 2009, we confirmed that our units were received in the Port of Houston on May 5, 2009, at 7:11 a.m. Our containers were on the Maersk Idaho, which was fully loaded by 5:27 that morning. The Maersk Idaho was scheduled to leave the Port of Houston at 10:00 and arrive in Algeciras, Spain, and be unloaded on May 19 at 8:00 a.m. Our containers would then to be loaded on the Maersk Claes, which would

No Turning Back

be fully loaded and ready to sail at 2:00 p.m. on May 25, 2009. Our shipment was to arrive at the Freeport of Monrovia on June 3, 2009, by 3:00 p.m. The technology that makes this possible is amazing—a stark contrast to the *lack* of technology we were about to encounter.

With the United States to Liberia shipping logistics sorted out, I could now focus on all that needed to happen once the containers and the team arrived in Liberia. I was becoming obsessed with finding a cost-conscious (free) way to get the material out of the container once it arrived in Ganta. Sam Dixon suggested I contact the country director of the Peace Corps in Liberia. No help from the Peace Corps, but they recommended we contact the chief of civil-military coordination for the United Nations Mission in Liberia. Sam forwarded one of my many e-mails to James Glass, who had served in the US Military and was acquainted with several officers stationed in Liberia who were assigned to help Liberians rebuild the country. James was confident that the United Nations Mission in Liberia (UNMIL) could help us dig the trenches and unload the containers. Hopefully that would be the solution to our biggest remaining problem. Of course, there were quite a few smaller problems left to solve. I was bombarded with a steady stream of questions, but I had very few concrete answers. We didn't have confirmed travel dates, and some team members couldn't fully commit to the trip until we did. Frank Daniels had a knee replacement operation but planned to go, but he wouldn't be at 100 percent.

The good news is that two new team members were joining us. Harrell Burr, a part-time electrician and jack-of-all-trades, would work with the Ganta electrical staff to mount the conduit and meter bases on the walls of the buildings and homes and then show the Liberians how to connect the power to the inside wiring. Pinkie Pinkston was highly experienced with generator installation, and he had worked on relief projects in Africa with the Texas Baptist Men, a volunteer disaster-response group.

We now had our team of experts *and* experienced professionals.

Loose Ends

Summer 2009.

James Glass was still trying to help us secure on-the-ground assistance in Liberia. He made a request for support to John Innis of the United Methodists of Liberia. The e-mail he sent was so elegant and complimentary that I began to think what we were doing was a big deal! And reading the fast response from Bishop Ennis, I thought maybe we were going to get someone with diplomatic muscle to help us find the equipment we needed! If we just worked hard and were bold, good things would happen!

James Glass e-mail to Bishop Ennis, May 20, 2016:

> Dear Bishop Innis,
>
> Greetings to you, my brother in Christ.
>
> I am writing to inform you that a very large and important shipment of electrical equipment is headed to Liberia this month for installation at Ganta Hospital. Yesterday I met with the CEO of the organization responsible for this. The estimated value is over $500,000!

When Faith Lights the Way

Mr. Stephen Vincent has been working with UMCOR and with Victor at Ganta to coordinate the shipment. You may indeed be aware of this undertaking. However, in the interest of ensuring that you are fully briefed, I have, with Mr. Vincent's knowledge, offered to contact you for this purpose. I will also be informing the Liberian desk officer at the Office of the Secretary of Defense and her counterpart at the Department of State because this fabulous gift deserves recognition in keeping with the partnership between our two nations. I have requested the assistance of Lieutenant Colonel Jeff Stansfield in contacting the commander of the Bangladeshi UN Battalion at Ganta, who may have a forklift that will enable the two very large and very heavy generators to be positioned on slabs at the new hospital site. So far, my attempts to reach him have failed—he may be away—but I will continue to try.

In the meantime, I encouraged Victor to approach the UN Battalion on his own because you and I both know there has been an openness and willingness on their part to be of help to Ganta Hospital. Through your contacts, you may have a better solution to offer. Whether Victor has made contact and/or has been successful, I do not know as of this writing.

Mr. Vincent is bringing with him a skilled team of professionals to facilitate the installation of this equipment. I am given to understand that Mr. Vincent's generosity includes cargo shipping and travel costs for the group. This is a remarkable and praiseworthy action and attests to his Christian faith and character. It is my personal hope that while he and his team are in-country, you would receive them.

May I say that Mr. Vincent et al., would very much benefit from having someone from your office meet them upon arrival and ensure that local accommodation and transportation issues are properly handled. I have a personal concern that the details of the transfer of the cargo from the docks to Ganta have the proper supervision,

Loose Ends

that the cargo is cleared promptly and without fees, and that the estimated costs of land transportation ($5,000) are indeed valid. You may wish to inform the Ministry of Health and the Office of Her Excellency President Ellen Johnson-Sirleaf of this project. I am sure you would agree with me that what Mr. Vincent and his organization are doing for Ganta will fundamentally affect the ability of that hospital to perform its mission and save lives.

John, obviously this is a mission of great importance to the people of Liberia and to the Liberian Annual Conference of the UMC. I will keep you informed of my contacts with State and Defense and how they might wish to support it as well.

I pray that you are well and enjoying time with your family. Please call me if you have any questions or requests.

Jim

Bishop Innis e-mail to John Glass, May 20, 2016

Dear James,

Thanks for the uplifting information. We will do our best to give Mr. Vincent the best of courtesy to make him feel welcomed and pleased. We appreciate all you have been doing for the ministry of the church in Liberia. Victor will be on top of everything. He will be at the airport to receive the team and will do his best to provide accommodation in Monrovia before going to Ganta. Hope you can also inform Col. Jeff to help us in getting the container from the Port. He has been a very helpful person since I got to know him.

I extend your greetings to Frances and others. I hope to return home in early July.

When will Mr. Vincent arrive in Monrovia? Victor needs to know this.

When Faith Lights the Way

Jim, we have been searching for a 2000kw transmitter for our radio. Can you find someone to help in this regard? Our Christian radio station is making a difference, but the present transmitter is so small that it does not cover much area. We want to be heard as far as Ganta.

God bless you.

With the materials on their way to Liberia and efforts underway to secure assistance with unloading, we began finalizing the trenching design, which we would send to Ganta for a team to begin work in advance of our arrival. We would need about four miles of trenches. Using Harry Andrew's maps, Frank Daniels drew lines where the ditches should be dug. We added notations on how deep and wide the trenches should be and how close to a road or a building they should be dug. We scanned the drawings and e-mailed them to the Ganta administrators.

The plan was to hire fifty to seventy-five workers to dig the trenches with shovels. They would start before we arrived and continue to dig the ditches during the three weeks we would be in Ganta, staying ahead of our cable-laying operation. The trenches for the primary cable needed to be thirty-six inches deep and twelve inches wide. And the 240-volt service cable needed to be eighteen inches deep and the width of a shovel. It would be difficult, but the soil was sandy and easy to pierce, so we thought the schedule might be possible.

A week before we were scheduled to leave, we received confirmation from the United Nations Mission in Liberia (UNMIL) that a team of Bangladeshi engineering battalion based in Ganta would help with the trenching. Any concern we'd had about the getting the trenches dug was history. However, they did not have any equipment to unload or move the transformers.

I shared the news with Jim Glass, and we discussed other potential options. Based on his military experience, Jim believed it was possible the Bangladeshi team just might have some lifting equipment on site. We would hold out hope. Looking at the difficulties we had overcome already, somehow we believed it was going to turn out well.

Loose Ends

Organizing this entire process had been a logistical headache. Prioritizing tasks that are equally important, and with time and cost factors, is like a football game; there are so many different things going on at once, but the clock is ultimately in control. And the clock said it was time to confirm our travel plans and figure out how to get the PFS work crew to Liberia. We had been doing online research on flights since early April, but we decided not to book our flights until we knew when the container was scheduled to ship, and we planned to arrive in Monrovia about a week after the containers.. Hopefully, this would be enough time for the container to clear customs and be transported to Ganta. It wouldn't make sense for us to arrive before the material and equipment.

With the container scheduled to arrive at the Freeport of Monrovia on June 3, we settled on a June 6 departure date, arriving in Liberia on June 8. We had limited flight options, as there were only three flights a week to Monrovia available to us. The tickets for nine people cost $18,360.00. The visas cost $1,180.00.

There was only one last loose end to tie up. I wanted to take a token of appreciation for the Bangladeshi military team who would be helping us. Our entire team was from Texas, so I thought a two-by-three-foot Texas Flag would be the perfect gift. We would make them honorary Texans.

As Linda and I packed my bags, making sure I had the right things—towels, soap, battery-powered fans, batteries, snack food, work clothes, shower shoes, boots, hats, and safety sunglasses, we continued to monitor the progress of the ship carrying our container. It arrived at the Freeport of Monrovia on June 1, two days ahead of schedule. Things were looking good.

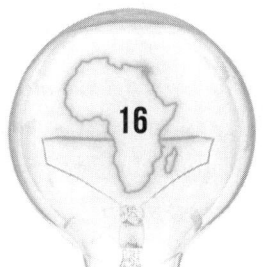

Into the Stormy Seas!

On Saturday, June 6, 2009, Terry Thornhill and Gary and Wes Wilson boarded flights from San Antonio and flew to Dallas/Fort Worth to meet Chris Olson, Frank Daniels, Ry Mosser, Pinkie Pinkston, Harrell Burr, and myself. It was the first time the entire team had met. We gathered outside the secured area and had our first team picture. After saying our goodbyes to family and friends, we headed to security. It was showtime. Our Continental flight left at 11:50 a.m., bound for Newark.

We landed in Newark at 4:42 p.m. We had an hour to grab something to eat and find the gate for our next flight. At 6:10 p.m., we left Newark for Brussels, Belgium, on a packed flight scheduled to last seven and a half hours.

The flight was calm until about forty-five minutes out from the coast, when we hit turbulence. Not just a little shaking, but *get me out of here!* turbulence. I've been on domestic and international flights with turbulence for over thirty-six years, but I can't remember another flight where the shaking was so bad, with the up, down, and sideways feel of a big roller coaster.

Harrell was remarkably calm, considering he'd never flown in his life. He showed no signs of panic or sickness, and he jabbered away about nothing, as usual. I remember looking at Chris, the accountant, who was

When Faith Lights the Way

engrossed in reading what appeared to be a manual. The young lady seated next to me reached for her relief bag and filled it up. We flew on, and the rough air continued. The lady next to me asked for her friend's relief bag. She filled it up. I thought maybe a bit of conversation might take our minds off the problem, so I asked where they were going. They told me excitedly how they were on their way to Europe to spend their vacation traveling around Europe, no plans, just taking life as it comes.

Chris, meanwhile, was still poring over his book. I turned to him. "Chris, doesn't reading through all this make you sick?"

"No," he replied. "It takes my mind off what's going on."

"What are you reading?" I asked.

"International Versus US Accounting: What in the World Is the Difference?" I knew that any accountant who could be that engrossed in an international accounting principles manual during a life-and-death situation was the best choice for Power from the SON.

Then the lady next to me asked, "Can I have your relief bag?"

"Do you need some medical help?" I asked.

"No, it's okay. I'm a doctor."

Good to know, I thought as I handed her my bag.

Finally, after about thirty minutes, the flight calmed, and we dozed a little as we waited for Belgium. We landed in Brussels at 7:45 a.m., or 12:45 a.m., Texas time. Of the nine of us, only two had traveled overseas in the last thirty-five years—Terry, who had been a Marine at the time on his way to Vietnam, and me. As the de facto tour guide, I was pleased that I had gotten them all this far.

We disembarked from our plane, went up many escalators and down long halls, located the gate number of our departing flight, went down more long halls, went through a comprehensive security checkpoint, went down escalators, waited in line to board a bus, rode to our departing terminal, went through another security checkpoint, and located our gate. That tedious description does not include bathroom breaks. Somehow all the "children" made it in one group.

Into the Stormy Seas!

Terminal T was rather spartan, with large glass windows looking out on the runways and a roof the color of aluminum, shaped like a Quonset hut with all the superstructure and piping in view. We did have access to a restroom, but people scheduled on our flight were kept in a secured area, separated from the other end of the terminal where the shops were located. There were uncomfortable chrome and synthetic material chairs. Our journey across the airport took about an hour, so we still had about two and a half hours to kill. We curled up on the floor and took turns napping, while those who remained awake kept a look out for our boarding time. At about two in the morning, Texas time, our enthusiasm began to wear off. The thrill was gone.

We boarded our Brussels Air flight for our next stop: Accra, Ghana. I'm sure these Texas boys were feeling like fish out of water. First, the flight attendant announcements were in French and English, and the ethnicity of the passengers changed from our flight across the pond. We now saw a predominance of Africans speaking many languages, and the second largest group of passengers were Chinese, which was most surprising to us. Texas is diverse with Caucasians, Black Americans, and Hispanics, all Texans, but it was a real treat to be immersed in all these different cultures.

Our flight left at noon Brussels time, and we settled in for a long, nine-hour journey to Liberia. Crossing Europe took a while—first the Alps, then the Mediterranean—before flying over North Africa and the Sahara Desert. The size of the Sahara startled me, as we seemed to take forever to get across this wasteland with nothing but rock and sandhills stretching as far as I could see.

Finally, we moved into Sub-Saharan Africa and began to see a little vegetation. As we made our way to Ghana, the sparse vegetation turned to tropical jungle. We were glad to land at the Accra airport, as it gave us a chance to stand up for a while after the almost five-and-a-half hour flight. Looking out the airplane window at Accra, I couldn't help but be impressed by the well-kept multistory buildings around the airport's gleaming white terminal, which was surrounded by well-manicured grounds dotted with palm trees. Many passengers had Accra as their destination—no doubt their home.

Security came onto the plane, and the remaining passengers were required to identify their carry-on luggage. The guards did a good job of searching the plane, running their hands in-between the seat cushions to look for unwanted items. Finally, they loaded the passengers from Accra that were headed to Monrovia and those who had plans to return to Brussels after our stop in Monrovia. After closing the doors, the flight attendant made an announcement that they would be briskly passing down the aisles of the plane, releasing a fog from an aerosol can that would kill any bugs that might have entered our plane during the stop. They said we would not be harmed. Maybe so, but the fog from that bug spray certainly smelled like it could harm us.

About an hour later, as the setting sun glimmered over the Atlantic Ocean and the hundreds of ponds and pools, we could see the lush forest surrounding Roberts Field, a little over thirty miles from Monrovia.

On board the Silver Sea in China in 2006 with President George HW Bush, wife Barbara, and the Aggies on the trip. Linda is beside Barbara.

TO GAIN INSIGHT INTO GANTA HOSPITAL, AN APPROXIMATE COMPARISON WITH HARRIS HOSPITAL, FORT WORTH		
BUILT	1926	1930
COMMUNITY SERVED	450,000	700,000
PATIENTS SERVED	24,000	33,000
NUMBER OF BEDS	80	710
EMPLOYEES	115 EMPLOYEES (3 PHYSICIANS)	OVER 800 PHYSICIANS
SERVICES	EMERGENCY ROOM, PEDIATRIC CARE, PRENATAL CENTRE, LABORATORY, OUTPATIENT CARE, EYE CLINIC, GENERAL MEDICINE, BASIC SURGERY, WOMEN'S HEALTH, TUBERCULOSIS TREATMENT, MALARIA & LEPROSY TREATMENT, HIV TESTING	EMERGENCY ROOM, PEDIATRIC CARE, SPORTS THERAPY, CANCER, DIABETES, EPILEPSY, GASTROENTEROLOGY, HEART & VASCULAR SERVICES, INFERTILITY, NEUROSCIENCE, REHABILITATION, STROKE CENTER, ORTHOPEDIC MEDICINE, PHYSICAL THERAPY

PFS newsletter

Water supply tower.

Material staged for loading onto the container for shipment to Liberia.

Departing DFW Airport.

SECTION THREE

Leading by Faith

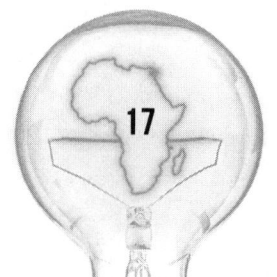

I Don't Think We're in Kansas or Texas

Day 1: Monrovia, Liberia

Sunday evening at 7:30 p.m., the Power From the SON volunteers landed at Roberts Field outside of Monrovia, twenty-six and a half hours after we'd left Dallas-Fort Worth Airport. Roberts Field is named after the first president of Liberia, and the airport played an important role in the Allied effort during World War II. Then it had been very dangerous to ferry men and supplies across the Atlantic by ship, so Roberts Field was essential to the North African Campaign. The United States and Britain flew supplies and men from Miami to Natal, Brazil, then on to a storage depot at Roberts Field. From there, supplies were flown to Morocco, Tunisia, and Algeria. Liberian natural rubber and Roberts Field were so essential to the US war effort that President Roosevelt visited Roberts Field in 1943.[7]

After World War II, there were many American, European, and African commercial airlines that serviced Monrovia from Roberts Field. The field was well maintained and had a very nice hotel only a few hundred yards from the terminal, where the airline crews stayed. It was a

When Faith Lights the Way

hub for good times until the Civil Wars started. We didn't find the airfield to be the welcome respite that travelers had experienced before the war.

It was dark when we deplaned. There were few lights around the terminal, and those we did see looked tired and dim. No lights could be detected in the surrounding countryside. We walked down the portable stairs from the plane to the tarmac. It seemed a remote and foreboding place. We walked through a door to the immigration checkpoint. The whole experience reminded me of what a rat must feel like in a maze—stiflingly hot, closed in, unsure about what waits around the corner. The immigration room was small and narrow and painted white; it had seen many years of wear and tear. Room lighting was not a priority. There was only one, slow-moving line for all of us passengers to clear immigration. We spoke in hushed tones. I'd traveled to several countries around the world, and I'd landed in some very small airports in the Caribbean. But this place made me uncomfortable. You can imagine how the rest of the group felt, having never traveled outside the United States. I tried to act cheerful and calm like it was no big deal, but I was sure they wanted to get back on that plane, and I didn't blame them.

Everyone lined up against a wall in a narrow corridor. We waited until it was our turn to step to a window about two-feet-wide and three-feet-tall, opening from a wooden protrusion in the wall the size of a telephone booth. When each person's turn came, he or she stepped up to the window, and a voice said something inaudible. If that person asked, "Beg your pardon?" and tried to lean in the window, the retort from the official became more agitated.

When I arrived, I handed the officer in the box the yellow vaccination card. He wrote on it and handed it back. He did this for each one of us, so I guess we all managed to pass. We went through a door and out of the maze, and *Oh, my gosh!* We'd reached baggage claim!

Every passenger on the fully loaded plane was crammed into a—you guessed it—dimly lit, drab room that had an old baggage carousel on one end. For every passenger, there were at least one and a half Liberians

I Don't Think We're in Kansas or Texas

wanting to help you with your bag. "Which is your bag? I will help you," each one would say.

"I don't need help."

"I was told to help you!"

"By whom?"

"The man outside, waiting for you!"

"What's his name?"

"You know, the man here to meet you!" He'd grab for your bag.

"I don't need help."

"Give me a dollar!"

We were elbowing our way through the crowd as our bags came around, trying to keep anyone from grabbing the bags we'd already retrieved.

"I will help you!" another man yelled, standing directly in my way.

Here we go again! I thought. Finally, we retrieved the last two checked bags and our two carry-ons, and we headed for customs. Thankfully, customs was uninterested in us all, and we quickly burst out into the steamy, dark night.

Looking around I thought to myself, *Boy, this place could use some lighting!* We gathered our bags in a circle, like a wagon train under attack, and tried to find someone named Victor who was coming to pick us up. He found us and directed us across the gravel street to two old, twelve-passenger vans that had seen better days. Guys grabbed our bags as we tried to make it toward the vans, and we had to back them off. Victor pointed out two or three guys who worked for him and told us he'd directed those particular men to help us with our bags. We made it to the van and started loading up our luggage. Some of the bag guys had infiltrated our assigned team of helpers, and they began pestering us for money. Ultimately, though, our luggage made it into the van.

Relief is getting into a beat up, hot, twelve-passenger van packed with luggage and people for the hour ride to Monrovia. Leaving the

When Faith Lights the Way

airport, we exchanged pleasantries and told Victor how excited we were to be in Liberia and how we looked forward to working with the Liberians on electrifying the hospital. Without alarming us, Victor gently told us the container was still in the port. It had not been cleared by customs. It was a small paperwork problem, he said, that we would work on the next morning. *Oh, great,* I thought. We were starting out behind schedule. Then I reminded myself that that was okay; it certainly wasn't the first problem we'd had.

The road from Roberts Field was a two-lane road, very similar to the country roads you find between towns in East Texas. The road was in good shape but a little narrow, with quite a few curves and small hills. Vegetation was growing up onto the road. Most of the trees were not over twenty-feet tall, but the brush underneath them was thick. There were no street lights and no lights on in or around the houses, either. We weren't the only ones on the road, and that was the scary part. Sitting in the second row of seats, looking out the front windshield, the van's headlights gave us a preview of coming attractions. Many times, as we topped a hill, we could just pick up the outline of something big, dark, and not moving nearly as fast as the van: a loaded truck without lights in our lane.

In Liberia in 2009, there were no load limits, size restrictions, or requirements on secure loads. Trucks in Liberia might be twenty years old, all rust and smoke. Few had enclosed containers for carrying their cargo. Trucks carrying vegetation to charcoal-making sites were quite common, just as they were in Haiti. Vegetation used to make charcoal is stuffed in woven fiberglass bags, like the burlap bags of yesteryear. At one time, the bags were a gleaming white. By the time I saw them, they were dark brown and black with embedded dirt and charcoal. The full bags were about three feet in diameter and about five feet in length, weighing maybe fifty to seventy-five pounds. They were stacked on the truck beds, which were surrounded by sideboards or wooden fence sections standing about four feet above them. The bags were stacked inside the fence sections until they reached about twenty feet off the ground, and they hung over the sides of the trucks by as much as three to four feet.

I Don't Think We're in Kansas or Texas

The way the loads dangled over the sideboards gave the appearance that the law of gravity didn't apply to the vegetation sacks. If it weren't for the ropes tied across the bags to hold them in place, the trucks would only hold about a third as much. Who knew the conditions of the ropes or how many ropes were used to strap down the bags of branches and leaves? Not me. Riding atop the unsecured bags were usually about twenty workers and their belongings.

For the first few miles, all we saw was darkness and a few lights on cars, trucks, or motorcycle taxies. After about ten miles, we noticed people walking down the road. It was about nine o'clock, and we wondered what was going on. As we drove on, the number of people walking down the road in the dark increased. We reached a point where a lot of people were gathered, just standing around, and as we drove on further, we still saw people walking in the dark. The numbers decreased the further we drove. Down the road, though, it happened again.

It continued, even as we neared the outskirts of Monrovia. Everyone was going somewhere. We began to see strings of lights and hear loud music as we passed some places. These lighted, rocking places were packed with people. On the side of the road, dilapidated yellow taxis emptied out their passengers or took on way too many new ones. Motorcycle taxis picked up fares and dropped riders off. Each of these hangouts had their own small gasoline generators to power the strings of lights and the blasting music.

After riding in the van for an hour, we turned left off Tubman Boulevard onto 12th Street and drove four blocks to the United Methodist guesthouse compound. It was surrounded by a high concrete fence, maybe ten feet high, topped with coils of rusty barbed wire and broken glass. The walls had not been whitewashed in many years and had been abused by the tropical weather, mold, and hard times. We pulled up to big, rusty metal doors that were nicely painted with a United Methodist emblem. As the van driver honked the horn, a guard opened the gate for us to drive in.

When Faith Lights the Way

Inside the walls, we encountered five structures built in the fifties or sixties. In the light the next day, we saw they were all painted a pale yellow with chocolate trim. The compound was right on the beach, and we could hear the ocean waves crashing, but the high wall prevented the longed-for view and the reviving breeze. It was a tease being so near to a cooling breeze without being able to feel it and being so close to waves crashing but unable to witness them.

We climbed a flight of outside stairs to our quarters. Our hostel included a large sleeping room with five single beds, four of which were taken over by Terry, Gary, Ry, and Wes. Frank and Chris took a two-person room, as did Harrell and myself. Pinkie slept in a single-occupancy room. All the sleeping rooms were on the ends of the building, and there was a toilet on each end. The middle of our quarters contained a chocolate Naugahyde three-cushion couch, a matching love seat, and a single chair in the exact style of the couches. The same couches were still there when I returned in 2016. I suspect they'd been there since the eighties, maybe longer. The kitchen had a dated refrigerator, stove, and sink, all very compact. A dining table that could seat eleven stood outside the kitchen.

The toilet facilities were identical, with white tile floors and a toilet, sink, and four-foot-high tiled wall that delineated the shower area. There was a large plastic bucket filled with water, a medium-sized bucket, and a half-gallon pitcher. In 2009, there was no running water. In the mornings, water was pumped for about an hour, using an onsite gasoline generator, to a water tower behind our building. The large buckets in the facilities and the kitchen were filled via the building's plumbing. If we used the toilet, we dipped the medium-sized bucket in the large full bucket and threw the water into the toilet bowl to flush. For showers, we filled up the medium bucket, placed it inside the shower area, and used the small plastic pitcher to pour water on ourselves. Most of us were not fond of cold showers, but to quote the Rolling Stones, "You can't always get what you want, but sometimes you get what you need."

I Don't Think We're in Kansas or Texas

The water in the kitchen buckets was heated on the stove for washing dishes. I doubt this water was potable, and we tried hard not to have to find out. It takes a conscious effort at first to make sure nothing touches your lips but bottled water, but it's incredibly necessary.

After throwing our gear in our rooms, we sat down to a good dinner prepared by Nowai and her daughter, Nyamah E. Dunbar. Nowai, or Ma, as elderly women are affectionately known in Liberia, was born in 1957. Her parents were agribusiness people. Her mother, Nyamah, died during childbirth when Nowai was very young, and Ma Nowai feels this tragedy shaped her sympathetic heart and helped develop within her the nurturing spirit of a caretaker. Her daughter, Nyamah, says Ma Nowai has used this gift from God to serve people all her life. She worked mainly as a trader in local markets and as a cook and domestic, including taking care of missionary or work teams staying at the seminary guesthouse in Gbarnga, Liberia. Ma Nowai was adept at preparing delicious Liberian dishes or adding a Liberian twist to American-style dishes. Our first meal was just-like-home spaghetti, some type of greens—possibly spinach—bread, and fruit. "I love to feed people," she often said with her dimpled smile. "That is just my part of the gifts that God has divided among all of us."

Nyamah E. Dunbar is the eldest of Ma Nowi's two girls. As a child, when the civil war broke out, she left Liberia and was raised in the United States while maintaining contact with her mother and her native home. Nyamah graduated from college and served in the Peace Corps. However, she always yearned to return to her native home to serve. Working with UMCOR via the United Methodist health programs in Liberia, she received that opportunity. We were immediately impressed with the quick smiles and laughter of both Ma Nowai and Nyamah. We felt as if we'd known them all our lives.

During dinner, we briefly discussed with Victor our options for getting our container out of port. Then he gave us a brief dos-and-don'ts session. Victor cautioned us about taking pictures of the Liberian military or any of their installations. It was okay to photograph or film the

When Faith Lights the Way

UN forces, but we could have our cameras confiscated, or worse, if we were caught taking pictures of the Liberian Military. Also, we needed to remember to maintain quick access to our passports at the various checkpoints we would encounter on the road to Ganta. We would be asked to show them numerous times.

Some of us showered using the buckets, and some decided to wait until morning. Finally, we got to sleep in real beds. Each room had a fan, but it was so humid and hot that even that didn't make me comfortable. We slept without mosquito nets because, according to the locals, mosquitoes avoid the beach area. We were told that they couldn't fly in the strong breezes created by the ocean. (Later, in 2016, after Ebola had infected over ten thousand Liberians, I saw mosquito nets over the beds when we stayed at the Methodist guesthouse.[8]) That first night in Liberia was long, hot, fitful, and thought-filled.

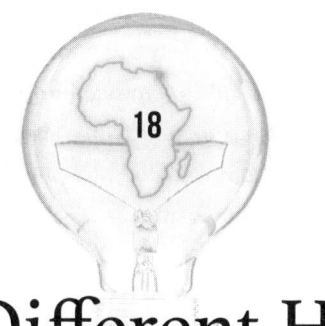

It's Different Here

Day 2: Monrovia

On the morning of Monday, June 8, we woke and enjoyed a breakfast of pineapple, instant coffee, and scrambled eggs. The pineapple was tremendous—so much better than what we bought in the stores back home. Despite the lack of good sleep, we were in good spirits, anticipating all the wonderful things we were going to accomplish. We loaded into two vans and went to downtown Monrovia to buy SIM cards and/or phones to call home. Downtown Monrovia was a macabre ghost of a once prosperous and thriving city. I could close my eyes and, in my mind, see an opaque image of modern buildings that had been crippled by civil war. In reality, none were untouched by the war. The fighting in Monrovia resulted in most structures having bullet holes through their facades and huge hunks of concrete torn away, exposing the now rusted rebar. All of them were unpainted, moldy, and dirty, but people did their best to operate their business out of these damaged buildings.

At government buildings and other strategic points in the city, the UN Military presence was conspicuous. On Tubman Boulevard, the main street heading into town, we saw a multistory building labeled "UNMIL Headquarters." There was no mistaking that UNMIL was prepared to

When Faith Lights the Way

defend their positions. At the presidential office, two or three armored vehicles resembling tanks or armored assault vehicles were parked in the driveway entrances, and a contingent of blue-helmeted soldiers with full combat gear and weapons stood in plain view. Driving along the roads were many stark white trucks and off-road-capable SUVs with the large "UN" letters stenciled on the doors.

The traffic was dense and uncontrolled, as all traffic signs and signal lights were gone or, at best, ignored. There were no police around to enforce traffic rules. Pedestrians didn't follow road rules any better than the vehicles. Motorcycles zoomed everywhere—everyone under thirty had one. Industrious guys had welded, taped, glued, and wired together parts of motorcycles they'd found along roads and engineered them into working modes of transportation. None of them were the progeny of a motorcycle manufacturing plant. These guys used their bikes as taxis to make money. A few bikes had solo riders; most likely they were between fares. Sometimes we'd see whole families on just one bike—up to five people and their treasures. The cars were all small and belched smoke, and the rust made every car two-tone.

Power lines strung from poles and buildings looked like a mass of black spaghetti on top of the city. It was amazing there were any lines still there, but it was doubtful any of them were in service. The electric generating plants had been destroyed in the civil war, so there was no electricity. During the chaos of war, people would climb the steel towers and poles that ran from generating plants to the cities to cut the wires. They would then hook the end that dropped on the ground to the back of a truck and pull down as much wire as possible. They intended to sell the downed conductor for scrap, hoping to find copper lines, but a lot of the conductor, especially on the transmission lines, was a combination of aluminum and steel. They didn't make much money, but when you're starving and trying to feed yourself and your family, you'll do a lot of work for very little money. Even today, there are still many large steel towers that are standing, both inside and outside of Monrovia, with the green glass insulators hanging limply from the poles, with no conductor

It's Different Here

strung between them. These steel towers, set in concrete, will cost Liberia millions of dollars to remove, but they must be taken down eventually. They're useless.

In 2009, if the existing electric system functioned at all, it was only for a few hours a day. And electricity was so expensive in Liberia! In the United States, electricity had varied from approximately $0.06 to $0.13 per Kilowatt hour over the last ten years. In Liberia, the cost was between $0.55 and $0.65 per Kilowatt hour! Employment in Liberia was 18 percent at that time, and wages were a fraction of those in the United States. How could anyone in Liberia pay five times the cost of US electricity when only the very fortunate had income at all?

Our vans parked on a busy main street in downtown Monrovia, and we exited to look at cell phones in a small shop that contained dark wood and glass display cases. The cases reminded me of those I'd seen in small Texas towns in the 1960s, but the phones were different from what we had available in the United States. Smartphone sales were beginning to ramp up but had not yet captured the market here. In the United States, flip phones were still in wide use, and if you bought one without a plan, you might expect to pay fifty or sixty bucks. In Liberia, phones cost about twenty-five American dollars. These were very basic phones, but they were ahead of us in some respects. All their phones had SIM cards.

There were several in our group who weren't familiar with SIM card technology because it was still fairly new at home. In Liberia, you bought scratch-off minute cards for five dollars each. In those days, we could call the United States for maybe thirty minutes on five bucks.

Only three people on the first trip bought a phone and minutes to call the United States. In later trips, everyone would buy a phone and bring it back with them on return trips.

That first morning in Liberia, it was time to free our container from the port. We all went to the Christian Health Association of Liberia (CHAL),

When Faith Lights the Way

an organization operated by the mainstream Christian denominations of Liberia, including Lutherans, Episcopalians, and Methodists. CHAL procured drugs and medical supplies in bulk. Consolidation significantly reduced delivery time and costs, and Ganta was one of the hospitals they served. They were experienced importers.[9]

Our container was consigned to CHAL in Liberia, which meant we'd listed them as the party who would receive the container once it cleared customs. We all went into the building to hear, understand, and solve the problem. After talking to two different individuals there, we learned that the Methodist Church in Liberia had let a tax-free exemption expire, and they were going to charge us a duty on our material. The duty would be about nine thousand US dollars.

It goes without saying that this $9,000 duty wasn't something we'd planned for. Even more, we'd spent all this time, effort, and money trying to help suffering people receive better medical treatment. Shouldn't somebody in the Liberian government understand we weren't getting anything for this? Wasn't there somebody who had the authority and morality to void this fee?

We didn't need the whole group to resolve the $9,000 duty problem so we decided most of the group would leave that afternoon for Ganta. At least that group could get settled in, meet the electric departments of both the hospital and mission and inspect and oversee the digging of the trenches. Chris and I would stay in Monrovia to get the container released and then head to Ganta.

The rest of the group would leave that afternoon, taking two similar vehicles, one of which was a vintage Toyota Land Cruiser that was almost twenty years old by then, with a heavy luggage rack mounted on top and large, heavy, off-road tires. It was white with a faded and scratched United Methodist symbol, a cross and flame, on the front doors with the words "Ganta Hospital" written underneath. Most Liberians are Christians, and most Christians in Liberia are Methodist. To the Liberians, anyone riding in a vehicle with this logo could be trusted.

It's Different Here

One of the most notable accessories was a four-inch black pipe coming out of the engine compartment on the passenger side. It turned vertical and reached up to the top of the roofline, terminating with a black vented cap. In the dry season, dust is blown in from the Sahara Desert. The red invader gets so thick you can taste it, and the sky changes from a beautiful blue to a sandy red. The problem is compounded for vehicles because most roads are dirt, and any truck or car driving in front of you kicks up so much dust that you can barely see thirty feet ahead. In the rainy season, the creeks return and evolve into rivers. These snorkels allowed these four-wheel-drive vehicles to put cleaner, cooler, air into the car engine and gave them more power. They also provided peace of mind that, when fording a river, you wouldn't be stuck midstream with a drowned-out car.

Another desirable truck tool for our project was a winch. This is a steel cable wound on a round steel cylinder attached to the front bumper. The cylinder is held onto the bumper by a frame that allows it to rotate on a shaft. To cross a fast-moving stream or get a stuck vehicle moving again, you unwind the steel cable from the drum and secure the cable around a tree, post, or another vehicle in the direction you want your vehicle to move. The winch is powered by the battery. When switched on, the cylinder begins to turn, winding the steel cable back onto the winch. This gets you out of the sand or mud or across a flowing stream. The alternative is to carry boards and place them under the slipping wheels or string a rope across the water and have people pull the vehicle across. I've done both, and the winch is by far the best solution.

We said goodbye to our team, who were crammed into the two vehicles. One person could ride in the passenger seat, but the back seats had been removed to carry equipment, people, etc. For carrying people, wooden benches with a little padding had been mounted on the sides so we could seat about six in the back, riding facing each other. Our small mountain of luggage was tied to the rack on top.

After the crew was gone, Chris and I rode with Victor Taryor, the Ganta hospital administrator, back downtown to the Ministry of Finance

When Faith Lights the Way

offices to see what we could do about getting the container released. The Ministry of Finance, located on Broad Street, was in a multistory building in downtown Monrovia. Broad Street has a nice boulevard down the center, and the Ministry of Finance was across the street from where we'd bought our cell phones earlier in the day. The official we met with was located on the fourth floor.

The stairs were a smooth granite, and the treads were worn down by all the foot traffic they had endured. At the center of a tread, the leading edge was worn down about two inches from the back. The building must have been grand before the war. Now, it struggled to be serviceable. So much had been lost during the conflict.

We had been told to expect to be solicited for bribes. I was completely committed to refusing to pay bribes. I felt it was not ethical or fair for appointed or elected officials, who were supposed to be there to serve the citizens of Liberia, to collect under-the-table money from us. They were paid to do a job. It was not my duty or responsibility to supplement their income on the sly. If Liberia was to return to its prewar vibrancy, the people must be honest and ethical in their transactions.

Ah, it is so comforting to have all the answers while standing on the moral high ground. I have never experienced what these people have endured: war and poverty. I might have had a different outlook if I had a difficult time keeping my family alive. There are few black and white answers in the world.

The Ministry of Finance couldn't help us without a specific form. The form was at the port, so we left there and headed for the Freeport of Monrovia, crossing the bridge that stretched over the Mesurado River on United Nations Drive. The bridge was a sturdy, four-lane, concrete construct that looked like it had been built in the sixties or seventies. As we drove across it, we noticed large chunks of concrete had fallen out of the bridge. Many of the holes were clustered together and were somewhat round. Bullet holes. If we looked out the back of the SUV toward downtown, we could see the spooky remains of once-grand multistory

It's Different Here

buildings rising as dark gray, decaying skeletons over the downtown area. All along the water's edge, we could see hundreds of rusty tin roofs partially covering tiny shanty shacks. *What a grand site Monrovia must have been in the past,* I thought. Now it slumped to decay, a sad example of man's ability to destroy.

We retrieved the form from the Safmarine shipping company's office at the port and returned to the Ministry of Finance. We sat down in a waiting room to see the taxing official, and after thirty minutes we entered his office. His dark, wood-paneled office was very spacious, with the windows open and sheer pinkish drapes blowing in the breeze. The windows looked out over the tree-lined boulevard onto Broad Street. The furnishings and the walls transported us back to the 1970s. We spend almost forty-five minutes there, discussing our duty problem on the container, the family in the framed pictured on his desk, and where the taxing official went to school in the United States. It was pleasant, but as it turned out, a waste of our time. He was not going to help us, and he only passed us to someone else. He said the Ministry of Health might give clearance to release the container duty-free. On to the next government body.

The Ministry of Health was in another building on the edge of downtown, likewise housed in a dark, rundown building. The minister wasn't there, but we spent some time with the Assistant Minister of Health, who Victor seemed to know quite well. He was agreeable to giving us a form that stated that our supplies were to be used for medical help for the people of Liberia. He told us that the form might help, but that it probably wouldn't be enough to override the problem of letting a permit expire. We went to a small office outside the assistant health minister's office, and he instructed one of the guys to type up the form. I've never seen anything like this in all my days in business. The typist must have been in his late fifties.

Growing up, there was a television show called *The Honeymooners,* starring Jackie Gleason and Art Carney. One of the routines was Jackie Gleason waiting for Art Carney to write something down or sign a paper.

When Faith Lights the Way

Carney would adjust his shirt sleeves, lick the pencil, stare at the paper, adjust his hat, and get a drink of water. He would do everything but write. Just when you thought he was going to finally write, he would start the procrastination antics all over again. Jackie Gleason would start out, patient, calm, encouraging, but the impatience and frustration would get the best of his character, Ralph Kramden. The oblivious Art Carney would just keep adjusting. Finally, Jackie would boil over and shout, "Come on!" and beat the shocked Art Carney with his hat.

It took this guy forty-five minutes to type a half-page form. He typed with both hands but only used one finger on each hand to type. He had no idea how the letters were laid out on the keyboard, so he had to search before each stroke. The keystrokes came about thirty seconds apart. He would type a line, roll the form up to look what he typed and then roll the paper back down and try to find the next line. At one point, he pulled out the form and started over. All the while he was typing, the other two guys in the room were carrying on conversations about everything imaginable. Chris and I were afraid to look at each other for fear we would burst out laughing! You had to give the typist credit, though; he was doing his best. Finally, he finished, and the assistant minister of health signed the form.

We went back again to the Ministry of Finance with the signed form from the assistant minister of health. The Ministry of Finance told us to go see the port manager—maybe he would help. We didn't have time to go to the port that day and went back to the Methodist guesthouse for the night. It had been a busy day. After getting the phones, Chris, Victor, and I had made a trip to our receiving agent, CHAL, the port, the Ministry of Health, and the Ministry of Finance three times. We got the impression after the first day that the standard answer to everything was, "There is nothing I can do. That is the way it is." Victor, the administrator of the Ganta Hospital, worked hard and did a great job coping with all the twists, turns, and dead ends. This wasn't his first rodeo.

Radio Stars

Day 2: Monrovia, continued

The port offices didn't open until later in the morning, so Chris and I went with Victor to the hardware store in downtown Monrovia to buy a water pump to replace a failed one. The pump was used in the lake at Ganta Hospital to supply the hospital with water. Driving down one of the streets crowded with clothing stores, we saw numerous small shops with entrances no wider than ten feet. The steel garage doors had been rolled up as they opened for business. Most stores were crammed with clothes, and more clothing was spilling out onto the sidewalks. Merchandise was delivered to the stores by wheelbarrow. We snapped a picture of a young, muscled-up Liberian wearing an old tattered t-shirt, long pants, and flip flops, pushing a wheelbarrow loaded with blue jeans.

The hardware store was an amazing place. It had everything you could ever want in a hardware store, all crammed into the space of a double garage. The last time I'd seen such a treasure was in a locally owned hardware store on the square in Coleman, Texas, in the eighties. It had wiring, plumbing, shovels, cement, tools, and just everything, including the pump we needed for the hospital. I had a great time squeezing through the aisles crammed with equipment, looking at all the stuff

When Faith Lights the Way

from all over the world. One of the employees loading bags of cement in a wheelbarrow had on a brown shirt with the word "MARFA" written in blue block letters. I walked up to him with a big smile and in excited voice asked, "Have you been to Marfa, Texas? Not many people even know where that is!" I knew the answer to my question—I just wanted to see his reaction. He looked at me like I was crazy. I'm sure he didn't know about Marfa and probably didn't even know what his shirt said.

After we bought the water pump, Victor and I headed to a scheduled appointment at the offices of the United Methodist Conference Center, two blocks from the Methodist guesthouse. The United Methodist bishop's office is there, along with the church's various departments that serve the entire conference of the Methodist Church in Liberia. The conference offices are on a busy street corner in Monrovia, occupying a city block surrounded by a concrete security fence. The only entrance into the compound is through a metal gate that covers the opening in the fence, and the opening is just wide enough for a medium-sized truck to squeeze through.

Before reaching the gate, our vehicle had to navigate a path through the crowd. The street where the gate was located served as a hangout spot and a place to do business. There were multiple stands, some shaded by bright-colored, red-and-white umbrellas with vendors eager to sell you scratch cards for five bucks that would add talk minutes to your cell phone. They were paid on commission, so they were very eager to help. There were also fruit stands with mangos, bananas, and pineapple. If you were there at the right time, a gentleman would come by pushing a rusty wheelbarrow with coconuts. For a dollar, he would cut off the top of the coconut with a machete so you could drink the milk.

After running the gauntlet in our car and squeezing through the gate with people walking in and out, we drove on packed dirt and concrete and parked in front of the three-story concrete building painted many years ago in pale mustard and chocolate brown. There were at least five people sitting on the steps or in plastic chairs in the shade around the covered main entrance of the conference center. They sat out there in

Radio Stars

the "cool breeze" because there were air conditioners in only one or two offices of important church officials. At the conference center, electricity was produced by a generator, which only operated a few hours a day. The guys hung around in the air-conditioned offices whenever possible, but if they were inside all the time and underfoot, they tended to get on the bosses' nerves. To escape, they would "disappear" to the building's front steps. In the following years, I visited the center numerous times, and each time I climbed the steps to the front door, we gave each other the Liberian handshake and had a hearty laugh about something...or nothing. I thought of the theme song from *Cheers*: "...where everybody knows your name."

The Liberian handshake is special. Any secret society would be proud to own it. It also morphs into a different choreography, depending on whether you're seeing a guy for the first time in a while or are seeing him for the fiftieth time that day. Liberians get a big charge when us *'wi mn'* (white man) can do it, but for some magical reason, only Liberians are experts. The handshake is a multistep hand dance that ends with a snap, using both parties' middle fingers. I was told that the handshake came about as a proud symbol of freedom for Liberians. The story goes that the middle fingers of slaves were cut off to identify them as slaves without affecting their ability to work. The Liberians, on the other hand, were free men returned to Africa. *They* had their middle fingers to make the snap. The story sounds as if it could be true, but some Liberians that were more likely to know the truth have told me that it's not. It doesn't matter where the handshake came from, though. What matters is that it's deeply embedded in the culture.

We arrived at the conference center to do a radio program. The Methodist radio station broadcasts to Monrovia and the surrounding towns. We went into a small, air-conditioned room—the first air-conditioning we had found since we arrived. Liberia is hot and sticky, even for someone having grown up in Texas. Entering the cool, dry air improved our whole disposition. We went into a small, windowless, dark-colored room and were asked to sit in wooden chairs and at a wooden table that

When Faith Lights the Way

looked like the same style of table and chairs I encountered in school in Dallas back in the 1960s. On the table were two large microphones—one for Victor and one for me—and we were each given great big headphones. In a room behind a glass wall sat the sound technician, in front of a soundboard, and the talk-show host.

In the 1990s, there was a popular television show about a psychiatrist, Dr. Frasier Crane, who did therapy for his call-in listeners on the radio. I envisioned myself as Frasier. I felt cool, doing my first broadcast to the nation. Well…maybe to a city where no one knew who I was. Victor and I laughed and wondered if anyone would be listening to the broadcast. Even if they didn't, it was still cool to do a radio talk show in Africa. We all got quiet, and the sound technician cued the music. After the music faded away, the host announced his name and his topics for the day's show. Next, he introduced Victor as the administrator of the United Methodist Hospital in Ganta and began to ask questions about why we were in town and what we hoped to accomplish. I remember the guy had a smooth "radio voice" and was engaging to listen to. Victor described our overall mission, then the host began to ask me questions. I was proud to explain we were going to install the only modern underground electric system in the country as our gift to the people of Liberia. I looked at Chris, and he had this big grin on his face. I don't know if he was smiling with me or laughing because I was on the radio.

The host's next question, though, seemed to have a bite to it.

"So, after you install this system to help our people, are you going to be available to keep it operating, or are you going to leave it with us and go home?"

Ouch.

Up until this question, everyone had seemed thrilled with what we were doing. The people we had encountered made us feel like a godsend. A little taken aback, I explained we were going to have the Liberians work with us on the installation. If we could get our container out of the Freeport of Monrovia reasonably soon, we hoped to teach the electrical staff at the hospital all about the maintenance that would be required to keep the system working for many years. In other words, it wouldn't just fall apart once it was constructed, if that was his concern. The staff at the hospital would be self-reliant.

To myself, I reasoned that we had been asked to fix the electricity by the United Methodist Bishop of Liberia through the United Methodist Committee on Relief. We didn't arbitrarily pick out Liberia and this hospital and decide, *Well, we'll just go there and give the people of Ganta what we think they need.* In truth, I was more than a little hurt by the insinuation that we would do our work, celebrate our accomplishment, feel good about ourselves, and then leave them with a useless monument to our own egos. I knew what he was getting at, but I also knew that was not our intention at all. We had arrived here upon someone else's request, and we were determined to do the best, most sustainable job we could possibly do.

What soon became obvious to me was that, as a savvy talk show host, he had a pulse on the thoughts and feelings of his audience. Upon reflection on his terse question, I came to realize that many Liberians didn't appreciate the aid that had been given them in the past. That might have been because the aid had arrived with either disingenuous or self-centered motives and resulted in negative consequences. This radio host ultimately made me consider how much of the work we do as Christians under the guise of helping other people is really just to make us feel good about ourselves.

He had planted a question that I would discuss with others many times in the coming weeks: *How do we judge the value of our gift?*

"What is the problem with the container?" our host eventually asked.

Victor and I diplomatically explained a problem with the paperwork necessary to get the container released from the port, explaining that we planned to visit more government offices to get the paperwork straightened out so we could get on with our work. I thought I had come up with a clever rallying cry, and I spoke it into the mic.

When Faith Lights the Way

"Moses told Pharaoh, 'Let my people go!'" I said. "Let our container go!" The talk show host, in response, simply stared at me. There was no reaction whatsoever. I felt embarrassed.

Near the end of the interview, he bombed me with, "Are you going to eat fufu and dumboy while you are in Liberia?"

I didn't know what fufu and dumboy were. Why I wondered, was he trying to prove on the radio that I don't know everything about a culture I'd only encountered days before? I thought to myself, *Look, dude, I'm here to help, not be made a fool of.* I smiled and tried to recover with, "I'm sure if our good friends at Ganta feel that's something I need to experience, I will eat fufu and dumboy!" I ended the radio segment with a laugh, not knowing what I was talking about.

The end of the radio program drew near, the music played, and the program ended. Victor and I said thank you and moved out. I left feeling a mixture of elation and humiliation. *What was his deal?* I wondered. We were out of our boat, trying to help the people of Liberia, and yet somehow this talk show host resented us? I comforted myself by thinking, *Oh, well, probably no one listens to the show anyway.*

The day before the radio broadcast, we'd been given a helpful hint from the minister of finance: "Go visit the manager of the port." We intended to do so, but we had the radio show scheduled, and we also knew that the port would be closed for lunch. We drove through downtown Monrovia toward the port and stopped in the area where several government buildings were located. There, we had lunch in a small local restaurant like one might find in the more remote areas of the Caribbean islands. We went upstairs, where there were a few tables, and sat looking out a big open window toward the Ministry of Justice: an impressive, seven-story gray building that exemplified what Liberia might have looked like before the many civil wars. On the side of the building, in large gold letters, was written the phrase, "Temple of Justice," with a picture of the scale of justice and the words, "Let Justice Be Done to All."

Radio Stars

Victor offered to order for us, and due to the talk show host's question, he ordered either fufu or dumboy for us to try. In truth, I can't remember which one he ordered because there are few differences between them. Both fufu and dumboy are doughy whitish balls, about the size of a baseball, pounded and strained from the cassava root, which is similar to yams. The roots have a brown skin that covers the edible white inside. The pounding is usually done with a large, wooden mortar and pestle and then strained with a cloth into a large bowl. Fufu is made from *dried* and fermented cassava root while dumboy is made from *fresh* cassava. Liberians eat these delicacies by pinching off a portion of the doughy blob and forming it into a small round ball. Soup with chicken, fish, or rice may be poured over the ball, or it may be dipped in the soup. You're supposed to swallow the small ball without chewing.

Chris and I tried it. We agreed it was okay, but it certainly wasn't chicken fried steak with gravy. As I ate, I felt a little guilty for thinking the radio talk show host was trying to make me look like an idiot. I thought to myself that perhaps I had taken what he was saying the wrong way and had gotten defensive when I didn't need to.

After lunch, we went to visit the CHAL agent located on United Nations Drive, close to the Freeport of Monrovia. The agent represents his clients, including CHAL, inside the Port. He had the authorization to enter the Port, and our plan was to enter with CHAL's agent, and together we would plead our case with the Port Manager.

We picked up the agent, drove to the massive steel industrial gate at the Port entrance, and waited for the uniformed security guard to come to our SUV. At some point, he had probably looked crisp and smart, but now he was a gruff-looking man who didn't seem happy to see us. He had a round stick about a yard long with a mirror taped to the end.

Moving slowly and methodically, he began looking with the mirror under the front of the car, moving to look under the driver's side, inspecting the underside of the vehicle, and looking inside the back window. All our windows were rolled down because it was hot, but even so, he

When Faith Lights the Way

spoke to no one. He moved to the passenger side, where I was sitting, and stopped. When he looked at me, I was almost to the point of being scared. He asked to see my ID, and I gave it to him. He looked at it and handed it back. Without speaking to us again, he walked to the gate, opened it, and waved us through. I let out a sigh of relief. Then he asked me something that amazed me. As we passed, he said, "Are you going to get the electrical system installed at the Ganta Hospital?"

My mouth fell open. How did he know? I looked around at the others. We were all shocked! It took a minute or so to figure it out. The Land Rover had the Cross and Flame on the side and said "Ganta Hospital." That meant he had listened to the radio broadcast earlier that morning! He had heard the broadcast, and that had made the path a little smoother for us. What a great affirmation of our effort.

To my knowledge, there was no television there in 2009, and I now know that radio is a big part of the lives of Liberians. But it still amazes me that the radio show—where I felt I had come across as somewhat egotistical and had done such a poor job—had actually built a bridge between our group and the port entrance.

We arrived at the port manager's ranch-style office building and started toward the door. It was near closing time for the port, and the wooden door was surrounded by a whole bunch of agents pressing close to the door and yelling, trying to get in. It reminded me of pictures I'd seen of the trading floor of the New York Stock Exchange during a rally. Somehow, our agent got the attention of whoever was in charge, and we squeezed into the building and were taken to the manager's office, which was decorated with 1970s-style dark wood paneling and contained a large wooden desk. The manager was very gracious and nattily dressed, and he asked us how he could help. We explained our situation. As he listened, he was very polite and asked several questions, but he eventually responded in a diplomatic tone. "I am sorry," he told us. "There is nothing I can do." This was something, in truth, I had not expected.

Radio Stars

I had dealt with everyone in Liberia by applying my best and most effective salesmen skills, meaning I was courteous, even while being persuasive. In the face of the port manger's reaction, though, I lost my *savoir-faire*. "Sir," I said, "there's a hospital in Ganta that serves twenty-four thousand patients a year, where the surgeons finish operations with flashlights in their mouths when the power goes out. The anesthesia machines don't work because of poor power. We've spent a year designing a modern underground electrical system to help these people. We have donated the material and paid for our transportation, and we are here to help with the installation on our own time without pay. We care about Liberians! Does anyone in this country care about Liberians?"

There was silence. A long silence.

He swiveled his chair around to the desk behind him and made a phone call. We could not hear what he was saying, but his tone, thankfully, did not sound like we were going to be arrested. When he was finished, he set the phone down and looked straight at me. "You have an appointment at ten in the morning," he said, "with the assistant minister of finance. She will be able to help you."

For a moment, I stood there in shock. Then I breathed a sigh of relief. Neither Chris nor I could thank him enough; we had become so frustrated with the process. I thought to myself, *perhaps there are indeed some in the Liberian government who want to do the right thing.*

The next day was Wednesday, June 10. That morning Chris and I woke, took bucket showers, ate breakfast, and packed our stuff. We hoped we would spend the next night in Ganta with the rest of the Power From the SON crew, having completed our goal of getting our containers released from the port of Monrovia. We loaded into the Range Rover and made our way to downtown Monrovia, heading back to the Ministry of Finance building.

By that point, we were getting very familiar with the building. Again, we walked up the several flights of well-worn gray marble stairs. This time, we walked into a part of the building with an enclosed air shaft

When Faith Lights the Way

courtyard. Black wrought-iron fences about three feet high stood sentry on each floor between the building walls and the open-air shaft. A roof overhung the walkways on each floor. A lot of business or socializing was conducted by workers leaning over the fence, talking to people on other floors.

We entered the office of the assistant minister of finance. Victor, Chris, and I took up residence in the three wooden chairs squeezed together against the wall facing two workers behind worn wooden desks. Behind them were aged bookshelves with many blue, cloth-bound bookkeeping ledgers—books about eighteen inches tall and a foot wide—a staple in all offices before the 1980s. I passed some time reading the labels on the spines of the ledgers. There was book after book with "Firestone." This impressed me. Later, I did some research and learned that Firestone—an American company known for natural rubber products—made up 40 percent of the Liberian economy at that time. I knew so little about the history of Liberia. The ledger books described a country whose economy was still in critical condition, with a barely detectable pulse. Liberia had been "Little America" before the civil wars. Back then, its economy had been somewhat diverse and vibrant. Now, one non-Liberian company was keeping the country alive.

We sat there for about twenty minutes, waiting to see the assistant minister. Aside from having to stand up and squeeze together as people came and went from the office, we had no way to entertain ourselves but to stare at the two workers across from us. Surprisingly, there were computers on each desk. They were older, desktop models, but they were the first computers I'd seen in Liberia.

We quietly observed the office workers, who spent most of their time on the computers. After leaving the assistant manager's office, visitors sometimes stopped at one of these desks in front of us and conducted business with them. When work demanded their attention, the workers would always leave the computer, stand up, and take one of the blue, cloth-bound accounting ledger books from the shelf, open it, and fill in columns with pertinent information. Then the worker would return the ledger book to the shelf and sit in front of the computer.

After spending many years trying to make Priester more efficient and serving as a member of an industry-changing development team, I couldn't help but evaluate how to put efficiency and accountability into the systems we saw. If we could somehow partner with the government in this process, Liberia might be returned to its former glory. It became a quest that would consume me for the next three years.

We went into the assistant minister's office after about twenty minutes and met an educated, intelligent young lady. She was very businesslike but cordial, asking what she could do for us. We explained as succinctly as possible that we were there to get our container, which was filled with supplies to help Ganta Hospital, through customs, duty-free; however, it was difficult to tell our story due to the continuance of people coming into her office, interrupting with their own problems and subjects.

We were delighted, though, when she gave us the good news. I suspect she was already aware of our situation and had already made up her mind to help. She was going to give us a duty waiver and make sure our containers were released and on their way within three hours—with one stipulation. She told us that the United Methodist Church of Liberia had sixty days to file the proper forms to receive renewed duty-free status; otherwise, the duty would be levied. We thanked her profusely for promising to release the containers and walked out with smiles on our faces and joy in our hearts.

We took care of some errands, picked up our suitcases at the Methodist guesthouse, and left about noon. Ganta was a short, five-hour drive away. We were in our old Land Rover; Victor and the driver were in the front, and Chris and I faced each other on benches in the back. I'm not sure seat belts had made their debut in Liberia when we were there. The air conditioner was a rolled-down front window.

On to Ganta!

Day 3

All the small homes we passed in Monrovia, and even the larger business, had high cinderblock walls adorned with broken glass and razor wire on the top. There were hotels, bars, and a lot of churches. We passed JFK Hospital and Third Rock Chinese clinic. On about every fifth block, we saw a brightly colored umbrella giving shade to a person selling cell phone minutes. Then there were the broken-down yellow taxis—some running, some dying, and some that had died and decayed, abandoned alongside the road. Most of the taxis had a religious statement painted on them, like, "Jesus is My Lord," or "Redemption Taxi."

Past Spriggs-Payne Airport—a temporary quarters for many UN cargo planes and Russian-made helicopters—set back two-hundred yards from the road, there was a huge, abandoned building maybe five stories high, surrounded by lush green, unkempt vegetation. The building was originally planned as the Ministry of Defense but was never completed. There was nothing left of this menacing concrete building but its shell, now gray, black, and splotched with moss. The black cast was due to weathering and, I suspected, mold. On the corners stood rounded spires that resembled the towers in medieval castles. The building had a

When Faith Lights the Way

front-entry porte-cochère of concrete that was formed from six protrusions in smooth curves, suggesting a futuristic weapon from a science-fiction movie. The whole aura of the area was one of destruction. It stood silently, waiting for instructions to come to life and threaten the existence of mankind.

We were just about to leave the city when the road made a slight turn to the left, and then everything slowed down. As we poked along in traffic, we moved slower and slower. Eventually, we discovered what was holding us up. What I saw reminded me a bit of something I had seen in my own country. In Texas, we have an event in Canton called "First Monday," a swap meet where you can buy just about anything you can imagine. What I saw before me in Liberia was First Monday on steroids. As far as I could see, there were cars. People were everywhere, darting in front of the cars, jumping into and out of taxis, five and six people at a time. Cinderblock buildings were set back from the road maybe a hundred feet, and between the cars and the buildings could be seen the greatest collection of dresses, blue jeans, soccer balls, sunglasses, car and motorcycle parts, handmade furniture, and anything else one would ever—or never—want in the world. People with candy, cookies, and other sweets walked up to cars and tried to sell their goodies. Girls strolled along, talking to each other, balancing buckets, fruit, and all kinds of things on top of their heads. This was a market called "Red Light." It was as if a black hole had positioned itself in the center of the market and was sucking everything in the world into Red Light. If one was hungry, there were people cooking fish, rice, and fufu right among the goings-on. To add to the extravaganza, it had rained earlier in the day, and the red dirt that supported all this activity had turned to mud and dirty pools of water. The swirling colors were stunning. The motion was overwhelming, mesmerizing. And Red Light apparently happened *every day*. Some days were more out of this world than others, but it was, and is, indescribable.

After spending forty-five minutes negotiating Red Light's ten blocks, the traffic thinned out, and we picked up a little speed on the two-lane road. One building, painted a crisp red and white, lifted our spirits. The

On to Ganta!

grounds were well manicured with strategically placed palm trees. By the look of the building, it was obviously some sort of factory, and it was easy to figure out who owned it. There was a twenty-foot-tall bottle of Coca-Cola in the middle of the front lawn. Seeing this production plant in Liberia, with a huge Coke bottle in the front, gave us hope for some strange reason. After experiencing Monrovia, all the poverty and desperation in a once-great city, the massive bottle of refreshing pleasure was an almost cartoonish image of something desirable, something that made us feel it would all be better. It seemed almost Disneylandish, arising out of all the sorrow and destruction the Liberians were enduring.

Before leaving Monrovia, all cars were required to pass through the UN Military checkpoint. The traffic began to slow again and then came to a full stop. Up ahead, we could see people in a crowd maybe ten vehicles ahead of us. We would stop for a minute and then move up, stop again, and move up. When we got to the front of the line, there were weathered guard shacks on each side of the road. A beam, three feet high, crossed the road, stopping traffic in both directions. It was only mounted on one end at the shoulder of the road so the unmounted end could be raised to a vertical position to let vehicles pass when the guard approved. Soldiers with rifles stood watch over the checkpoint. A uniformed UN Peacekeeper came up to the passenger side, looked at the four of us very closely, then asked for Chris and me to show him our passports. Once we handed them to him, he looked them over, looked us over again, handed us back our passports, backed away from the car, and motioned for the pole to be raised. We drove on.

We asked Victor why the checkpoints were operating. He explained that Liberia was still concerned about violence, and the checkpoints were there to detain undesirables or people carrying weapons. Chris and I felt like they hadn't spent enough time with us to discover if we were a problem or not. Victor explained, "Our license plate is UMC. Since maybe 85 percent of the country is Christian, and most Christians here are Methodists, the soldiers see the plate and are sure we are okay. But

When Faith Lights the Way

those cars, trucks, and people over by the soldiers at the checkpoint are being thoroughly searched."

We moved out of the urban area and passed jungle growth on the side of the road. We began to pick up speed as we moved more into the center of Liberia. Suddenly, we were in an area where the trees lined up in rigid order. Each tree was about the same size as its neighbor, spaced about ten feet from the next tree in the row, with about twenty-five feet between rows. Looking closely, I could see a spiral groove cut in the bark of the trunk that began about where the branches were first attached to the trunk and wound its way down to about three feet off the ground. At the bottom of the spiral groove, a pot hung on the trunk, collecting sap from the rubber trees. This was a Firestone farm. Firestone had been in Liberia since 1926, producing natural rubber.[10] The rows of trees went on for a few miles, and then the rubber plantations would skip for several miles and then resume. These rubber plantations were a shady, cool, orderly forest. I wanted to stop and wander through and forget all the disorder and poverty surrounding this oasis.

The road had been paved long ago, maybe in the 1970s, but now the potholes and washouts were enormous. Drivers mostly stayed on the paved right side of the road, except when the road was smoother on the left side. Wherever the road was smoothest, that's where they were, whether it was on the shoulder, on the right, or on the left. The drivers went fifty to seventy miles an hour in the rural areas, and our drivers drove these roads almost every day. They knew where all the potholes, water hazards, and side-of-the-road ruts were located, so they drove like they were heading through an obstacle course. Our driver would start out on the right side of the road in his lane, but we learned to anticipate a runaway mine train ride because he would quickly jerk the steering wheel side to side as if he was getting a feel for how the car was going to respond to his game. As if trying to avoid a goat in the road, he would fly the car into the left lane, then back to the right shoulder to drive for a while, back to the left lane, to the left shoulder, and finally back into the right lane. Of course, the pattern was never the same because the

On to Ganta!

potholes were not uniform. Sometimes there was a truck in our lane, or maybe an oncoming car driving as haphazardly as our driver was. Other times, there would be an abandoned car or truck in the smooth part of one of the shoulders, and our driver would be forced to slam on the brakes and then slam into some ruts or potholes.

We overtook a lot of slow-moving trucks carrying cargo. We passed twenty-year-old trucks, all rust and smoke, carrying vegetation to make charcoal. The bags were stacked on the bed of the truck, held in with wooden fence sections surrounding the truck bed. The bags were loaded to a height of twenty feet off the ground, hanging three to four feet over the sides of the truck. The dirty brown mound was tied with ropes. Between ten and twenty workers, with all their earthly belongings, rode on top of the bags. It was best not to think like an engineer and analyze the potential for failure of the truck or the rope, or what would happen in an accident. I think back to a time in America, not one hundred years ago, when you would see the same conditions on our roads. How fortunate we are that our forefathers sacrificed and innovated, allowing us to enjoy a higher quality of life.

Slow-moving motorcycles presented another hazard. Some were stacked with five woven fiberglass vegetation bags, three feet in diameter and about five feet in length, weighing maybe seventy-five pounds each. Others were carrying families of five. Cars painted yellow—taxis—carried five to ten people, struggling to maintain forty miles an hour.

Sometimes the menagerie of slow-moving vehicles would line up five in a row, requiring great skill, or no common sense, to pass them. Add the walkers on the side of the road and the pothole obstacle course, and you've got a ride that will cause you to shoot God some quick pleas for help.

It was a typical upper-eighty-degree day in the back of the SUV, and a five-hour drive, so it wasn't easy not to get motion sickness. Sometimes it was best to lie down on the bench, close my eyes, and pray; that is until I was thrown on the floor of the truck bed during a maneuver.

When Faith Lights the Way

In Liberia, the universal sign for *caution, trouble ahead, slow down*, was a hunk of tall grass pulled up by the roots and stuck in the middle of the road. When a truck ran off the road or broke an axle because the vehicle was overloaded, the driver would leave the accident, pull up several hunks of tall grass, and put them in the middle of the road. When our driver topped a hill, driving on the left shoulder of the road because he was passing a car, and saw the grass, he would come to a screeching slowdown. This warning was ingenious because flares and warning triangles cost money, and one would have to retrieve them and stow them in one's vehicle when one left. The grass, on the other hand, cost nothing. But after a few hours, the warning would disintegrate.

A lot of the breakdowns were a result of potholes. And who repaired all those potholes? Well, enterprising kids, of course! Driving along, when we came upon hunks of grass, our driver would often slow down to find children with digging tools. As our SUV came closer, I realized these tools were actually old pots and broken shovels the children used to carry sand from the roadside and fill the holes. Some of the holes were as big as our car, so it took a lot of work. In addition to this, we were in the rainy season. The passing storms were not kind to the repairs, as torrents of water washed away all the sand and filled up the holes with water, and the water holes were not our friends when our car hit them at highway speed. At the same time, the storms were a blessing to the youthful road-repair crews. They gave them a steady stream of work, and for this work they sometimes received money.

As we drove slowly through this "work zone," the kids would run up to the car and yell, "Gimme a dollar! Pay for my work!" Sometimes, we couldn't resist turning their demands into smiles as we gave in to them. Some of the bigger kids, though, extorted money by copying the UN and police checkpoints along the road. We'd see grass on the road and slow down, but this time a long bamboo stick would be stretched across the road, held up by two shakedown artists. Again, as they approached the car, they would shout, "Gimme a dollar!" Victor and the driver were not sympathetic to pay these kids for their coercion, so our driver would

On to Ganta!

creep forward until, at the last instant, the entrepreneurs would reluctantly remove their bamboo pole to prevent our car from breaking it. A broken pole would have put them out of business.

Eventually, we entered a stretch of road where we saw trees and lush green foliage clear to the horizon. After traveling through this tranquil forest for several miles without seeing a house, we noticed two women in beautiful red, green, and yellow African clothes walking toward us down the side of the road. They walked straight and tall with perfect posture and grace. Ballerinas would envy such grace. One carried a large, colorful dishpan on her head filled with fruit. The other had a stack of cloth and dresses balanced on her head and a baby on her back, secured with a cloth wrapped tightly around her upper body. Both women swung their hands gracefully, moving their heads to look and talk, all while balancing their burdens on their heads.

Another hundred yards and we encountered a woman walking down the road with three children. She was dressed like the previous two women, except in blues and oranges, and she was carrying a wooden board on her head. Two of the children also carried boards on their heads. With each mile the flow of women, some with children, some in groups, all carrying burdens on their heads, increased until it was constant. As we entered a village, the mystery of what they were doing became clear. They had been to the market, which resembled Red Light but much smaller. The women had walked from their homes in the early morning to the market to sell their goods and buy what they needed for the week. The women we encountered as we approached the town were returning home. As we left the small village, we saw women with the same great posture and purchases balanced on their heads, moving in large groups in the same direction we were traveling. They must have lived on the other side of town and were returning home. There were many consumers as we left, but the numbers grew smaller and smaller as we moved away from the village, until there were no women at all. Then, after a few miles, women walking toward us began to appear, and the process repeated. It seemed to us the trading villages were spaced about

When Faith Lights the Way

ten miles apart. We guessed that doing the morning chores, walking five miles to the market, selling and buying goods there, and then walking the five miles back, put these women back home in time to cook the dinner meal and finish their chores before bed.

All along the sides of the road, I saw skeletons of abandoned cars and trucks. Sometimes it was just the rusting frame of the car; sometimes all that was left of a burned car—maybe remnants of the war. Some had not been on the roadside for long, like one truck I vividly remember. The truck had a broken front axle, its nose buried deep in the mud. The thing was beaten up and old, resembling some once-majestic animal that had grown haggard with the scars of many fights. It seemed as if this great animal had been rushing at something or someone and had been shot midcharge, its front legs buckling and its face burying itself in the mud as it died. All around, people were unloading what was salvageable, stripping the meat from its bones and leaving the skeleton to decay. Printed under the windshield in yellow letters was the name of the truck: "God Will Provide."

What an experience to ride the Monrovia-to-Ganta Highway. The wonders, previously only available to me in books and magazines and on television, were repeated over and over. The only major towns we passed through were Kakata and Gbarnga. Kakata was the location of a technical school, Booker T. Washington, which marked the educational path of many well-known Liberians. Vibrant, intelligent people graduated from this school, like the former United Methodist bishop and former vice president of Liberia, Bennie Dee Warner, who would become a close friend in the coming years, as well as the Liberian ambassador to the United States, Jeremiah Sulunteh.

About halfway to Ganta, two and a half hours into the trip, we stopped at the CooCoo-Nest Café outside Totota. After our long ride, all of us needed to use the facilities. Chris and I were beginning to feel a little more comfortable in this strange land, so we opened the front door of the store and went inside. It was dark because there was no electricity, but in time, our eyes adjusted and we could see. As the darkness

On to Ganta!

gave way to obscure vision, we quickly made our way to the bathroom. The restroom was small and stained with years and years of no running water. There was a small window that let in some fresh air, but since there was no window pane, the rain had poured in, bringing with it dirt and muck. Like almost everywhere in Liberia, we had to use a bucket to flush the toilet. Bathrooms like this do not exist in the United States. It was gross, and it smelled; I had the sensation of herds of germs jumping from everywhere to attack me. Wandering back into the store proper, we all decided to have a Coke. We each paid our dollar and went outside and sat on the porch, where there was at least a little breeze blowing. There was a large building across the road that looked like an abandoned 1960s hotel. Victor told us it was once an amusement park with waterfalls, swimming pools, and kids' outdoor playground equipment, built by former President Tubman, whose "getaway" mansion wasn't far away. Victor told us one of the properties even had a zoo. During the wars, all the animals in the zoo and all the other animals, domestic and wild, were killed for food. It was sad to think what Liberia was like before the wars and what it had become. Liberia had the highest standard of living in Africa before the wars. The instigators of the wars were willing to destroy everything to possess the power to force their will on the people of Liberia instead of effecting change through the law. How many lives were forever destroyed by the desire for power?

Somewhat refreshed, we piled back in the Land Rover and continued the second half of our journey. We were finally leaving the congestion of the city and the suburbs and traveling into what felt like an untouched land. Of course, a lot of the areas around the road had been cleared for habitation, currently and/or in the past, but now there were long stretches of magnificent bush. One feature stood out over all the rest: the cotton tree. Across the landscape, cotton trees towered high above the rest of the green vegetation. These trees were eight to ten stories high, twice as tall as the surrounding jungle. Their branches twisted and contorted in odd shapes, with tufts of green sprinkled randomly. I

When Faith Lights the Way

wondered to myself whether the trees in Dr. Seuss's books were inspired by these amazing specimens.

In the tropics during the rainy season, we learned to expect afternoon rain showers to boil up and drop deluges. The short-lived storms leave the land with spectacular sunshine, the sweet smell of clean air, and thankful vegetation. We rode along at seventy miles an hour with the windows down, smelling the just-washed air and looking at the majestic cotton trees standing guard over the land. The rain brought tranquility. I refused to believe all this happened by chance. A deep peace overcame me, and I thought to myself, *thank you, Lord, for giving me a glimpse of your glory.*

Someone told Victor that the regional commander for the UN Peacekeepers was stationed in Gbarnga, a town seventy miles from Ganta. It was our understanding that the command center had recently been moved from Ganta to Gbarnga. Since we had to pass through there to get to Ganta anyway, we decided to drop in without an appointment and see if we could solve our problem of getting the container unloaded. At that time, I didn't realize that five years later we would return to Gbarnga to electrify a seminary and high school, a project which would become one of our greatest successes.

The guard at the gate allowed us into the UNMIL Compound, where the UN Bangladesh Peacekeeper Battalion, BANENGR-12, office was located. We were directed to a portable building, the command headquarters, to meet the officer in charge. The inside of the building was well equipped and practical, with modern décor—just how you would picture a US Military mobile command post. We were escorted to the second in command, who informed us that Major Sultana, the officer in charge, was away. The second in command was very impressive, spoke excellent English, was well-educated, and had the bearing of a fine military officer. He told us that Major Sultana had gone to Ganta for the day and was expected back, but they were not sure when. We exchanged pleasantries for a while and learned this UNMIL unit was composed of soldiers from Bangladesh. I knew nothing of Bangladesh except they were once a part of British Empire, then part of Pakistan, and I remembered George

On to Ganta!

Harrison of the Beatles had written a song and done a benefit concert to help the people after a horrible natural disaster in the early 1970s, during their war for independence from Pakistan. I was impressed by the level of sophistication of the people I was meeting. When you meet different cultures face to face, sometimes they're not at all like you had pictured them in your mind.

Since we still had a one-and-a-half-hour drive to Ganta, we decided to leave and make an appointment at a future time to see the officer in charge. We had just walked outside when an all-white off-road vehicle with a UN symbol on the door pulled up beside our vehicle. The officer who walked us to the car told us this was Major Sultana's vehicle. She came over to us, introduced herself, and asked in an assertive tone who we were and what our business was. Though small in stature, she was large and in charge. We told her our names and the names of the organizations we were with and described our purpose. As I recall, it took a few minutes of questions and discussion before she felt comfortable with us and our intent. After the preliminaries, she asked if we would like some refreshment. She had a small white plastic table brought out, and we sat on the well-manicured green grass and enjoyed the late afternoon temperature drop. Her staff brought us fruit drinks, and we all enjoyed getting to know each other. She was delightful. With our improved relationship with the officer, we inquired if she could authorize the use of some unloading equipment. But she was not aware of any such equipment in the Ganta area.

We said our goodbyes and climbed back into our Land Rover to finish the last leg of our journey to Ganta. How were we going to get the material out of the truck in the morning? We were running out of possible saviors to unload the containers, but there was comfort in meeting the Bangladeshis. They were impressive.

We had visited with UNMIL in Gbarnga for about an hour and a half. It was getting dark, and we still had a long way to go to reach Ganta. There were plusses and minuses to driving after dark in Liberia. On the plus side, almost no one drove after dark, so we could go fast. The minus

When Faith Lights the Way

was the roads were clear at night for a reason—it was too dangerous. The roads didn't become straighter, and the potholes weren't suddenly repaired. Just as in the daytime, the driver would jerk the steering wheel side to side as if trying to avoid ghosts in the road. He would fly the car into the left lane, then back to the right shoulder for a while, and back to the left lane, the left shoulder, and finally back into the right lane.

At night, the few vehicles on the road didn't have taillights. Abandoned cars or trucks on the smooth part of the shoulders were only one of many obstacles. For some unknown reason, women walked along the side of the road at night. Several times, we zoomed around corners at seventy miles an hour, driving on the left shoulder to avoid hazards, and suddenly came upon women carrying bundles on their heads, walking on the left shoulder beside head-tall weeds. When they saw us, these poor women grew terrified. We could see their eyes widen and their mouths open in screams, and we watched, shocked, as they dove head-first into the bushes to avoid us. We never went back, never slowed down, just kept barreling down the road. Traveling really did tax my ethical sensibilities. What I thought was right and wrong could put me in an infinitesimal minority in a country that was not my own. I had to learn to focus on the big issue and let go of my need to disagree with smaller customs and events.

21
Plan B

Day 3, continued

Finally, we arrived at the guesthouse on the grounds of United Methodist Church of Ganta. It was good to see the rest of the team and get out of that vehicular torture chamber. The guesthouse, a single-story ranch house, was built in the 1950s or '60s, and the half we occupied was brick with a screened-in porch. The other side was a concrete block structure, covered with plaster and painted pale yellow. The whole house had a tin roof, and the windows were jalousie style with a layer of chicken wire and screens to discourage mosquitoes and critters. Crumpled white drapes adorned each window, tied in knots to let in the breeze.

Chris and I walked in the front door and took in our new living room: a large, white-plastered room with an overstuffed, furry, brown chair, a matching couch, and a loveseat. We also had a wooden coffee table to put our feet on. Near the fireplace stood a wooden table with eleven wooden chairs with rattan bottoms, most of them matched. On the other side of the fireplace sat a small table topped with a large industrial coffee pot. The furniture would have been turned down if we'd tried to donate it to a thrift store. Each room had one bare light bulb fixed to the ceiling and an electric fan, but only about half of the fans worked because the electricity was so anemic it burned out the motors quickly. The only bathroom could be found between the two large bedrooms.

The bath featured a multicolored grayish tile floor set with white grout infused with indigenous red sand, a turquoise porcelain bathtub, Pepto-Bismol colored four-inch square tiles surrounding on the walls, and a small porcelain sink and toilet. The red sand infusion in all the grout joints, as well as the grout that was smeared all over the floor, was styled by those who had reset the toilet many times—not by professionals. The bath plumbing received running water about two hours a day when the pumps were started in the three wells on the property. The running water was used to fill up two large plastic tubs that were steel gray in color. One was to be used for a bucket shower and one, with a pail, to flush the toilet.

Terry, Gary, and Ry had dibs on one of the bedrooms. The bunks were single-sized beds that stood about a foot off the floor, with mosquito nets hung from the ceiling over each one. Pinkie and Frank chose another room, and Chris selected the remaining bed in that room. There was only one bed left for me, and that was in the room with King Harrell.

Harrell was having a delightful time in Liberia. He never met a stranger, and once he arrived in Ganta, he wanted to establish immediately that he was in charge and to be respected. He declared himself king, and after that, everyone in Ganta addressed him as such. He constantly kept things stirred up by flirting with all the women. They flirted back.

We were starving after our long journey, so Chris and I ate while we all sat around the table and went through the events of previous days. There was good news and bad news. Chris and I were pleased to share the good news that the containers had been released and would arrive in the morning. For the bad news, we told the team that we were unable to locate any unloading equipment for the transformers in the container. We would be forced to use plan B.

Plan B was this: over several months before we'd left Texas, we concocted every scheme imaginable to remove the six thousand-pound

Plan B

transformer—a big green box of iron, steel, and oil—from the back of the container. This monster was almost five feet tall, five feet wide, and five feet deep, and it weighed more than most pickup trucks. We planned to go old-school and copy the Egyptians. Maybe if we dug a pit that gradually sloped down and ended in a dirt wall, the delivery truck could back the container down into the pit until the floor of the container was level with the top of the ground. Using a hand-operated hydraulic forklift we brought with us in the container, we could raise the transformer up—seven inches was all we'd need—and then we would put four-foot-long, six-inch diameter, heavy steel pipes under the unit. If we could get it on the ground, maybe we could move it using the heavy steel pipes, like how the Egyptians moved the blocks of stone for the pyramids. We could push the unit forward, rolling it on the pipes. As the unit moved forward, a pipe would be uncovered at the back. We could pick up that pipe, run it around to the front, and push the transformer onto the newly placed front pipe. We would repeat this as often as necessary. We had fifteen smaller transformers to move that way, and some of them would have to be moved over a mile uphill.

The trip to Ganta must have been an adventure, according to the first team to make the journey. One of the tall tales from the trip involved Frank, who was never distracted by his clear vision of electrical principles and laws. Frank is a devout follower of the laws of engineering. As for Frank's ability to follow man's laws…not always so much. If he didn't see a clear purpose behind a rule, he did what he wanted. We were told the first night it was okay to take pictures of the UNMIL people and equipment. We were also told *not* to take pictures of the Liberian Military!

There were two checkpoints like the one on the outskirts of Monrovia at two additional towns along the road to Ganta. When our first group made their trip to Ganta, passing through the checkpoint outside Monrovia that was staffed by UN Peacekeepers, things went smoothly. But things were different for our first explorers at the Kakata checkpoint, which was manned by Liberian Army soldiers. Frank rode shotgun due to his recent knee replacement. As the Land Rover moved up to the

When Faith Lights the Way

pipe blocking the road, a soldier approached. Frank, being a self-proclaimed cameraman, started filming the Liberian soldier coming up to the passenger-side window. Others in the group said in a low voice, "Frank stop. You're not supposed to film the Liberian Army." When he wouldn't put away the camera, they got a little bit louder: "Frank! Stop!"

The soldier began to get angry. Our group escalated their pleas. "Frank, Stop! You'll get us arrested!" Since they were now safe in Ganta, they were rolling on the floor with laughter as they told the story. The soldier was really mad when he got to Frank, and Frank insisted he wasn't doing anything wrong. It was Frank against the Liberian Army, and they had guns. The driver got out and somehow talked the Liberian army into letting them pass. I suspect the Cross and Flame on the side of the vehicle had a big influence in convincing the guard that our team intended no harm.

The crew then gave Chris and me bad news. The Mission and Hospital electrical departments didn't get along. They wouldn't speak to each other, and they even stole tools from each other. This meant that our plan to build a single system to support the two facilities was in jeopardy. When we were preparing for the project, we'd insisted to the hospital and mission administrators that the local people would need to sacrifice to make the system a reality. Having the electric teams at Ganta Hospital and Mission help build the system was a great way to develop pride among the people that would operate and maintain the electric grid in the future. We planned to encourage the Liberians to watch the Power From the SON team as we began the installation of the system, then we would work together, and finally, the Liberians would do the work while the PFS team advised. This would ensure they had skin in the game. The hospital system across the road had a generator, an electric system, and an electric department. The mission side, where we were, had its own generator, electric system, and electrical department. We planned and brought the material to run the whole campus off one generator, located on the mission side, and install and operate only one electric system to

Plan B

improve efficiency. With all the adversity we'd overcome, and all that still confronted us, we needed something to go our way on this project.

To add to our problems, we had given the administrators a plan for digging the trenches for the cable before we arrived. UNMIL was digging the deep trenches for the primary cable, and the mission had hired thirty-six local workers to dig the smaller ditches. The mission provided shovels to these workers and paid them the standard hourly rate in Liberia of two American dollars per day plus a meal. Not too much of the shallow trench had been dug in the days preceding our arrival, and our plan disintegrated earlier that afternoon. We quickly learned that we didn't get a lot of trenches dug when the mission paid people by time instead of production. The diggers complained to the Liberian foreman about their pay, she started yelling back at them, and a shouting match ensued. It almost escalated to a fistfight—or, rather, a shovel fight. The workers all walked off the job.

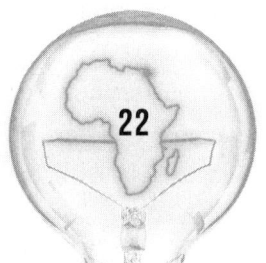

Where Is the Calvary?

Day 4: Ganta

On Thursday, June 11, we woke early. Our Egyptian-inspired plans for unloading the containers would not be needed that day; the containers had not arrived. Not only this, but only *eight* Liberians had returned to dig trenches.

I began to think again that we weren't going to make it happen. Despite our best efforts for the past year, we would have to return home without providing reliable electricity to this hospital that was desperately needed to help its twenty-four thousand yearly patients. We were on an island, surrounded by the African bush, in arguably the most destitute area in the world, away from everyone we loved and everything we were comfortable with. That morning, the world seemed far darker than the night before. All our laughter and joy was gone.

Thinking back on everything we'd already gone through, the very threat of losing all we had accomplished made us sick. We'd faced down obstacles at every turn, and we had solved problems that we'd never encountered before. We had almost a hundred grand invested, not counting donations. For over a year, we had done the design work and bought and shipped the material. We'd used up two and a half valuable

When Faith Lights the Way

days engaging in withering and discouraging negotiations, finally getting the containers released from customs. We were left with trying to unload the containers using the backbreaking, time-wasting, Plan B. We had lost the local people who were supposed to dig our trenches, and we had two electrical departments, who didn't like us or our plans, engaged in a cold war. We were good, but not super-hero good. These developments could flatline all our efforts.

Sitting and sweating without the safe water and food we had packed in our containers, we had no way to get anything we might need, and we were wondering where to turn. We all realized we were going to fail if something didn't change. Right before breakfast, we all drowned our hands and arms in hand sanitizer. Then we stood around the table, only touching elbows, with arms extended straight out from our shoulders, our forearms turned upward at the elbows at ninety-degree angles. Several years ago, there was a popular wall poster of a kitten hanging for dear life on a wire with only his front paws, and the caption read, "Hang On!" Our hands were cupped like we were the kitten hanging in there, and that morning's prayer went something like this: "Dear Lord, we have done our best, but we can't do this. If you want this done, you are going to have to make something happen. Amen." It became a ritual that we still do.

We stepped out of our boats, let go of the sides, and gave up control of the project. At that point, we had to acknowledge we weren't smart enough or committed enough to overcome these obstacles.

We finished breakfast and ventured out so Chris and I could see the grounds and the project. It was a bright, sunny day, and as I looked toward the school, I could see ten or so elementary school children with long knives. The knives had handles they held in one hand, and they were swinging the blades back and forth like the pendulum of a clock. The cutting end curved up, the curve bringing the blade horizontal to the ground. They were cutting the two-foot-tall grass on the football pitch, and they were having such a good time performing their hard work.

Where Is the Calvary?

After watching these children, we walked out of the guesthouse and ran into Sue Porter, Barbara Tutton, LiZa Eisner, and Wulle Wö coming to introduce themselves. Sue was the dean of the nursing school, and Barbara was the administrator on the mission side. Both women were tall and slim with dark hair, and they'd been friends for quite some time. Sue had spent some time in Afghanistan during the war and had encouraged Barbara to leave the "normal" behind, come to Liberia, and do something that counts. LiZa and Wulle were German, in their twenties, and on a mission exchange program. It was nice to put faces to the names of the people we'd corresponded with during the preparation.

With the disappointment in the previous day's events in the backs of our minds, we decided to start our tour on the hospital side of the campus. We walked on the side of the Miller McAllister United Methodist Church, situated between the guesthouse and the two-lane country road that served as the highway between Monrovia and the country of Guinea. Miller McAllister Church was unique for this part of the country, in that it looked like the old mission churches found in Texas. It was a traditional, tall, rock church—as tall as it was wide. The roof was a steeply pitched tile roof, once red, that formed an equilateral triangle perched upon the walls. A bell tower stood as a sentry high above the front entrance. Everywhere we looked, the church needed repair. Some of the colorful, old stained-glass windows were broken, and the roof was decrepit.

Moving across the road, we passed the hospital and walked north on the dirt road past the house Sue, Barbara, LiZa, and Wulle occupied. There was a hill to climb to reach the area where the girls' dormitory was once located. As we walked, we heard a truck engine. We moved to the side of the road as two trucks painted white with the UN letters on the door approached where we were standing. One truck appeared to be a tanker.

"What's the deal?" we asked. "Who are they, and what are they doing?"

When Faith Lights the Way

Sue replied, "That's the local UNMIL Peacekeepers, going to our lake to draw water for their camp. They do that about every other day." A plan bloomed in the back of my mind as I stared at those tankers. I replied that I sure would like to talk to them when they came back.

We kept on walking up the hill, looking around, then started back down the hill about the time the UN trucks returned, loaded with water. Sue flagged them down and introduced me, and I started my sales pitch. I told them who we were and what we were trying to accomplish, and I asked if they had equipment that might help us unload two containers. They radioed the camp, discussed it with their superiors, and said one of their majors would be available at ten o'clock to meet with us. He would come to visit us on the crest of a hill, close to an abandoned girls' dormitory.

Before ten, we saw two UN trucks pull up to the spot where we had been told the meeting would take place with the representative of the UNMIL battalion stationed in Ganta. A gaggle of soldiers in camouflage uniforms and blue UN baseball caps piled out of the trucks, unloaded a bunch of equipment and material, and began to work like frenzied ants erecting two tents. On one tent, the army-green canvas formed a triangle with the ends open. Tables and other equipment were loaded inside, and this became the outpost during the meeting for the soldiers that did the tent erection.

The other tent structure was for our meeting. The soldiers placed a waterproof brown tarp on the ground and then made a lean-to structure. Three sides were open, with a green canvas roof over our heads and more canvas covering the remaining side. The lean-to made me feel like I was looking out a big picture window. They placed a plastic table and chairs inside.

At ten o'clock Major Touhidul (Touhid) Islam arrived with a driver and escort. Major Islam was a tall, well-proportioned man in his thirties, who exuded a military demeanor. Our group consisted of our new German friends, LiZa and Wulle, and the whole Power From the SON

Where Is the Calvary?

team, excluding Frank and Pinkie. Major Islam took a chair at the head of the table, and the two soldiers who had arrived with him in his vehicle stood at attention behind him. They didn't speak a word. We were invited to the meeting room tent and offered a chair, some candy from Bangladesh, and water. All my life I've been mesmerized by military movies, and this made me feel like I was in one. What an adrenaline rush. I chose to stand, as I felt I could be more effective by pacing. We exchanged small talk and then got down to the purpose of the summit. The PFS team and I explained who we were, why we were there, and how we were going to accomplish our mission. We thanked them for their help with the trenching, but we said we needed one more thing from them. We needed help with something that would save our project.

We described the transformers in the containers and our need for some mechanized equipment to unload the units and distribute them around the UMC campus. To my surprise and elation, Major Islam, very fluent in English, let us know that he would carry our request back to his commanding officer. He didn't offer any hints about the availability of the equipment we desperately needed, though. The meeting lasted maybe thirty minutes, and he said he would get back with us. The major and his two aides left; the rest of the soldiers broke down the temporary camp, loaded everything, and left in their trucks.

Soon after the major left, Barbara Tutton received a cell phone call from the Bangladeshis. Apparently, we were invited to come to their compound at one that afternoon, to discuss our inquiry for equipment. At about 12:45, we loaded into the SUVs and headed for the UNMIL complex located on the southern outskirts of town. The soldiers at the entry gate checked to confirm we had an appointment, and as we drove to the parking area, we got excited. They had all kinds of equipment needed to make our project a reality. We just had to convince them to help us.

When we arrived, we parked by a well-maintained portable building and were guided up the stairs into the entry of a large meeting room. Ah, air-conditioning. The room was immaculate white, with chairs along the

When Faith Lights the Way

wall and a large TV. The room was filled with officers enjoying a World Cup football match. We were introduced and began to work the room as if at a cocktail party. The drinks were not cocktails, but the same sweet and tasty light yellow fruit juice we'd been served by the major earlier that morning. I was steered by Major Islam to enjoy light conversation with Lieutenant Colonel Md Nurul Huda, the unit commander.

Colonel Huda asked if we would be interested in being their guests for dinner, and of course we were pleased to accept the invitation. Colonel Huda was trim, in his forties, and a little shorter than five-nine—my height. He was distinguished looking and very much a refined gentleman, as were all the Bangladeshi officers.

The first course, dessert, was the same candy we'd enjoyed with Major Islam: a petite, soft, sweet morsel that gave the meeting a genteel atmosphere. After dessert, enlisted personnel came into the room and set up tables in a U shape. The UNMIL officers sat on the left side of the U, Colonel Huda and I sat in the middle, and the Power From the SON crew and those from the mission sat on the right side. It was a delicious meal, very Mediterranean, consisting of kebabs and rice.

Looking out over the group gave me one of the most vivid memories of the trip. Terry was sitting quietly, eating rice. I was shocked! Ever since I'd known Terry, he'd been adamant in his committed Marine tone: "I will not eat rice! All I ate in Vietnam was rice. I will *never* eat rice!" On the flights to Liberia, we harassed him by constantly reminding him that all they ate in Liberia was rice. He said, "I don't care. I'll go hungry before I eat rice!" We'd had rice every meal since we arrived in Liberia, but Terry wouldn't touch it. At this dinner, when his eyes caught mine, a scowl appeared, but he was getting it down. I admire people with conviction, especially those who have a reason to follow their commitments. But when it came to doing the right thing and not offending the Bangladeshis, he put aside his personal commitment for the benefit of the Liberians and us all. He ate rice. Much later he would admit it wasn't that bad, and he has eaten rice since then.

Where Is the Calvary?

During dinner, the colonel asked me about our request for help from his unit. I described how we needed a forklift or crane to unload and transport the transformers. I gave him a short history of the hospital, including how badly it was damaged during the war, the number of patients they treat, and how the poor electricity affected the treatment and recovery of the patients. He listened politely without saying a word, and then he asked where all the material came from.

"We had it sent on two containers from the United States," I said.

"Who paid for the equipment?" was his next question.

I told him some was donated by individuals and companies in the United States, and some was paid for by Power From the SON.

"Who pays these men?" was his final question.

"They are not getting paid. They are volunteering their time. This is our gift to try to help these suffering people."

There was a short pause. Lieutenant Colonel Md Nurul Huda asked for attention from the group. He looked at his soldiers and said very convincingly, "Gentlemen, you will do everything you can, as long as it does not interfere with your regular duties, to help Power From the SON complete their work!"

Unbelievable!

All the UNMIL officers seemed to have cameras on them, for they retrieved these immediately and began taking pictures of the happy occasion. After this was over, we all went outside together to look at the equipment on site and take a lot of pictures in front of the equipment, with our arms around our new best friends. Admittedly, they did have some reservations as to whether their huge forklift with its all-terrain tires could handle the six thousand-pound transformer. After looking at the load-lifting rating of the forklift, though, we had no reservations as to whether it could do the job.

The day had started low and ended high. We all felt great on the ride back to the hospital/mission. We agreed to call our new best friends, the UN Bangladesh Peacekeeper Battalion (BANENGR-11), as soon as the

When Faith Lights the Way

containers arrived, and they would drive the forklift over. We felt that, by the time we drove back to the mission/hospital, the containers should be there. We planned to put eyeballs on the containers, call BANENGR-11, unload that afternoon, and start pulling wire the next day.

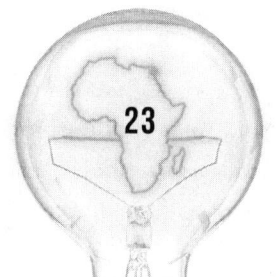

Time Is Wasting

Day 4

After a successful meeting with Bangladeshi battalion, we were at our highest, but the news that greeted us at Ganta Hospital and Mission brought us back down.

When we got back to the hospital and looked around the campus, the containers were nowhere to be found. *Are you kidding me?* I thought.

So many things had come together for it all to fall apart. I thought back, clearly remembering how the Assistant Minister of Finance promised us the containers would leave the previous day from the Freeport of Monrovia. It had been over twenty-four hours. What was going on? Where were our containers?

We had already overcome a few huge hurdles, so I wasn't going to let this latest one derail us. We put our trouble behind us and stayed focused. Our mission was to provide the necessary electrical equipment from the generators that were already at the hospital to all the buildings on the property. We hadn't yet seen the electrical facilities in person, so our group spent the afternoon on a walking tour with the two electrical departments, plotting a course of action and identifying any problems.

When Faith Lights the Way

There were maybe six electrical workers on the hospital side who were managed by Mr. Harry Flomo, the head electrician for that team. Flomo was a slight man in his fifties who was confined to a wheelchair and required an assistant to push him everywhere. His office was in a dark corner of the grimy generator house, made black from years of diesel-engine exhaust smoke. The building housed three old generators, and only two of them worked. Coming outside the mud brick building with a tin roof were ten white pipes with about fifty wires coming out. The wiring was in multiple colors—red, green, white, black, and blue—all taped together or crisscrossing each other. It looked like an out-of-control spaghetti factory. The thin copper wire inside the plastic insulation—about twice the size of a pencil lead—carried electricity all over the hospital. The wires hung limply on an old wooden support structure, some parts of which were broken off as a result of many years without maintenance. Branching out from the support structure, the wires were separated and nailed to trees or other old structures that looked like the weathered wooden clotheslines I used to see in pictures of rural America in the 1930s. We couldn't figure out how this all worked, and we didn't want to try, but we had to give the teams credit: their system worked, to a limited extent. Now we had the unenviable task of bypassing this colorful, tangled mess and connecting the generators inside the house to the new system we planned to install.

Adjacent to the generator house stood an outdoor wash station—without running water—and an old-fashioned clothesline used for washing clothing, bed linens, and rubber surgical gloves. Items we never thought twice about using and disposing of because of contamination concerns, were in short supply and were thus washed and reused. The individual hospital building structures resembled building blocks containing massive magnets that had been scattered around the grounds. The magnets caused some blocks to touch or be separated from the other blocks in random patterns.

The hospital was a mixture of architectural styles, each reflecting the era of its construction. Some buildings had wood siding and some native

Time Is Wasting

brick. The main building had a tin roof and, looking at the front, the equilateral gable of the house was punctuated with three windows. But the most eye-catching feature of all was the teal blue siding on the large gable. Outside, on a four-by-ten-foot plaster-coated wall, were written the words, "Ganta United Methodist Hospital."

The Harleys, the Methodist missionaries who had established Ganta Hospital and several other buildings in Liberia, had made huge sacrifices for the people of the country; it would have broken their hearts to see the damage done to their lives' work during the fourteen years of civil war. That being said, the current staff at the hospital were doing wonderful work with what they had. Truth be told, the whole time we were there, we avoided going into the hospital. The condition of the patients made us want to cry and made our skin crawl at the same time. The patients were not there to get treatment for colds or flu. The civil war had been brutal on the people in the Nimba County, and most were deathly sick or maimed. Many had lost limbs, digits, or eyes. Worst of all, at that time the only ambulances were motorcycles. If someone was in a car accident or fell from a tree, they were strapped to a motorcycle and transported many miles to Ganta, arguably the best hospital in Liberia at the time. There wasn't much to do for many of the patients except make them comfortable. Doctors simply didn't have the resources to help them. Liberia had a huge obstetric-fistula problem, partially because of the war, and a lot of women in and around the hospital were waiting to receive surgery to correct the problem. Our avoidance didn't stem from callousness, but rather a necessity to control our emotions and protect our compassionate hearts. The work we were doing would help these suffering people, and we needed to remain focused on our work.

On the hospital side of the road, there were many more buildings: offices, hospital supply storerooms, houses, and, up the hill, a girls' dormitory that had been destroyed in the war. Down another hill from the girls' dormitory lay an old dirt runway. In the 1960s, commercial flights used this runway for regularly scheduled flights. In 2009, the runway was merely a dirt strip, overgrown with grass and weeds.

When Faith Lights the Way

There were five electrical workers on the mission side, managed by Mr. Zuu, the head electrician. Zuu was also in his fifties and, like Flomo, had worked his way up through the ranks and learned electricity by doing, not by education. Both were naturally smart and practical and could be counted on to make good decisions. The mission side had two generators. One was running, but the other large machine, donated by Caterpillar, had never been installed because the local administration felt it would use too much fuel. It was a real struggle to help them understand that the amount of fuel used was proportional to the electrical load on the machines. These generators were housed in a tin shack at the edge of the mission. The mission side had the guesthouse, where we stayed, as well as the church, gymnasium, mission offices, boys' dorm (also destroyed), a high school and elementary school, and many houses for teachers and principals.

The tour around the hospital and mission showed us more than the facilities. It was apparent the two groups didn't work together or speak to each other. They only agreed on two issues: one, they didn't like our plan to combine the two systems; two, they didn't trust us. We explained our system to both electrical staffs, and they were not happy. "Who will be the boss?" they asked. "How many people might lose their job because of the new system?" We could hear them thinking to themselves, *how can these guys come over here, all the way from America, having never been here, and improve on what we have been doing for years?* We couldn't blame them for being concerned. We were going to have to convince them by actions and results, not by words.

In the afternoon, we brainstormed how to get the trenches dug for the secondary cables without any workers. LiZa and Wulle had some experience working with the Liberians on previous digging projects and suggested changing the pay to a dollar per foot of trench—shovel width, eighteen inches deep—plus a noon meal. This seemed a reasonable pay scale and was certainly worth a try.

By the end of the day, the containers still hadn't arrived. We evaluated our predicament and concluded there was no way to install all the

Time Is Wasting

equipment and complete the project in time if the containers weren't there the next morning. Texas A&M University has many catchphrases. One is, *Aggies never lose, though they may run out of time.* Time was going to run out; but in this game, the patients of Ganta Hospital were going to lose.

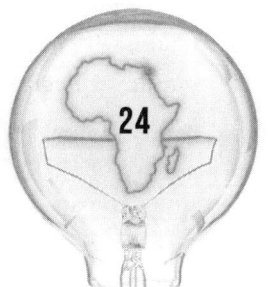

I Can't Believe My Eyes!
Day 5

On Friday, June 12, we all woke about 5:15 a.m. As the faint hint of sunrise crept into our tropical paradise, we could tell something had changed. Two large blue boxes on wheels sat on the road by our guesthouse. The impossible had happened—the containers had made it!

We threw on clothes and rushed out to celebrate, looking for the truck drivers to thank them. But they had vanished into the morning mist. After searching around and in the truck, we finally found them underneath the trailers sleeping in makeshift rope hammocks. Our commotion woke the drivers who, we learned, had arrived at about two o'clock that morning.

Someone explained that the containers had left Monrovia after dark so the drivers could better navigate the bad roads and avoid all the crazy daytime traffic. Only the trucks had brakes—meaning there were no brakes on the trailers—which made it was hard for them to stop. This explained why, on our way to Ganta, we'd passed several large trucks that had crashed into bridges or had burrowed nose first in the mud on the side of the road. They had no brakes.

When Faith Lights the Way

We let Sue, Barbara, and Victor know the containers arrived. They called the Bangladesh UN Battalion, who had agreed to help us, and we hurriedly ate breakfast and began to strategize about the unloading. As we ate and talked, spectators began to arrive. The arrival of the trucks was a big deal. Children of all ages came to see the show, and after about an hour, the UNMIL arrived in a caravan. There was the huge forklift and four or five other vehicles, including a ragtop truck carrying UNMIL troops in the back. It was a parade. Everyone had come to see what was inside the huge, steel containers.

We unlocked the padlock and opened the doors to find our six-thousand-pound green-metal transformer sitting there, just as we had left it. Harrell climbed up into the container and reported that nothing appeared to be broken by the transatlantic journey. We sighed with relief. Harrell reported the same for the second container. The shipment was in good shape, including eight of the team members' personal containers; everything, that is, except Harrell's personal container of clothes and snacks. It had been squashed. Our resident clown's misfortune made everyone laugh.

The members of the UN Bangladesh Engineering Battalion at Ganta came out in force for the unloading. There was a lot of discussion by the officers about the best way to unload the largest transformer. It was their unloading equipment, so it was their show, and the PFS team, including several who were more than experts in running this type of unloading equipment, watched impatiently.

It took a lot of time to get the big unit off, but thanks to the safety-conscious UNMIL personnel, there were no mishaps. UNMIL continued to assist with unloading the first container, which also held the fifteen single-phase transformers and half the supplies and equipment needed for the project. We moved the heavy items to the back doors of the container so the forklift could get the forks under the palletized material. The pallet jack we'd included in the first container facilitated moving these heavy pallets to the back. A pallet jack has two arms, resembling forklift blades, which can be raised or lowered about eight inches using

I Can't Believe My Eyes!

the steering handle to pump up a hydraulic cylinder. The ends of the arms have wheels, as does the back of the pallet jack, where the steering handle is attached. When someone pumps on the steering handle, the wheels will raise a pallet off the floor, and one can move heavy loads with the wheels. It took all morning to get the first container emptied, and after we had finished unloading it, the Bangladeshis broke for lunch off the grounds of the mission.

When the Bangladeshis took a break, so did we, and we hurriedly ate lunch before we tackled the unloading of the second container. During this lunch break, Chris phoned home, so the call came into the States at seven in the morning central time. Chris told his wife, Cathy, that we had received the containers and were in the process of unloading them, and that everyone was eager to get to work. Chris also told his wife that the people of Liberia were wonderful—very gracious and eager to help. "Everyone tells us, 'God bless you, thank you for all your hard work,'" he said.

Since the first container took so long to unload, we were doing a lot of standing around while the forklift—otherwise known as the gift from heaven—did its work. The unloading of the containers marked the first time our Power From the SON team had an opportunity to do some actual work. We were pumped to be working. It reminded me of how eager we were to get to work in Haiti, except this time we planned before we started. We didn't want to wait for the soldiers to return from lunch to get started, so we devised a plan to unload the second container without the use of the forklift, using only our pallet jack and ingenuity. There was also probably a little bit of competitiveness coming out. We planned to shock the Bangladeshi UNMIL soldiers with how quickly we could unload a container.

The main dirt road in front of the guesthouse had a driveway cut into the road at a ninety-degree angle so vehicles could pull up to the guesthouse. The rounded corner where the guesthouse driveway intersected the road had a two-foot mound of soft dirt piled up at the side. We had the driver of the second truck back the open end of the container up

When Faith Lights the Way

to the mound. This second container held all the wire and the balance of what we brought. The reels of secondary cable weighed a thousand pounds each, and somehow we worked the reels that were stacked on top down to the floor of the container, where we rolled them to the back and out of the container onto the soft dirt mound. We used the same basic method on all nine secondary cable reels.

The seven reels of primary cable, sixteen hundred pounds each, had been loaded in the container in Arlington so they could be rolled to the back. As we rolled them out onto the mound, we worried that what we were doing might break the wooden reels. But we took the risk, and it was worth it: all the reels survived. We unloaded the second container in two hours. When the UNMIL soldiers returned, all that was left was the second large transformer. They were adequately impressed.

"How did you get that container unloaded so fast without a forklift?" they asked. We happily told them everything we'd done.

Both drivers had to start back to Monrovia that night, so we had to unload the empty containers off their trailers. We PFS engineers brainstormed the problem among ourselves, but we couldn't come up with a solution. Major Islam asked calmly, with a hint of competition, "Where on the ground do you want the containers placed?"

"One in front of the guesthouse and one in the vacant lot beside the administration building," we told him.

"Very well," he responded.

We took up positions out of the way and watched everything unfold. They had a really old truck that looked like it was used to tow dead eighteen-wheelers. Using rusty chains to connect the tow truck to the container, they told the delivery driver to start his engine and put on his brakes. When they started the tow truck, it began to move, and the container groaned and squeaked in protest, then began to slide off the trailer!

I Can't Believe My Eyes!

When the empty container, weighing about five-thousand pounds, got a little over half off the trailer, the bottom of it—the end that was tied to the tow truck—tipped down until it rested on the ground. They left the chains connected between the tow truck and the container and told the UNMIL tow truck driver set his brakes. This time the delivery truck driver pulled forward. The container end chained to the tow truck stayed in place on the ground, and we could hear a metal-on-metal scraping sound as the delivery truck inched forward. There was a loud *boom* as the container slid off the trailer and hit the ground. *Wow*, I thought. Everything had gone according to plan.

After getting the containers on the ground, most of the wire and PVC water pipe was reloaded into the container closest to the guesthouse for safe storage. Three larger reels of wire were left out, as they could not easily be stolen, and we had the onsite security staff keep an eye on the goods for twelve hours a day during our stay. The chief of security was a wonderful man named Peti, maybe four feet tall, who carried a five-foot-long stick for a weapon. He took a lot of pride in his job and was very serious about making sure no one walked off with our supplies. His associate was six feet tall, had a scruffy stubble beard, and always wore the same faded purple jumpsuit and floppy blue hat. I'm sure the jumpsuit had never been washed. This man always wanted to help lift and carry things—or just be part of the party. He was also fairly old. During one of the first days, we started joking around about age, and we asked him how old he was.

"153!" he said with a big grin that showed missing teeth.

After that, he was known as Methuselah. We never got his real name. He was probably younger than we were; life in Liberia wore you out quickly.

For the duration of the project, Power From the SON and BANENGR-11 would alternate roles, each acting as teacher and student in turn. We became brothers as we toiled together to help the people of Nimba County, Liberia.

When Faith Lights the Way

Fulfilling our promise had seemed impossible until we turned the entire project over to God. We released our control and declared, "If it is your will, we will be your hands and feet." It was the only by God's grace that we had gotten as far as we had. We were laughably poor on planning, long on naivete, and sorely lacking on experience working in the developing world. Who uncovered all the hidden pieces of this puzzle of a project? The answer is God.

I've been spiritually moved by God many times, but I was never one to believe that God intervened in my physical life. For an engineer like myself, it's not logical to believe that God answers prayers. I sometimes wrestle with what I believe, what I do not believe, and what I still question. I was trained to use the scientific method in my quest for answers or solutions, so I tend to want concrete, doubt-proof explanations. But I also know from experience that cold, hard logic can't explain everything. To be honest, I never felt like what I did was worth God's time. But, as one who has experienced assistance beyond my capabilities, I am convinced the most rewarding path for me is to obey God by stepping out of the boat and onto the water when he calls.

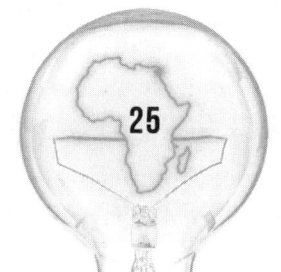

We Make Progress
Day 6

On Saturday morning, June 13, Major Islam arrived with a copy of a letter Lieutenant Colonel Huda had prepared to send to the UNMIL Command of Liberia, headquartered in Monrovia. In the letter, he stated that BANENGR-11 was going to work with Power From the SON to construct a modern underground power system for the Ganta Hospital and Mission. He included the necessary details. I must confess I'm a skeptical person who tries to look at all the possibilities that may occur in a situation, so I was concerned, due to my experience with bureaucracy, that the UNMIL bureaucracy might appropriate the project, and then it wouldn't be completed. I asked the major if I could add a sentence to the letter, and he agreed to take it back to Colonel Huda to see if he would approve the change. I added, "Power From the SON has designed, engineered, procured the material for this project and has the experience to assume the responsibility for the Ganta Hospital/Mission electrification project." Major Touhid, as we began to call him, said he would deliver it to Colonel Huda.

Shortly after noon, Major Touhid returned with the colonel's answer. My heart sank as I unfolded the letter and saw my sentence

When Faith Lights the Way

scratched through. Then, I noticed, a handwritten sentence had been added below my work, and I bent close to read it. "BANENGR-11 will take orders from Power From the SON," it read. I choked up. Colonel Huda had more experience working in these conditions than anyone I had ever met. To recommend to his superiors that his unit should follow the instructions of a civilian with no experience was a leap of faith on his part. The trust and honor Colonel Huda bestowed upon us was more than I could imagine. In the coming weeks, I witnessed even greater faith and kindness from these incredible soldiers.

We began the day by laying the wire in the trenches in the mission section, and by the time we were through, we had most of the primary wire in the ditches on that side of the campus. It rained most of the day, and that made it hard to walk, but at least it was cool—Liberian cool, that is, which means it was eighty degrees. On rainy days and at night, the Liberians broke out jackets and stocking caps. We were sweating in tee shirts and jeans, but they were cold.

Putting the cable in the ditch amounted to a group trust-building experience. The first man took the end of the cable, began pulling it off the reel, and walked into the end of the trench. If we let this cable drag on the ground, it would scar the outer plastic jacket, and the cable would fail in a short time. If it got damaged, we didn't want anyone to have to dig it up, repair the cable, and cover it back up—especially in Liberia, where a shovel is generally the only tool available. So before it dragged on the ground, another person would step in, put the cable on his shoulder, and walk into the ditch. Since some of the cable runs were six hundred feet, it took a lot of people to carry the cable. This was fun for both the Liberians and us. They had never seen anything like this, they all got to help, and everyone was shouting and laughing.

The compensation rate change from per day to per foot of dug trench did wonders. We had so many people wanting to take part that we didn't have enough shovels. It would take the contract diggers three more

We Make Progress

days to finish, but there would be no problem having all these trenches completed on time.

Each day yielded experiences we didn't have back home. Near the hospital, but standing separated from everything, was the morgue, a twelve-by-twelve-foot mud-brick building with a tin roof that had bricks left out in strategic places to create airflow. We were glad we didn't have to run electricity to that building. At about ten o'clock that morning, word spread like a fire through the campus that a Nigerian Peacekeeper soldier had died in the hospital that day. He'd been transferred to the morgue, and the Nigerian UNMIL were coming to retrieve the body. We sensed fear among the local population.

Around noon the Nigerian contingent arrived, and people scattered. The place was deserted. We all moved back and stood maybe a hundred yards away, watching as two or three very large, fit soldiers went into the morgue and retrieved the body. The soldiers left—they were only there about ten minutes—but the reaction of the people has always been a curiosity to me.

In the years since this first trip, I've made four more trips to Liberia and tried to understand the things I've experienced while there. Liberians who lived through the war have described the Nigerians as efficient soldiers who accomplished their main objective: to defeat Charles Taylor militarily. But they also tell stories of rape and pillaging. One well-respected furniture manufacturer survived the war only to have half a million dollars of equipment stolen and taken to Nigeria by the UNMIL Nigerian contingent. His factory was then burned to the ground, and he died of a heart attack due to a broken heart. Rumors have it that 250,000 children were fathered by the Nigerian Peacekeepers. I take no stand as to the truthfulness of these claims. I can say that these stories, so common among the people of Liberia, explain why the locals fled when these Nigerian representatives arrived to recover their comrade.

Everyone returned to work after the visit from the Nigerian UNMIL, and we began to disperse the primary cable throughout the hospital side

When Faith Lights the Way

of the compound. The electric cooperative where Gary Wilson worked had made a great tool for us to use: a wire stand for the primary cable. The reels that contained the primary cable were designed to be energized at 7,200 volts and weighed 1,600 pounds. We needed some way to pick up the reels, carry the wire to the area where we were doing a pull, and then have the cable easily "pay off," or unwind, from the reel. The stand was made from heavy, galvanized pipe and had a thick steel pipe that passed through the center hole of the wooden reels and then attached to two cables. A hoist was used on the cables to winch the steel pipe up on the stand where the wooden reel was suspended on the bar that passed through the reels. This would allow the reel to turn freely on the pipe when the assembly was locked on the steel stand. The stand had a skid bottom, so we attached a chain to the back of a pickup truck and pulled the stand with the wire down the dirt roads to the location where we wanted to start the wire pull. You can't take the kid out of the man, so we took turns riding to the site with our feet on the skids, holding onto the stand's vertical uprights. The Liberian boys joined in on the ride, and everyone had a great time moving the cable. At the site where we would start putting the cable in the trench, we unhooked the chain from the stand holding the wire reel and began walking the wire into the ditch.

More than once, we used the less proper method and stuck a pipe through the hole in the center of the wooden reel, put three people on either side of the reel, and just rolled the wire reel where it needed to go. We knew we were asking for trouble, since we had already dropped the 1,600-pound reels out of the truck onto soft dirt, possibly damaging the inner core of the wooden reels. Rolling the reels could exacerbate the situation because one of the wooden reel sides might collapse under the strain and leave us with a tangled mass of spaghetti. Nevertheless, to be more efficient, we decided to take a chance. We did this several times when we needed to get reels across the main road to the hospital. The main paved road was down in a depression about ten feet deep, so we had to roll the wire as fast as we could down the embankment and then up the other side. If we didn't have enough speed, we couldn't get the reel

We Make Progress

up the other side. Also, we couldn't see the traffic coming down the road in either direction because of the dirt walls that lined the intersecting road where we rolled the wire.

We sent Pinkie out onto the paved main road to stop any traffic as we gave a big push. The reel rolled so fast everyone had to run just to keep up with it. The motorcycle drivers, though, didn't respect Pinkie as he stood in the road with his hand up—a white man wearing his overalls and baseball cap, yelling in a high-pitched East Texas accent. "Stop! Stop! Stop I said!" What *did* get the motorcycle drivers' attention was when a five-foot diameter reel of cable came barreling down a crossroad with a metal pole stuck in the middle, pushed by six people—some Liberian and some white—running as fast as they could go.

The ditches for the large cable needed to be about thirty-six inches deep and a foot wide. We were fortunate that the Bangladeshis had done some digging before we came, and they managed to always have open trenches for us to lay the primary cable. The shovel on their excavator was probably four feet wide—too large for this job. In sandy soil, they got carried away. In some places, the trenches were seven feet deep. We tried to let them know that all that depth wasn't necessary, but the enlisted personnel running this equipment enjoyed the experience, so we finally just let them have at it.

The most important thing we did that day was to encourage the hospital and mission electrical crews to get excited about the project. They disliked each other, but by the end of the day, they were working together to complete a wire pull across two roads. It was a first step in getting them to trust each other and to trust us.

But even though they were talking to each other and working together, the two Ganta electric departments still resisted installing *only one* electrical system. They held on to their misconceptions about fuel usage on a large generator and brought up other issues that were easily countered. We wondered if the problem was really that it would not take as many people to operate one system as two. The number-two guy on

When Faith Lights the Way

the hospital side seemed to have the biggest objection to the idea of a single system. Was he afraid he wouldn't be in charge one day? True feelings and motives were difficult to read.

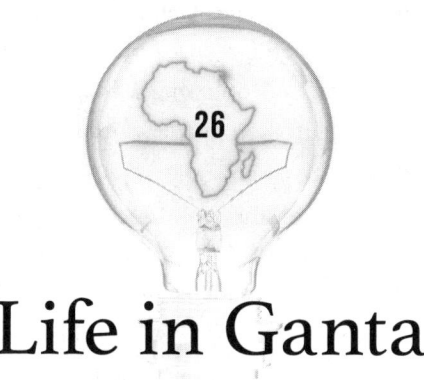

26

Life in Ganta

Day 7

On Sunday morning, June 14, we postponed work until after church, attending the Miller McAllister UMC located by the guesthouse. We walked in a little apprehensive, not knowing what to expect. The ladies were dressed beautifully in traditional long wrap skirts with loose tops. All of them wore head wraps. West African clothes are famous for their brightly colored and patterned fabrics, and these ladies knew how to dress. The men wore western suits or African shirts known as *dashikis*, loose and brightly colored. Everyone was so kind and welcoming. We wanted to sit near the back so we could slip out, as we were warned the services normally went for two or three hours, but we were ushered toward the front.

The service was very comforting to me, as the order of worship was the same as the Methodist Churches back home. I noticed the old hymnal was from the United States, given in honor of someone's mother and father in Ohio. It was tattered and worn, but it warmed my heart when I thought about how Christians and Methodists are connected throughout the world.

When Faith Lights the Way

When the singing started, that's where the service departed from the churches at home. These brothers and sisters sang with enthusiasm! At first, we sang the same way we would sing at home, with reserved dignity. But it didn't take long to catch the spirit and raise our voices along with the crowd. It felt right.

After ten or more hymns, they introduced us and asked us to come forward and explain our mission. The church was so excited. They offered a prayer for our project's successful completion and for our safety. We went back to our pew and stayed a short while longer. I looked up toward the roof and saw small shafts of God's light shining down on us. My mind wandered, and I pictured what it must be like to be all dressed up, standing in the rain inside the church. At home, even now, I miss the wonderful, uplifting African services and the zeal of the worshippers. During my later returns to Liberia, I always looked forward to attending services.

Well into the second half of the church service, we quietly slipped out. As we went about our work the rest of the morning, we could still hear the service going strong. We had installed most of the primary wire in the ditches, and by late afternoon we began to pull some of the secondary cables in the shallower, shovel-dug trenches. Since these reels weren't as heavy, we could roll them to the places where we would begin to pull the wire off to lay it in the ditches. We used two old wooden school chairs—the ones with single arms for writing—stuck a pipe through the center of the reel, and lifted the pipe to rest the assembly on top of the writing arms. This lifted the reel high enough off the ground that it would turn freely. We didn't need as many people to carry the wire, either, as the outer insulation on this cable was tougher, so we didn't have to worry as much about dragging it on the ground.

We still had a lot of local spectators from the younger crowd. One, in particular, was always there watching, never saying a word. We tried to talk to him, but he wouldn't speak. We judged him to be between eight and ten years old. After he'd watched us for an hour, we asked him if he wanted to help us by turning the reel so the cable would come off easily. Without a word or change of expression, he ran to the reel and

Life in Ganta

began to help us turn it. When we had reeled off the proper cable-run length, we would go pick up the cable cutters, cut the wire, and move to another location to start a new cable pull. The boy would go right with us, working alongside us without saying a word. Next, we asked him to bring the cable cutters when we had the proper length. He ran and picked them up and brought them to us. After a few cable runs, he would help turn the reel, and when he saw we had enough cable, he would run and get the cutters without our prompting. This was all done without him speaking a word. At the end of the day, we thanked him for all his hard work. He turned and silently ran home.

While we were surrounded by young spectators a great deal of the time, other kids were going off into the jungle in groups of four or more and hunting for fruit to knock down from the trees, playing in the river, or helping wash clothes in the river. The only shoes we ever saw on the kids were old flip-flops. As fast as children's feet grow, in a place like Liberia, it made sense to have a cheap shoe that could be easily passed down to another child. What we couldn't figure out was why one of them always had machetes, thick-bladed swords about two feet long that could cut through steel nails. We asked Barbara why each group always had a machete. "Is it for protection?" we inquired.

"Sort of," she replied. "There is a green mamba snake in Liberia, one of the most poisonous snakes in the world. Once bitten, you die quickly unless you stop the spread of the venom. Fortunately, the snake has a small mouth and can only bite you in places like your fingers or toes. They carry the machete so that if someone is bitten, they can chop off the finger or toe before the venom spreads and kills the child."

Every experience added to our understanding of Liberia and the Liberians. Trying to do work on the infrastructure in Liberia, with its lack of almost everything available in a civilized, developed country, made us rethink our grumbling about Dr. Labala asking us to bring him brake shoes for his Subaru Outback. If we didn't bring our equipment with us, we weren't going to find it in Liberia. It's hard for anyone to understand this lifestyle without having spent time living it. Dr. Labala's request for

When Faith Lights the Way

help with the brake shoes didn't mean he was trying to get us to do something he could do himself. Without our help, he would not have had brakes on his car.

While we were pulling and cutting cable, "King" Harrell was busy with three young Liberians, going from building to building, mounting the circuit breaker boxes and the conduit onto the buildings. Our wire would run underground up to the building, then up inside the conduit and into the circuit box. Harrell's team then ran the wire inside plastic pipe up to where the inside wiring came out of the building. The plan to change from the old system to the new was to leave the current overhead system supplying the buildings after the PFS crew finished installing the new system. The hospital and mission electricians would change the wiring at each building from the overhead to the new underground system when it was convenient for them. Electrically, we could only have the overhead or the underground system connected to a building—not both.

Harrell's guys stayed busy getting the wiring on each house ready to change from the overhead to the underground, and they provided a lot of entertainment. At first, Harrell would show them how to make the connections, then he would slowly give them more and more of the work until, during the last few days, they could do all the work by themselves. They were a band of four, including the "king," and they were constantly laughing and clowning. But they were very efficient. They installed all fifty-two service entrances in the time we were there.

For everything we did, an entourage of kids followed us. There were probably five or six in a group, five to ten years old. At first, they stood back, watched, and giggled, not wanting us to hear them. When we put something down and walked away, they would sneakily go look at what we were working with. They never bothered what we were using.

Except for our empty water bottles. It was so hot, we carried bottles of water with us in our back pockets to stay hydrated. After we would guzzle down a bottle, if we were away from the other children, one of the kids would shyly come up and ask us for the empty plastic bottle.

Life in Ganta

You would have thought we had given them a state-of-the-art cell phone. We wondered why they were so excited, so we asked Sue about it. She explained the children didn't have any way to carry water to school. With these water bottles, they could get water from the river and have water to drink during the day. She advised us to be careful and not give a smaller child a bottle any time a larger kid was around. If the larger kid wanted something, they would beat up the younger child and take what they wanted. Sometimes the beatings were severe.

This reminded me of the Haitian missionaries telling us that it doesn't help anyone to give to people without requiring something in return. Sue's explanation of what happens to the kids, and what I've personally witnessed in my travels to other countries, helped me understand those missionaries' advice not to give to beggars, including children. Behind their beautiful smiling faces is a sad existence that is difficult to escape, and nearly impossible to fathom. In many countries, parents send their children to beg. It's not uncommon for the parents, siblings, or older children to take by force whatever the smaller children managed to collect. It's a way of life. These children grow up and have children. They send their children to beg. The cycle continues. It took me a while to lose my naivete. It's hard to turn away little children, but the cycle of poverty isn't broken by rewarding begging.

Things are different in America. That's not to say there is no poverty in the United States. Of course there are poor communities across the country, but the level of poverty in America isn't as severe as one sees in rural Haiti or rural Liberia. In the United States, most children are able to go into stores and and pick out items they want, even at thrift stores. There are no such stores in these poor countries. Logically the only thing they can do with money is surrender it to someone with more authority or power. Sadly, the one who gives the money or candy feels good about themselves for having given, when ultimately it has the potential to harm the receiver. Giving the money to trusted local missionaries who understand the local situation is a much better use of a gift.

When Faith Lights the Way

It was apparent to us that many Liberians harbor negative feelings about the people who come to their country to help them. They would often say to you, "God bless you. Thank you for all your hard work." But the unspoken part of the statement was, "Hurry up and finish and give it to us so we can do what we want with it." We felt that some people were clearly trying to play us. They had learned that Christians will give them big handouts as rewards for making us feel truly magnanimous, so they would bow and act overly thankful. But this kind of Christian charity is not helpful; it is harmful.

Generally, Liberians resented Christian mission workers for acting as the masters who handed out favors. That was never our intention. We wanted to provide the opportunity to learn, to work alongside us in an effort to better their situation. They were our equals. No one wants someone from another culture to come and tell them how to live their life and what they should value. "Christians love to swoop in and give people Bibles, and the Afghan people love Bibles," Sue commented during a discussion about Christian charity. After a pause, she added, "The pages make the best rolling paper for smoking."

The Power From the SON team had decided before we left the United States that we would respect Ganta's electrical workers, consult with them on designs and plans, and work with them, but we would not do all the work for them. We wanted everyone who participated to understand that PFS could learn from others, and they could learn from us. As we worked and sweated together, laughing and getting to know one another, their resentment appeared to fade. We were growing in respect for the Liberians, and they seemed to be feeling the same about us. But we kept coming back to the fact that this was their system. We were there to help, but when we left, they would do with it what they wanted. How do you determine the cultural value of a state-of-the-art electric system? We still had no answer.

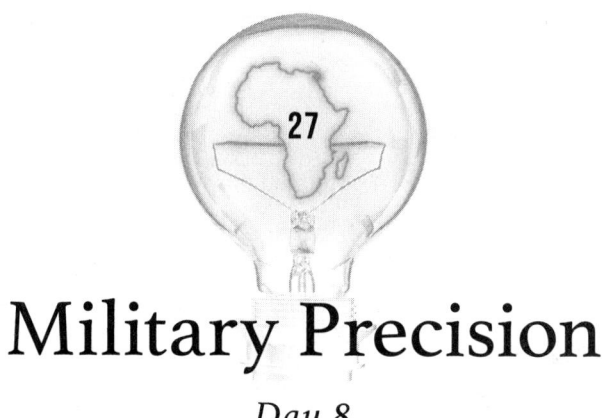

Military Precision

Day 8

Malarone, the anti-malarial pill we took every day, kept us hyper. No one could sleep much, even though the days were long and the work was backbreaking. We could keep working forever, it seemed. Our normal schedule settled into waking up at four-thirty or five in the morning and working every day until five or six in the evening.

On Monday, June 15, everyone got up early because we had a big project planned for the morning. Cables needed to be laid under the paved road that bisected Ganta Mission and Hospital from the main highway between Monrovia and Guinea. We were going to cut a four-foot-deep trench through the road, stopping traffic and causing chaos. We had been preparing for this event for several days by digging two pits right up to the road's edge on each side.

Our primary cable, buried thirty-six inches deep, would run from the generators on the mission side up to the edge of the road, then enter plastic conduit for the journey under the road, exit the conduit below ground level, and continue on to serve the hospital side. Three cables were needed—one in each pipe. We would put bags of cement over the

When Faith Lights the Way

pipes, and they would harden in a short time, encasing the conduit so it wouldn't move. We would then cover the road.

The day before, Barbara had gone to the police in Ganta and asked them to be onsite to direct traffic. They agreed, but only if we dug through one side of the road, completed our work, and repaired that side before we cut the road on the other side. The police wanted to be able to route the traffic through the construction instead of totally closing the road. The local police wanted the work to begin at 7:00 a.m. to minimize traffic interruption. Barbara agreed to these conditions; we didn't.

We had worked out the details of the operation the night before at BANENGR-11 headquarters. After work on Sunday, Touhid invited us to have dessert and a planning session. It was quite an enjoyable meeting, on a deck with a nice cool breeze overlooking a pond. On the red dirt surrounding the pond, the words *Bay of Bengal* were displayed on a white background in big, maroon letters. The smallish pond had a fishing boat, which dwarfed the pond; the small body of water lay beside a garden being tended to by the unit's Imam, dressed in a white robe and cap. A hill of red dirt sloped down to the Bay of Bengal, maybe fifty feet tall. At the top, the Bangladeshis had a rock circle with a trough of rock going from the circle down to the Bay of Bengal. The engineers pumped water from the pond up into the rock circle, and that water flowed down the rock trough back into the Bay of Bengal. It was all rather whimsical and clever. Days of peacekeeping can get boring, and building something to remind one of home makes the job more bearable.

We returned to the guesthouse after dark and filled in Sue, Barbara, LiZa, Wulle, and Victor on our plans for the morning. I guess they heard what we said, but the main response was, "You had ice cream! We've been here for months, and we didn't even know they had ice cream! They never invited us to have ice cream!"

During the planning session at BANENGR-11 headquarters, the Power From the SON team and the engineers from BANENGR-11 agreed there was no way to cut one side, do the work, and then cut the

Military Precision

other side. There wasn't time to argue with the police. We needed to cut the whole road at one time to keep on schedule. Power From the SON and BANENGR-11 agreed we would just do it and take the consequences. We planned to complete the task in one hour. The hospital and mission people weren't too keen on the decision but reluctantly agreed to go along. "Forward the Fight!" as The Salvation Army says.

PFS was on the hill overlooking the road at 6:30 a.m. when the Bangladeshis arrived with their huge excavator. They had several vehicles, including the ragtop personnel carrier filled with a cadre of armed soldiers dressed in bulletproof vests and helmets. Everyone involved knew their assignment, a necessity to complete the job in a single hour.

We were ready and in position at 6:50 a.m. 7:00 came and went. There were no police to direct traffic. At 7:30 Barbara headed to Ganta on the back of a motorcycle to get the police. At 8:15 or so, she arrived with a policeman. He would not come unless Barbara gave him forty dollars. There went my unwavering stand on bribery. I felt my footing slip on the loose rocks of the moral high ground. I quickly decided that I needed to focus on the bigger issue at hand.

The policeman directed traffic, and UNMIL began to cut the road. The excavator began digging a deep trench on one side of the road as traffic was routed to the other side. When the excavator finished one side of the road, he moved to the other side and began to cut that side as well. That's when people got excited. The policeman went into orbit. He jumped all over Barbara, saying there was no way for the traffic to pass. He was right. Cars and trucks on both sides of the road were at a dead stop. Our PFS team, the Ganta UMC electric department's men, and the soldiers moved into the ditch and began leveling the bottom and throwing out rocks as the excavator dug up the other side of the road.

I was standing on the side of the road with Major Touhid, on a hill forty feet above the action, with two armed soldiers on each side of us. Below, a riot was about to break out. The motorcycle riders with their passengers were racing up the hill into the hospital property and jumping

When Faith Lights the Way

our four-foot-wide trenches, but the trucks and cars were stuck. A crowd of about a hundred people was being held against their will. One car, transporting two Australians who had been in Africa for two months, was on its way to Monrovia so the Aussies could catch a flight back home. They jumped up and down and shouted at the policeman, who had basically given up.

I felt safe beside Touhid and the soldiers. I told them, "I'm glad I'm here with you guys and your weapons, in case I'm attacked." Touhid continued to stare at the scene below, with its chaotic motorcycles and angry people. He said with a sly smile, "We are Peacekeepers. We can only respond to people that attack us first. If they attack you, we can only watch and report the incident."

The trench was cut across the entire road, the pipe laid in, and the concrete sacks stacked on the pipe. The excavator covered up the ditch and packed the road. Traffic was released, and the road returned to normal. It had taken us fifty minutes. We were impressed with our planning and execution, not to mention the fact that a team from the United States, electricians from both sides of the road, and a group of soldiers from Bangladesh had worked together efficiently.

Working with the Bangladesh military was a treat in many ways. Their professionalism as a military unit, their work ethic, their humanitarian response, and their cultural traditions were such a joy for us to experience. Especially the daily tea break. Almost every morning and afternoon at ten o'clock and two o'clock, the ragtop personnel vehicle would pull up beside the guesthouse in a shady spot, and two soldiers would jump out and set up a plastic table and several chairs. Touhid and one of the other majors would have hot tea in white cups, with water and dessert. Power From the SON personnel were usual attendees at tea, as were Sue, Barbara, LiZa, and Wulle. Frequently, I was away working somewhere else on the property, and someone would come get me to join them for tea. The conversation centered around life in our respective homes. The event added civility, where six years earlier, there had been none.

Military Precision

After the circus surrounding the road cutting, Chris and I went to the campus school to talk about electricity and safety awareness. It was important that everyone know what the big green boxes were for and why it was necessary to take care of the system so it would last a long time. There were about 125 students dressed in yellow shirts and blue pants or skirts. Another twenty-five were dressed in white shirts and blue pants or skirts. Raising the Liberian flag while singing the national anthem was the first order of business. We were on the porch of the schoolhouse, and the flagpole stood between the students and us, making it easy to survey the crowd as they stood at attention and saluted.

The students were evenly mixed between girls and boys, ranging from elementary age to grown men. There were the clowns, smiling and making faces as we took pictures, and then there were some young men that had permanent frowns. Their expressions were disturbing and sad at the same time. You knew they had been child soldiers during the war and had seen and participated in unspeakable horrors. Now they stood with the younger children, learning the things they had been deprived of in their early youth.

We wanted to connect with the students and tell them a little about ourselves and our home. We told them that Texans were honest, hardworking, loyal, and self-reliant. We told them they had these same qualities and ideals, as represented by the similarities between the Liberian and Texas flags. The Liberian flag has eleven horizontal bars, alternating red and white, like the US flag, and in the upper left-hand corner is a field of blue with a lone white star. The Texas flag consists of a vertical stripe of blue, containing a lone white star, beside a white and a red horizontal bar. Texas is known as the Lone Star State, while the name of the Liberian football (soccer) team is Lone Star. We gave them a Texas flag and proclaimed them honorary Texans. We also told them Texans greet each other by holding up one hand, folding in the fingers, extending the thumb upward, and saying, "Gig 'em, Aggies!" We had them practice this several times until it became second nature. Sue or Barbara told us there would be visitors from Austin in Ganta the next week. I was pleased

When Faith Lights the Way

with myself when I returned the next year and several of the kids greeted me with thumbs up and a "Gig 'em, Aggies!" We took a picture of all of us with a Texas A&M flag and everyone giving the thumbs up.

After Chris and I left the school, we went back to working on the secondary cable, and the silent boy returned—but he was different! He started talking to us! He told us his name was Ronsay, and that he was ten years old and he liked school. And what a great worker! He was always there, always wanting to help.

As we made good progress on laying wire, with the Liberians doing more and more of the installation, the Power From the SON crew prepared to install the transformers. With our shipment, we brought polymer concrete pads to lay on the ground as platforms for the transformers to rest upon. This saved us time, eliminating the need to form and pour concrete platforms for each transformer. These had been delivered to all the designated locations on the property, and UNMIL used their forklift to set the thousand-pound transformers in place.

Sometimes, it's more efficient to run wire carrying 240 volts to a location, set a secondary pedestal, make connections inside, and run electricity from there to various buildings that are clustered together. The more expensive and wasteful alternative is to run every wire from the transformer to the various buildings. We had about ten secondary pedestals to install. This was an installation that could be completed with minimal experience, and it was a skill the Liberian electric department would use as the system grew. We taught them how and let them do most of the installations.

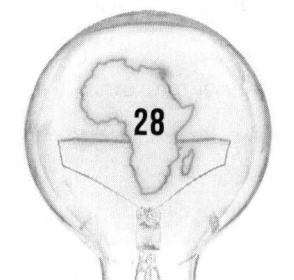

Is It All Worth It?
Day 9

On Tuesday, June 16, by the end of the workday, all the wire had been installed in the trenches. The Liberians finished this phase of the installation. Some of us watched, made suggestions, and answered their questions. BANENGR-11 was using their equipment to cover up and compact the dirt in the trenches, and together we finished putting the transformers and the secondary connection pedestals in place.

With the pace and physical demands of the work, we were beginning to take casualties. Gary was sick to his stomach, probably thanks to something he ate, and had to spend the afternoon in bed. Terry was having back pains and went to the hospital. The doctor gave him pills to relax his muscles. We were a small crew, so losing even one person might affect our timeline.

In our downtime, usually during evening meals, we often returned to the question of whether our plan was what was best for the mission and hospital. What if we were wrong? What if the system was too advanced for them to operate and maintain? Were we good enough instructors? Did the Liberians see the value and advantages of the system? We had no way to answer those questions, but we would know either way a year

When Faith Lights the Way

from now. If this system were still in place, we'd made the right choice; if it were abandoned, it would mean we'd spent a lot of money and time giving people something they didn't want.

On Tuesday afternoon we quit work with a little daylight left and took a tour of the boy's dorm. Most of the buildings had been rebuilt since the war, but not the boy's dorm. It was one of the last buildings completed before the war, and it still lay in ruin. The Liberians didn't want to rebuild it because, Barbara told us, it had "bad mojo."

During the final months of the war, two of the warring factions were camped on either side of the mission property. They fought each other across the property, and one of the groups used the boy's dorm as a prison. The dorm was a solid concrete structure, and with all the overgrowth by vines and caladiums, it looked like it had just emerged from hundreds of years of darkness under the African bush. It was a myriad of color: pale yellow, dark red, bare-aged concrete, and blackish-brown mold all painted the walls in grotesque patterns. The dorm was a gruesome reminder of the war. Vegetation had invaded the interiors, and bullets had gouged holes in the walls. Surely the dark red stains were rust or paint, we thought. But knowing what I know now, it may have been blood. A wide concrete stairway descended into a dark, concrete-walled basement. We were told this was where they tortured prisoners with knives and electricity. I have visited Soviet prison museums in Eastern Bloc countries and felt burning rage against the perpetrators while at the same time, feeling deep sorrow for the victims. I felt similar feelings here. We didn't want to continue to explore, instead exiting the other side of the building. We understood enough of what had taken place there, but I had many more questions. How can people commit these atrocities? How can other countries—and Christians—stand by and not stop the aggressors? Most people want to live their lives in peace in their lands, with their own customs and beliefs. They don't hurt others or drive innocent people from their homes. Why would we, as Christians, not support the rights of innocents to live on their land? Why would we not

Is It All Worth It?

confront evil in its infancy, so good people would have a chance at peace and happiness?

It was late afternoon, and a rainstorm was passing through just to the south of the mission. From the road in front of the guesthouse, looking back at the boys' dorm, I caught sight of one of the largest, most brilliantly colored rainbows I've ever seen.

After dinner on Tuesday, the PFS team walked to the administration building, which was the only place with Internet access. The building was locked after hours, but there was normally someone there until eleven or so—another person trying to communicate with the outside world. The building had three computers we could use, but I used the laptop I'd brought from home. Communicating by e-mail wasn't easy. To call the Internet there a dial-up system would be a compliment, and I won't be that complimentary. It wasn't uncommon to spend an hour trying to download a few e-mails. I would draft and save my e-mail messages offline at the guesthouse and try to send them once I had Internet connection. One night while waiting for e-mails to download, I decided it was time to initiate my most ambitious sales effort to date.

UNMIL had most of the comforts of home, including the great food from their homeland that was flown in by helicopter. There was an old runway on the hospital grounds that was used in the 1970s and '80s for commercial airline traffic. The runway was overgrown with weeds, but it was still a great landing pad for a helicopter. UNMIL would fly Russian-made helicopters in once a week with food and supplies. The road from Monrovia to Ganta was brutal, and we had every reason to believe the return trip would be just as bad.

I had names and e-mail addresses for American military personnel stationed in Monrovia, from the correspondence that took place when we'd tried to find a forklift to help with container unloading. I sent e-mails late that night from the Internet office, asking for assistance in

When Faith Lights the Way

getting a helicopter ride back to Monrovia. My request was humanitarian and truthful.

We needed to spend as much time as possible in Ganta working on the installation, and a forty-five-minute helicopter ride would give us four more hours to work. Three members of our company had fallen ill by that point, and it would ease their pain to not have to ride back by car. Additionally, the helicopter normally returned empty, so we weren't asking for a trip that would be an extra UNMIL expense.

There was one selfish reason for wanting to take a helicopter that I didn't mention. We simply *did not* want to travel that road. After the ordeal we'd been through over the last three weeks, we needed an easy trip to Monrovia. Also, I just wanted to see if I could pull it off.

The exercise was put in motion.

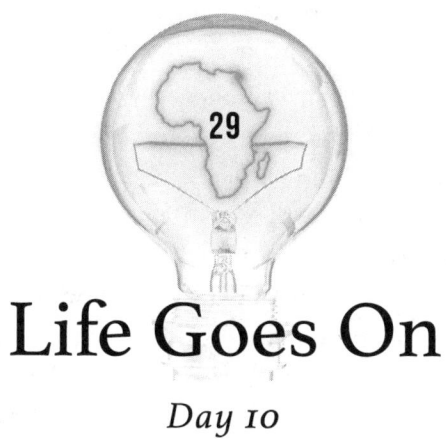

Life Goes On

Day 10

Wednesday, June 17, Gary was feeling much better and returned to work. But now Ry was down. Ry had become close friends with Darlington Dolo, a Liberian who was the partner of the juggernaut who almost went to war with the contract ditch diggers. It's not bad to become close friends, but sometimes it's not a good idea to go eat at a friend's house just because they invite you. Before he left for dinner on Tuesday night, we all told Ry to be careful of what he ingested, especially anything served in liquid. On Wednesday, Ry didn't report for work—he didn't report anywhere but the toilet for the rest of the day. When asked, he replied in a brink-of-death voice, "I know I shouldn't have eaten the fish soup, but it would have been rude not to."

The two large transformers were the last to be set in place. It was time to connect the wire to the transformers. The primary cable was used to carry the 7,200v to ground. The conductor consisted of aluminum, encased in three or four different, highly specialized layers of various plastic materials. Another layer of copper conductors was wrapped around the plastic and these copper conductors were encased in an additional layer

When Faith Lights the Way

of extruded plastic. This cable was highly engineered and manufactured according to stringent specifications in clean environments.

Preparing this cable with the fittings necessary to connect them to the transformers was a skill acquired only through education and repetition. First, you had to cut off the outer plastic layer of the cable, exposing the layer of copper conductors wrapped around it. The copper wires were then pulled back from the end of the cut cable and wrapped together to be attached to the system ground. Electrical tape would then be wrapped tightly around the interface that occurs between the copper wires and the plastic layer below the copper wires to ensure moisture didn't enter the cable between the two layers. Next, with a knife or insulation removal tool, you had to cut through all the plastic layers down to the conductor, two and one eighth inches—plus or minus one eighth of an inch—from the end of the cable. If you cut or scratched the aluminum cable, the cable would prematurely fail at that point. Next, you measured five and seven eighths inches, give or take an eighth, from the cable end and cut completely around the cable with a knife, taking *extreme* care to only cut most of the way through the outer, black plastic semiconducting layer. You then cut two straight lines from the circumferential cut to the end of the cable insulation left after removal of the layers down to the conductor, taking care to not cut into the white insulation.

The above describes about 40 percent of the preparation of primary cable to be connected to a transformer. It's not necessary to continue with these tedious instructions because the point has been made: this is a *very* exacting procedure.

Terry and Gary did this work in their jobs on an infrequent basis, and it took them about forty minutes to complete one termination. I could do one in about an hour. Wes did the terminations occasionally at work, but he was uncomfortable performing them, so he stopped after only a few. No one else in the Power From the SON crew had any experience with this. We had forty connections to make, and it took a lot of time, especially since it was just as important to train the Liberians to finish the system.

Life Goes On

To serve the hospital, we had to provide three-phase power, mainly to heat the autoclave used to sterilize the surgical instruments. We set three transformers in a row and began the cable preparation. Terry and Gary were in the three-foot-deep trench, side by side, working. Frank was connecting the secondary wires to the other transformer—the one that wasn't being prepared by Terry and Gary. The six primary connections took over three hours to complete. The hospital and mission electricians were fascinated. Mr. Flomo had his wheelchair parked at the edge of the ditch along with ten spectators, and you can imagine all the questions they asked. The distractions created stress and tension for Terry and Gary, who worked hard to avoid mistakes during this delicate operation. As questions were asked, I diverted the audience by describing what they were seeing and why we were doing what we were doing.

Later on Wednesday afternoon, at the guesthouse, we heard a huge commotion coming from near the high school: a great deal of high pitched yelling that sounded like what I could only classify as a war cry. In a minute, a teenage boy on a motorcycle came down the road, weaving and struggling to maintain his balance. He was being chased by a dozen kids with sticks, whacking him and trying to knock him off the bike. With each hit, he winced and swerved the bike, trying to escape. By the time he reached us, he was finally beginning to pull away from the crowd. He gunned the engine, roared down the road, and disappeared. As he turned onto the highway, three boys on motorbikes roared past us, followed by the crowd of agitated pursuers giving chase on foot.

We asked what was going on, but everyone was too excited to explain it so we could understand. Sue and Barbara were finally able to discover the problem: it seems the boy had stolen the motorbike, and the kids giving chase were attempting to get the bike back. Something exciting happened every day.

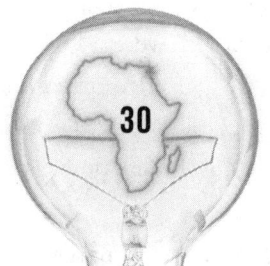

There Will Be Hiccups
Day 11

The administration at the hospital and mission had not developed a close relationship with the Bangladeshi team, so on Thursday night a few of us took the opportunity to go to the BANENGR-11 compound for a meet and greet and to plan a project completion ceremony for Friday morning. This was Colonel Huda's idea, and it was gracious of him to propose such an event. We planned the ceremony and spent some time getting everyone more comfortable with each other.

The Liberians seemed standoffish and intimidated, possibly due to the presence of soldiers and lingering emotions from the civil war. An interesting exchange occurred between one of the majors and Wulle. There were still some unexploded mortar rounds stuck in the trees on the hospital/mission campus. The major felt the mission personnel were responsible for clearing the grounds. Of, course Wulle wanted the military, who were the experts, to handle the situation. Ultimately, no decision was reached that evening, though we've been made to understand that, after we left Liberia, both parties participated in clearing out the dangerous shells. We received pictures of Wulle, dressed in a UN blue helmet and flak jacket, smiling from ear to ear during the clearing operation.

When Faith Lights the Way

After the meeting, we were all invited to the canteen to purchase any items we might want. There were a lot of clothes and hats with the BANENGR-11 logo, but we all settled on a green shirt with a nice collar and the BANENGR-11 logo, featuring the UNMIL globe in white. All the gear had been produced in Bangladesh, so we had to buy the largest sizes they had.

While there, I received an e-mail update indicating that our request for a helicopter ride was progressing nicely. UNMIL asked a few questions, and I responded, "Come on, let's do this!"

Thursday was a tough night for Terry. I woke at four-thirty the next morning and found him sitting on the couch, reading his Bible with a wet rag on his head. I told him he looked like Martha Washington with a mustache. He laughed but only out of courtesy. Although we weren't doctors, we both decided Terry had a kidney stone, and it was moving. He'd had the misfortune of experiencing a kidney stone before, and I'd been tormented with several in my life as well. Terry stayed in the guesthouse for part of that morning, and he was really hurting and very emotional. He apologized, thinking he was letting us down because he wasn't working. Nothing could have been further from the truth. Somehow, we would make it all happen. We continued our tradition of the "hang on" prayer before eating breakfast and went out to start our day.

Gary worked to get the cable terminations finished throughout the campus, and I completed the terminations on the big three-phase transformer outside the generator house on the mission side. Pinkie and Frank had been over at the generator house by the hospital, ensuring everything was ready to switch from generating separately at the hospital and mission sites, to using one generator at a time for the whole campus. The generators on the mission side were newer, larger, and more efficient. They would be the primary generators, and the hospital generators would serve as backups when the mission generators needed maintenance.

Before noon, I received a call on the walkie-talkie from Pinkie, saying he needed a connector.

There Will Be Hiccups

"What kind of connector?" I asked.

"A connector," he repeated.

Exasperated, I replied "*What kind* of connector? Compression, bolted, chair, *what?*"

"Maybe you should come look," said Pinkie.

Great, I thought. *Now I have to walk half a mile to babysit these guys.* I reached the old generator house and asked, "Okay, where?"

"Inside that cabinet against the wall," Pinkie told me.

I slid the door back and was at a loss. On the ground, I saw a ball of copper wire, made up of twenty or more wires of all sizes wrapped together. Pinkie and Frank laughed and said, "That's the system neutral. See on that wooden post, the block letter N written with an ink pen? How are we going to connect our wiring into the system neutral?"

It took a long time to come up with a (terrible) solution, and I'll take full responsibility. The aluminum wire we were using, when energized, heated and expanded at a different rate than the previous system's copper wires, which would still be in use. This might lead to a fire or keep the system from working at a later date. Our solution was to add to the mess by wrapping our aluminum wire around the older wires and then take copper wire and wrap it tightly on top of the aluminum. Then we wrapped it all up tight with electrical tape. That workaround was one of the biggest no-nos we've ever done, but it worked. And it's still working.

Around noon, we quickly broke for lunch. We received the wonderful news that Terry felt good enough to work. To ease the stress created by the onlookers—and to further the electric departments' education—I took the observers into a classroom to answer more questions. I explained to them why the cable was constructed as it was, why we were preparing the cable in a certain way, and what would happen if they didn't follow the same procedure. Finally, we paired up in teams and attempted to prepare a primary cable termination. Out of the six teams, only one was marginally acceptable. Hopefully, they wouldn't have a primary cable failure that needed repair when we weren't around. PFS

When Faith Lights the Way

had already decided we would come back if we were needed. I asked if they had any questions.

"If I jump up and grab hold of a bare wire, will I be electrocuted?"

"Why don't birds get electrocuted?"

"We heard a woman was washing her clothes in the river and, upstream, a power line fell in the water, and she was electrocuted. Her husband came by and tried to save her, but he, too, was electrocuted. Is that possible?"

"There's a big transformer in Monrovia that will suck you into it and kill you if you walk too close. Is that true?"

Some of my answers were long and complicated, but they seemed to understand. We had a great time. They quit at five most evenings, but that day, they stayed until six, asking questions. They had the mental capacity to hang with anyone. They were smart, experienced guys but had no formal education. I felt they had a new respect for us and no longer saw us as condescending Americans who made them feel inferior. Instead, we were there to help them help themselves, to give them an opportunity to improve their quality of life.

After class, the mission side was ready. King Harrell's guys had run the wire up to where the building wiring came out of the wall, but they'd made no connections to the inside wiring of any building. We couldn't wait until the following day to try energizing the mission side. We all gathered fifty feet away from three transformers by the mission generator house and closed the switch to energize the system on that side of the campus. We heard that familiar hum of the transformers. No fire— just a hum. We walked the mission side, and all the transformers were humming. We checked the voltages at all the breaker boxes, and they were correct. Unbounded joy! We almost had it! We would check the hospital side tomorrow. Time for a shower.

After bucket showers, which we were getting used to, several of us went to Sue and Barbara's house for dinner. We had a great social life while we were in Ganta. The administration building was close to their

There Will Be Hiccups

house, so I checked the Internet on the way. The helicopter extraction from Ganta was looking like a real possibility. We needed this, as Terry was in terrible pain because of his back. UNMIL in Monrovia reported they had passed my request on to the group in charge of the flights and would let us know.

Our spirits were lifted by the possible helicopter extraction, so that night, we enjoyed a great home-cooked meal and enjoyable conversation. While we were talking after dinner, Sue received a cell phone call from Bishop John Innis, the United Methodist Bishop of Liberia. He asked to speak to me, and when I took the phone, he was very appreciative of the work we were doing and thanked us profusely. We both agreed we would try to meet face to face as soon as we could. It was a great ending to a great day.

As we walked back toward the guesthouse, we noticed several Liberians about twenty years old, reading under street lights. Sue had told us it was exam time at the nursing school, and some of the students were walking five miles every evening to study under the street lights. It was a cool night, and as we walked down the dirt road, Terry and I admitted we had grown comfortable there. We thought we could live there and be happy, but we both agreed our wives couldn't. The place and the people really had taken over our hearts. Despite the sheer poverty, there was a great deal of happiness.

What makes people happy? In America, we chase after all the material possessions the world can provide. Sometimes, like a subway train stopping for a short time at a station, we pause our gorging to act benevolently. Most of the time we show our benevolence only in the ways that cost us the least amount of effort or resources. We certainly don't put in the effort to study what's best for those in need. We spend a little time, give a little of our money, share a Facebook like, and send up a quick prayer that our small actions will help those less fortunate to become as

When Faith Lights the Way

"successful" as we are. We've become so advanced that we have built walls in our minds, boundaries that isolate us from what could really make us happy: taking the time to enjoy the beautiful earth God has created or spending time with those around us. Our lives would be much happier and more fulfilled if we spent time laughing with others and hearing and understanding their joys and pain. It's so simple, living our lives to celebrate the joy of companionship with man and God. These poor Liberians possess something we desperately desire but don't remember how to obtain.

The Big Event
Day 12

June 19 was a Friday—a big day. We planned to focus on making the hospital side operational, but diversions took center stage. We would have to juggle a lot of balls that day and hope none hit the ground.

The hospital and mission, as well as the UN, had invited dignitaries and officials from all over Liberia to attend a lighting ceremony in the gym that morning at ten o'clock. At eight o'clock, Major Touhid arrived with a crew to help with last minute details like connecting the gym to the new system. The plan was to illuminate a big flood light we'd set at the bottom of the stage facing the crowd at the beginning of the program. Touhid was nervous that morning because the colonel had challenged him. He told Touhid that he bet it wouldn't work, and the colonel said he would hold the major accountable if it didn't. I felt a shockwave of pressure moving in my direction. I assured him it was no problem. I hoped that was the truth.

The wiring at the gym was completed by UNMIL, so we went to the generator house to have them start the generators and make sure everything worked as planned. Normally, during the day, the generators on the mission side were turned off to save fuel. The operator turned on the generator, threw the switch, and over the walkie-talkie, we heard

When Faith Lights the Way

the light was working. It was all good. We gave instructions to start the generator at 9:40 a.m. and headed over to the gym for the celebratory meet and greet.

Not all of PFS attended the ceremony. If we didn't put elbow terminations on the cable at every opportunity, we wouldn't finish the project. Much of the work we'd come there to do was yet to be completed.

I was surprised at the turnout. The local officials and UNMIL had sent the commanders from Monrovia to attend the event, and with the school kids, there must have been two hundred people in attendance and almost twenty speakers. Desserts were provided by BANENGR-11 and drinks by the mission. We even had a printed program. We double checked everything again at 9:50 a.m., but now there was no "juice" at the wall receptacle where we were going to plug in the light. I started to sweat. Major Touhid wasn't happy. He was sweating too.

We'd planned to plug in the light right before the program started, so we dropped the plug and headed out the door, smiling at the people that had gathered. We went outside and looked at the connections on the building. Nothing wrong there. Harrell and I trotted to the generator house and found the generator sitting silently. There was a new guy at the controls.

"Where's the operator we talked to earlier?" we asked.

He had gone home, we were told. He was the night shift operator. "I am day," the attendant added.

"Did he tell you to turn on the generator at 9:40 a.m. this morning?"

"No," the guy said calmly.

"Well, turn it on! We have two hundred people waiting to see the lights!" I replied, not so calmly.

"We have to go get fuel," he said.

"Move! Now!" I said, acting like anything but a meek Christian. I asked Harrell to stay there and make sure the generator was started while I rushed back to the gym, arriving right about the time the program started.

The Big Event

The program began with a prayer, but with no light. Several speakers talked about how wonderful it would be to have dependable electricity—while there was no light. Several politicians took a little piece of the credit for the project—while there was no light. I was on the stage, dying. Still, there was no light.

Twenty minutes into the program, Harrell slid into a chair at the back of the room and gave me a thumbs-up. Suddenly I could breathe again. I sat there a short time, wondering how to make the illumination of the lights dramatic, and then came up with a brilliant idea. The Bangladeshi major sitting beside me had a writing pen in his shoulder pocket. I reached over and grabbed it. The major jumped, startled, and I just smiled and began writing on the program.

I motioned for Harrell to come to the stage and handed him the program I'd written on, and he walked back to his chair and read what I had written. "The king" smiled and nodded his head.

The speeches continued, with no light. It was my turn, and I basically said the same thing I'd told the school the day before. We were proud to have been a part of a project that would benefit the people of Liberia, our brothers and sisters. Texans were honest, hardworking, loyal, and self-reliant. We told them they had these same qualities and ideals, as represented by the similarities between the Liberian and Texas flag. I presented Victor Trayor with a Texas flag and proclaimed the people of Ganta as honorary Texans.

We were in the home stretch; there were just a few other speeches. I motioned to Harrell at the appropriate time to plug in the light. When energized, this type of light flickers and then begins to glow dimly. Everyone stood for the Liberian National Anthem; the light fixture sputtered and flashed a dim, golden light. As we all sang the Liberian National Anthem with gusto, the light increased from a glow into a crescendo of golden light that lit the gym like the sun. It peaked right at the end of the last verse.

When Faith Lights the Way

Everyone clapped and smiled, then moved on to the water and desserts. Major Touhid looked like he wanted to hug me, and kill me.

On to the next adventure of the day. During lunch, we all got together and looked at what we had left to do on the hospital side. There were still a bunch of terminations left to complete, probably fifteen, and too many to finish in the daylight hours that were left. We decided to work on all the connections that supplied power to the buildings that were currently in use and save the terminations for unoccupied buildings until the end of the day. Frank was scheduled to put the battery backup system in the two operating rooms because no surgeries were scheduled on Fridays. This system would keep supplying power to the operating rooms, even if the underground system or the generators failed. It took all afternoon for Frank and the hospital electric crew to install the equipment, but it worked great when we tested it.

We really got busy, but we couldn't finish it all by sundown. The last two connections were finished by flashlight. There was cause for optimism because everything worked as planned on the mission side. We connected the hospital side into our system, and it all worked as designed, too, except for two locations. Some houses were without power on the end of one cable run, and, no kidding, the hospital didn't work. We had to stop because the Bangladeshis had prepared a celebration for us, set to begin at eight o'clock at their facility. We would try again in the morning before we had to depart for Monrovia. We couldn't leave the next day with so much left unfinished. If things went our way, we would have a helicopter ride on Saturday and more time to finish the remaining tasks.

What a gracious event BANENGR-11 had prepared for our last function together. Their officers joined the administrative staff from the UMC hospital and church, along with the Power From the SON volunteers. Dinner was a buffet of Mediterranean cuisine, with shish kebabs, lamb, beef, chicken, rice, and vegetables—and, of course, they had ice cream

The Big Event

for us. All flown in by helicopter. I sat with Colonel Huda, and this was our second time to chat about our personal lives.

Before spending time with the Bangladeshis, I'd had a wrong impression based on my own lack of knowledge. Bangladesh is not well-covered in American news. My impression of Bangladesh had come from George Harrison of the Beatles' *Concert for Bangladesh* in the 1970s. I'd concluded that Bangladesh was a poor country with little education and little value. Meeting the UNMIL Bangladesh was a revelation. I must apologize to Bangladesh after working with my Bangladeshi military friends. Their soldiers are very similar to our own men and women in uniform. They have a calling to protect and defend others. Bangladesh supplies more UN Peacekeepers than any other country. Most of them spend their lives going from one unsettled area of the world to another, in rotations of one-year durations. These soldiers sacrifice themselves to provide a better life for their families and for the next generation. Our parents and grandparents willingly sacrificed leisure and convenience to make our own lives easier than theirs. There will come a time when those living in the developed world will be challenged into service if they want to maintain a life spent in leisure and convenience. Hopefully, our progeny will be willing to sacrifice for others. And, hopefully, they will have inherited the fortitude and vision of our ancestors.

After dinner came the customary speeches. I told of the wonderful impression we had of the colonel and his command. We knew little of Bangladesh before meeting them and were left with a most favorable impression. We would remember them always. I gave the retread speech about Texans: honest, hardworking, loyal, and self-reliant. We told them they had the same qualities and ideals. I presented Colonel Huda with a Texas flag and proclaimed them honorary Texans. He responded with kind words about us educating them on electricity and underground construction and how they admired our efforts, which they saw as truly humanitarian. He gave us all pins portraying the flag of Bangladesh.

Before leaving, we talked to their doctor about Terry's back problem. He offered to see Terry the next day to try and relieve his pain.

When Faith Lights the Way

Saying goodbye to these men who'd worked alongside us, laughed with us, and become our brothers was hard and sad. The past few weeks, we'd worked together to accomplish the common goal of helping to make the world a better place. These Muslim peacekeepers embraced our quest and were willing to follow the lead of an American Christian and civilian. Neither parties beliefs had ever deterred us from our common goal. All over the world, there are people of great character who walk among us, though their deeds are not often the stuff of great media stories. Stepping out of our boats had led us to see the world with different eyes.

E-mail from Bishop John Innis, June 19, 2009

> I am excited. I am pleased. I am at a lack of words to express thanks to your team and Steve for the good work you have done at Ganta Mission. You guys are great, kind, and generous. What your team has done for us in Liberia, especially at Ganta Mission, will remain a history for us. Providing electricity at the mission is awesome.
>
> I wish God's rich blessing on all of you for your commitment in helping underdeveloped countries—Liberia, for example.
>
> I am away from home in the interest of the United Methodist Church in Liberia…I appreciate all you have done. Thanks to all. Yesterday I had a conversation over the phone with Mr. Vincent. He is a good man, committed to doing good. I hope to visit with him when I return to the States in October for the Council of Bishops' meeting. Take care, and may God bless you and the work you do that is helping humanity.
>
> —Bishop John G. Innis

Last Chance

Day 13

On Saturday, June 20, we were up early, with one full day left to get it all working. The houses without power were an easy fix. The lightning arrester in one transformer failed when we energized the system, but it didn't damage any other equipment. If something had to go wrong, that was the component we would have hoped would fail. The hospital problem, however, was a different story.

If you isolated the hospital from the rest of the system and used the small generators in the hospital generators' building for power, the hospital worked fine. If you connected only the hospital to the mission generator, the hospital transformers and everything else worked fine. You could even disconnect the hospital and use the small generators in the hospital generators' house to supply the whole hospital and mission. When you connected the hospital in with the rest of the hospital/mission system, however, the circuit breakers took the hospital offline. This was not a simple problem, and it drove us crazy.

We had planned to relax and go buy some wood carvings for presents to take home, but there was no way. Barbara graciously offered to go to the leper colony, about five miles away, and buy items for us to take

When Faith Lights the Way

home as gifts. There, people with leprosy made crafts to generate income. The PFS guys had gone there at the beginning of trip while Chris and I were still in Monrovia. They showed us some of the beautiful work and told us the inspiring stories of the artisans there. They carved wood and wove baskets using knives, and they lived in primitive conditions, even using outdoor fires to cook their food. Leprosy is caused by bacteria on the nerve endings, which makes it difficult to feel pain, often resulting in the loss of some extremities. How they did such amazing work without all their fingers is a lesson in perseverance and optimism. I was especially enthralled with the nativity sets they carved. The wood used was brought up from the bottom of rivers, and it was very heavy and hard, almost like petrified wood. The finished works were as smooth as polished stone. The figures' shapes were the most intriguing part: the carvers didn't have access to pictures, so they carved from their experience. All the figures had African features, unlike the Western-influenced faces one buys in stores in the United States. The camels were particularly extraordinary. Never having seen camels, they carved an animal that more closely resembled a hippopotamus. The nativity set I purchased there is a treasure for me every Christmas.

We tried everything to get the hospital online with the rest of the campus. But every time we tried, the circuit breakers would take it back offline. We began to suspect a wire somewhere in the generator house that carried power into the hospital was incorrectly tied into the strange system neutral. Many, many wires in that building ended up electrically connected in numerous places and found their way to that weird ball of wires under the cabinet called the "system neutral." For some reason, the hospital breakers were not sensing a problem when the local generator was connected, but only when we tried to power the whole system from the mission generator. We continued to work on the problem.

Terry went to visit the UNMIL's Bangladeshi doctor. The diagnosis: a bulging disc. We had our doubts about the diagnosis—we were still

Last Chance

betting on a kidney stone—but the doctor gave him some strong pain pills to last until Terry returned to the United States.

Barbara returned with our art treasures, and we remembered to ask if she knew the result of the motorcycle theft. The boys that went after the thief on their motorcycles had confessed that they caught him behind the mission property, killed him, and dumped his body in the bush, she said. We were startled, to say the least.

"Is that true?" we asked.

"You never know if it's bragging or if it really happened," she replied. "We've learned not to ask too much."

Years later, the story still haunts me. I think I'd like to know the truth, but I may not really want to know what happened. Liberia was the most developed country in Africa before the civil war. A quarter of a million family members, friends, and neighbors were killed by previously sane, rational people whom they may have known well. I realized that depravity could occur again, anytime, perpetrated by anyone. The Liberians, though, are not unique. They're human. If this society can implode, it begs the question whether our own society could descend into a *Mad Max* scenario? Evil is very powerful in our world.

That last day was a rough one. I began to wonder when the good news was coming. I received a call from my United States military contact in Monrovia about the helicopter ride. This should have made it all better, but it didn't. We couldn't be extracted by helicopter, even though we had health issues. I was dumbfounded. My UNMIL contact explained that the group in charge of the flights asked which group we were associated with, and the answer, of course, was the United Methodist Church. The Methodists, as it turned out, were on the no-fly list. It seems the Liberian Methodists had been using the UNMIL helicopters to take sightseeing flights around Monrovia with their families, so they'd been restricted from using UNMIL aircraft. I will admit that I was upset and disappointed by this, and I even felt a little righteous indignation that church leaders had abused the privilege so much that the

When Faith Lights the Way

use of UNMIL helicopters was being denied to Methodists, even when there was a humanitarian benefit to their use. I've seen many instances when Christians, not just Methodists, ignored their professed beliefs for personal gain. Wickedness has no label, color, or sex; goodness is the same. But if I'm being honest with myself, I have unknowingly caused hardship to others by taking a contested parking place or by playing golf or going to a football game when I could have used the time to teach someone who wanted to learn.

Truthfully, I can't claim to be more righteous than anyone else. And would I always do the right thing if I'd lived my life in Liberia the last twenty years? I've seen them lie, cheat, steal, act indifferently, and refuse to help others. But I've never had to forgive a neighbor who killed my child or stole food from me to save his own starving child. I've ultimately decided that to judge oneself to be more righteous than another is to aid darkness, not strengthen light.

We are not appointed to judge others; we are responsible for ourselves. Christians are not perfect. We do bad things. That's why we need to accept our failure, ask for forgiveness, and listen when the Teacher tells us to step out of the boat and focus on what he is telling us.

Our overworked, tired, and sick team members would have to ride five miserable hours on a hot, dusty road to Monrovia. But we were Texans, and we would survive. That afternoon, we toured the campus with the electrical staff, answered questions, and made plans for when we were gone. There were still two green plastic secondary connection pedestals that they would set after we left. We also needed to work on getting three-phase power to some equipment in the woodworking shop. Outside of that, the Liberian staff just had to make the necessary changes to supply electricity to the buildings with the underground system and remove the old overhead system. Oh, and yes, the hospital was still a problem.

Without giving another lesson in electricity, I'll just say that it's possible that not everything in the hospital or the generator house was installed correctly. We learned the generator had recently been rewound, making

Last Chance

us suspicious that the work had not been done correctly. But other clues unrelated to this indicated that not everything in the hospital was A-okay, either. We kept working into the night, but we didn't solve anything.

After dinner and showers, we separated the items we wanted to take home and those we wanted to give away. The items we left were given to the hospital and mission administrators to distribute to the right people at appropriate times. We were concerned about older kids beating up and stealing from smaller or weaker kids.

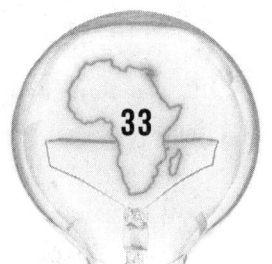

Hard to Say Goodbye
Day 14

It was Sunday, June 21, and we were up and ready to leave as the sun rose. As we walked out of our screened porch, we discovered a throng of Liberians had arrived to say goodbye. It was hard to leave, but we had served our purpose; it was time to go back to our families and lives. We'd made so many new friends. Flomo, in his wheelchair, gave us a great gift in the form of a compliment: he was thankful we had come, that he'd learned from us, and that we were his friends. Zuu, who would now maintain the main generator, was there for us as well, along with Victor, Ronsey, Sue, Barbara, LiZa Wulle, and many more. Terry had a fondness for Peti, our four-foot security guard, and gave him a yellow rainsuit to keep him dry while he was on duty. They had a picture made, which we labeled "Terry meets Big Bird." The Power From the SON crew took pictures as a group with the blue shipping container as our backdrop. The smiles were genuine.

The electrical crew—now one group, not two—told us that even though it was Sunday, their day off, they'd decided to look for the trouble with the hospital connection. Our gift of an electric system was appropriate. They had taken ownership and responsibility for the new system.

When Faith Lights the Way

We were given a round, mahogany plaque, carved in the leper colony, that read, "Ganta U. M. Mission, Liberia; Power From the SON; Joint Electrification Project." It also contained two palm trees and the Methodist Cross and Flame. In addition to this, we were given a carving of two hands in a Liberian handshake. These were marvelous, symbolic gifts coming from people who had grown to mean so much to each of us.

We piled into two Land Cruisers for the ride back to Monrovia. I rode in the first vehicle, and the dust we kicked up obliterated the one following us. In time, they had had enough and dropped back to where we couldn't see them, allowing them to breathe cleaner air. It was a really rough road. The day itself was much hotter and dustier than the day of the trip up. A lot of us got carsick, so we laid on the benches and truck bed floor with our eyes closed most of the way. We were relieved to get to Red Light, where the drivers had to slow down.

We arrived at the guesthouse in Monrovia, intending to enjoy some food, quick bucket showers, and a little relaxation before heading for the airport. But it wasn't to be. Frank, who'd had his knee replaced shortly before the trip, hadn't been able to move around much in Ganta. Now, after the arduous trip back, Frank was almost to the point of passing out. Nyamah Dunbar was at the house and had a nurse friend at JFK Hospital, which was arguably the second-best hospital in Liberia after Ganta UMC. The hospital was only a mile away, so we took Frank, and he was examined and admitted. He was extremely dehydrated. So dehydrated, in fact, that they would not let him leave the hospital for the return flight. Instead he was put in a room and given fluids intravenously. Finally we went back to the guesthouse, ate, showered, and rested until it was time to head to the airport. At six that evening, the others left for Roberts International Airport. But a medical doctor from Ganta Hospital, who was also on our flight, went with Victor, Chris, and me went to get Frank. It took more time than we wished, but we finally sprung him at 6:45 and raced for Roberts Field.

The check-in was no problem. It's amazing how a place can be so scary at first, but then after you've been there awhile, you adapt, and

Hard to Say Goodbye

things become natural and comfortable. We all went through security and into the un-air-conditioned waiting room to wait until boarding time. A lot of us wore our green UNMIL BANENGR-11 shirts, which elicited some questions as to who we were. The flight was late, and we waited impatiently, sweating. Finally, we were called to board. A cell phone rang; it was Flomo. The gang at Ganta had located a wire connected to the ground system that was causing the problem, and the hospital was now working alongside the rest of the campus. The project was officially complete!

Sometime during the flight, my mind wandered to Jesus telling the story about talents. The story goes like this: a ruler gave his servants custody of his valuables while he was away. When he returned, he expected the servants to return these "talents," but with interest. The story is a parable, explaining that we are all caretakers of gifts from God. We will be judged by the return on the investment we produce while we have custody of God's valuables. Some people will bury what God has given them, choosing to distance themselves from God and his love. But if we use these gifts as intended, we will invest them, thus increasing the valuables in our custody. To be successful and increase the valuables God has placed in our possession, we need to be representatives of God here on earth. We need to become his hands and feet. God will reward us with increased trust, love, and responsibility for work in his kingdom.

Then I thought of Moses, who was born of a Hebrew slave but raised in the pharaoh's household. I liked the romantic version of the old movies where Pharaoh gave Moses the education and experience to basically become the chief operating officer of Egypt. He would have spent his first forty years learning, experiencing, and refining his abilities to motivate people, as well as studying military tactics, logistics, and anything else one needed to know to successfully govern a country. Then, Moses killed an Egyptian in defense of a Hebrew and fled to the

When Faith Lights the Way

wilderness for forty years, learning, experiencing, and refining his abilities to live off the land. He lost all his arrogance and grew in humility. Basically, he was enrolled in God's finishing school to hone the techinques necessary to be a powerful servant leader. Subsequently, he had the expertise, demeanor, and skills to use every bit of the talents he was given by God. Now God called him. Who else in history had the experience and ability to lead two million people from Egypt, survive an attack by the world-class Egyptian Army, then lead all those people in the wilderness for forty more years, finally bringing some of them—mainly the descendants of the original slaves—to the land God had promised them? God called Moses to step out of his boat. When he focused and followed God, he could metaphorically walk on water.

Why us? I wondered. *Why now?* All the Power From the SON team were given talents. Had we been in school all our lives, until the Teacher decided our training was complete? When we were properly prepared, did he call us to step out of our boats to serve him by helping to provide the gift of electricity? Is that the way all of us should live our lives, experiencing and educating ourselves in preparation to do the impossible when God says, "It is time, I will be with you?"

We were back in America, and we sat eating in a fast food restaurant in the Newark Airport. There wasn't a lot of conversation. I made eye contact with each of my brothers, they smiled, and I returned the smile. Nothing needed to be said. We had all stepped out of our boats and let go of the side. We were transformed.

ELUM, The United Methodist Church's radio station in Monrovia. Steve Vincent and Victor Taryor Ganta United Methodist Hospital Administrator.

Red Light Market, Monrovia.

Power From the SON enjoying an evening meal around the table at the Guest House in Ganta.

Bottling plant on the outskirts of Monrovia.

First meeting with BANENGR-11 to enlist their help in unloading and installing the system (see additional).

At our initial meeting at BANENGR-11's compound in Ganta with Colonel Huda (see additional).

Truck driver's sleeping arrangement. This driver delivered one of two containers to Ganta UMC.

Power From the SON and the Ganta Electric Departments are laying primary cable in the huge trenches dug by BANENGR-11's hydraulic shovel.

The Liberians are installing secondary cable in the trench. Gary Wilson is supervising.

UNMIL's hydraulic shovel digging a trench for power cables to cross the road linking Monrovia, Liberia, and Guinea.

UNMIL BANENGR-11 Bay of Bengal on the grounds of their base in Ganta.

Work buddies Ry Mosser, Darlington Dolo, and Wes Wilson.

Methuselah says he is more than 100 years old!

Gary Wilson and Terry Thornhill clowning around in front of original wire exits from the Hospital Generating house.

Gary Wilson working with the Ganta Electric Department to load primary cable on to reel stand.

Terry Thornhill beside our favorite security guard, Peti.

The Ganta Electric Department gets involved with Gary Wilson, Terry Thornhill, and BANENGR-11 in setting a transformer.

Steve Vincent Teaching UMC Ganta school children a Texas A&M University tradition—the "Gig 'em!"

At 10:00 a.m. and 2:00 p.m. the Bangladeshis brought everything for tea time to be enjoyed by Power From the SON and BANENGER-11 officers.

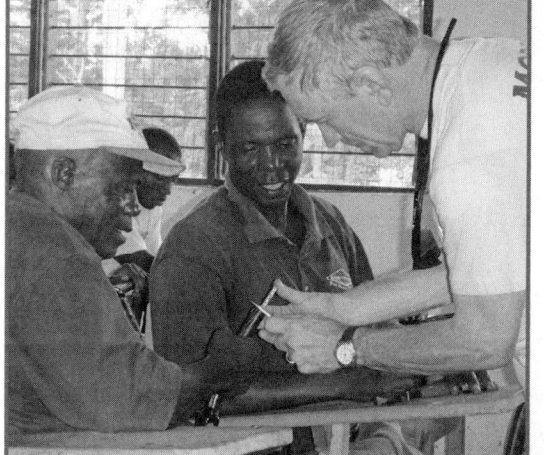

Steve Vincent instructs Ganta Electric Department in hands-on cable preperation.

Installing three transformers at Ganta UMC Hospital with plenty of interested Liberian onlookers. Terry Thornhill, Gary Wilson, and Frank Daniel were doing the installation.

We are finished in Ganta. One of the containers is our backdrop. Left to right: Harold Burr, Gary Wilson, Wes Wilson, Pinkie Pinkston, Frank Daniel. Ry Mosser, Steve Vincent, Terry Thornhill, Chris Olson.

Saying goodbye. Liza, Wulle, Sue Porter, and Barbara Tutton.

Departure day from Ganta. Left to right: Victor Taryor, Darlington Dolo, Flomo, and Zuu.

Epilogue

> Thousands, thousands of lives will be saved, and hundreds of lives have been saved already.
>
> —JOHN INNIS,
> BISHOP OF LIBERIA, UNITED METHODIST CHURCH,
> OCTOBER 19, 2009, ARLINGTON, TEXAS FOR WFAA NEWS

Since returning from Ganta, not a day has passed when Power From the SON hasn't tried to help the people of Liberia. I have returned four more times. In 2010, I went back to add a circuit to the Ganta hospital, and in 2013 and 2014 to map and electrify, respectively, a seminary and high school in Gbarnda. Most recently, in 2016, I went back to help with the construction of a school that is the dream of the former vice president of Liberia and simultaneously the United Methodist Bishop of Liberia, Bennie Dee Warner.

I became haunted by what Liberia was before the civil war and how to aid in its return to prosperity. Upon returning home after this first adventure, I reflected on the difficulty of getting our container released and the 1960s business procedures that were still being used in Liberia, and I realized where I might be of further service. My experience was in business, and I wanted to help Liberia become an economic force in Africa. In my view, Liberia offered very little the world was willing to buy, except its natural resources. It also had at least one whole generation who had been deprived of education by the civil war.

My passion led me to Oklahoma, where I visited Bishop Bennie Dee Warner. Bishop Bennie is a true rags-to-riches success story and has become a close friend. He grew up in an environment similar to those children we'd encountered who were thrilled to receive empty water bottles.

I presented my rough idea for the reclamation of Liberia for his critique and suggestions.

When Faith Lights the Way

Together we drafted a plan called "Arise Liberia," with eight basic points:

▷ Economically, the world wants to embrace the African markets. Companies long to establish factories and distribution systems in developing countries that have the necessary ethics, job skills, and infrastructure. Regionally, the first independent country that initiates and establishes these attributes will have the highest quality of life for its people.

▷ Liberia would be the owner of the process and control the direction and implementation of any action items.

▷ Develop Liberia's Freeport of Monrovia to be the prime importing location in West Africa for goods from Europe and the Americas.

▷ Modernize the import process.

▷ Develop distribution and transportation systems to circulate the goods through Sub-Saharan Africa.

▷ Texas A&M University and Southern Methodist University could provide doctoral and masters-level consultants to aid in the planning, and if requested by the Liberians, implementation. The consultation could be broadened to include agriculture, architecture, business, education, engineering, law, medicine, and other disciplines that are necessary to improve prosperity.

▷ The process would reach into all areas of Liberian society to advance Liberia up the economic ladder.

▷ Liberia would pay the expenses of the consultants using a small portion of the approximately $172,000 million given to Liberia by the United States in aid during 2009.[11]

I met with the presidents of Texas A&M and Southern Methodist University, and both agreed to participate in discussions with Liberia.

In 2010, after a trip to Sierra Leone to install an electric generator for a community-outreach center sponsored and maintained by Restore Hope of Arlington, Texas, UMC Bishop John Innis arranged a meeting

Epilogue

between President Ellen Johnson Sirleaf of Liberia and me so I could present the Arise Liberia idea. The plan was given to Education Minister Othello Gongar to evaluate and make recommendations. No response was received.

In June of 2012, President Sirleaf agreed to meet with Bishops Innis and Warner and me concerning Arise Liberia while she was in New York. She told us that Liberia did not have the financial resources to participate in the program. For the next few months, I met with US government officials, attempting to carve out funds for Arise Liberia from USAID funds that were allocated for Liberia. I was unsuccessful.

Arise Liberia was a plan of practical education that would "Teach a man how to make a fishing pole, show him how to fish, and then let him provide for himself and his family." It would have been a win for all Liberians, the United States would have benefited from the growth of a strong democratic and economic ally, the universities would have developed a master plan to improve prosperity in developing countries, and the students would have received an unparalleled practical experience. Arise Liberia has been one of the most passionate projects of my life. Because of its death, it's also one of the most disappointing efforts of my lifetime.

Power From the SON continues to work with the Ganta Hospital and Mission. Several years ago, an event destroyed the controls on the two main generators. For unknown reasons, PFS was not consulted about a solution. After a while, the Liberian Electric Corporation (LEC) built a line along the road bisecting the campus, and UMC Ganta began to purchase electric service from them, again reinstalling overhead lines. LEC was only able to provide single phase power, however, and this reduced the ability of the autoclave to effectively sterilize surgical instruments. As a result, much of the campus was underserved or not served at all. After a change in administration at UMC Ganta, school principal Priscilla Jaiah and Patrick Mantor took charge, and we were again contacted to consult. Power From the SON designed a simple way to connect LEC power into the underground system and, if the generators at the mission were repaired, to keep them as standbys in case of a

When Faith Lights the Way

power outage by LEC. We bought the equipment and did our part of the installation work to make this happen while we were in Liberia in 2014 to electrify the Seminary in Gbarnga. PFS and UMC Ganta have been in contact with LEC and its operations licensee, Jungle Energy Power, trying to get them to build a short line to reenergize the underground and solve the issues there. Currently, Jungle Energy Power has not been willing to accept Power From the SON's offer to fund the construction of the short line to save Liberian lives.

Our return to Ganta in 2014 was a homecoming. It was great to work with Mr. Flomo and Zuu once again. Mr. Flomo had received a motorized, almost all-terrain, wheelchair that gave him the freedom to roam the property without needing someone to push him.

We did some wiring on the switch panels in the generator house at the mission and set three transformers in place that will change the voltage used by LEC, now Jungle Energy Power, into voltages that will work in our underground system. It was humbling to hear Mr. Flomo tell the new electrical workers to "listen to these guys. They know what they are doing. You will learn something." We had done well in 2009. Our gift was of value.

Preston Kissman, a long-time business customer and personal friend, and I went to Liberia at the request of Donald Turner, then the development and partnership coordinator for Gbarnga United Methodist Mission Station. Donald had seen the Ganta system and wanted us to install an electric system for the Gbarnga Seminary and Mission. Power From the SON installed a system at the seminary in 2014, during the rise of Ebola. In 2015, Dr. James Labala, the pastor at Ganta's Miller McAllister UMC during our first trip, was now the superintendent at Gbarnga. He challenged the students to complete the electric system. They copied our work and finished our system. This was a confirmation that our gift was so desirable to the recipients that they were willing to learn about electricity and then do the work themselves.

Epilogue

I've been asked numerous times why I chose to work in foreign countries when there is so much work to be done in my own city, state, and country. Dr. David Mosser, our senior pastor, asked me to write an article on my reasoning for mission work abroad. The article, reprinted below, attempts to explain the reasons for my passion.

Pay It Forward…Away from Home.

You can read in the newspapers on a regular basis how people are beginning to pay it forward. You go into a restaurant, or in for a cup of coffee, and someone you don't know has already paid your bill. Is that great or what? You just got something for nothing. You got the best of that deal!

Acts 20:35 says, "…remembering the words the Lord Jesus himself said: 'It is more blessed to give than to receive.'" Really? If I am a Christian, am I to understand that the person who doesn't know me and just paid for my meal is being blessed more than I?

Okay, so, it appears God wants us to not just read his word, but to get up off the couch sometimes and give away money or stuff. That's a good takeaway from reading the Bible. There are helpful clues in the Bible. The Bible talks about taking care of widows and orphans, and after the disciples were anointed by the Holy Spirit, they went around healing people. Many people go to the Bible and consult with God to discover what talents God has given them and what they are supposed to do with them.

In Matthew 25:14-30, Jesus tells us the story about talents. The message is that we are given opportunities and abilities to serve our neighbor and bring glory to God. Some people will bury, or not use, what God has given them, basically adding nothing to God's glory—sort of "dust to dust.'" Others understand that Jesus is telling us to spend our time and efforts in advancing God's efforts.

If we develop a close relationship with God, we may find our calling is not what we expected. We may discover that God is also interested

When Faith Lights the Way

in what goes on outside our neighborhood, and he wants us to be his hands and feet in another neighborhood.

Have you ever read the book of Acts? What an exciting adventure story. These guys didn't stay home and just minister to their neighbors. Seeing how it all turned out, the descendants of their neighbors have remained anchored in the Jewish faith and did not make the transition to Christianity. Aren't you glad the disciples believed in paying it forward away from home?

And for those of you who are Methodists, there were plenty of souls to be saved in England in the 1730s. John Wesley and his brother, Charles, responded to an invitation to become chaplains for the colony of Georgia. Neither was happy in the colonies, and they soon returned to England. The American experience was discouraging and unsettling for John's faith, and the questions raised resulted in him having his "heart strangely warmed" experience at Aldersgate. The Aldersgate experience was the inspiration behind the Methodist Church.

The bottom line is, as Christians who love God, we are drawn to do his will, not our will.

About seven years ago, Power From the SON was formed to engineer, procure, and construct efficient electrical systems for hospitals, schools, and missions in the developing world. In that time, our members have journeyed to Liberia five times and have played a small part in saving the lives of many faceless Liberians through a war-torn hospital where the doctors had previously operated on patients without the use of anesthesia machines. We have electrified a seminary where future United Methodist ministers learn to preach the gospel to future generations. This June we will journey to Honduras to electrify a Methodist-sponsored orphanage. We have spent time trying to evaluate the value of our work. We have no way of knowing how many lives we have touched. We do know that our lives have been changed.

Epilogue

In September, Power From the SON and FUMC Arlington will go to Liberia to complete the dream of Former Liberian vice president and Methodist bishop Bennie Dee Warner. Bishop Bennie has donated the land and started building a rural school. It is 15,600 square feet with six classrooms, a health office, a teacher's lounge, a principal's office, lockers, a multipurpose area, and space for agriculture.

I agree there is plenty of good that needs to be done around here. But I am certainly thankful the disciples—and John Wesley—followed God's will for their lives. Because they chose to go where the Spirit led them and pay it forward away from home, we have been taught about Christ and his wonderful gift of saving grace.[12]

Appendix

Liberia's Politcal Context

Portuguese explorers established contact with Liberia as early as 1461 and named the area "Grain Coast" because of the abundance of "grains of paradise" (Malegueta pepper seeds). In 1663, the British installed trading posts on the Grain Coast, but the Dutch destroyed these posts a year later. There were no further reports of European settlements along the Grain Coast until the arrival of freed slaves from the United States in the early 1800s.[13]

The Haitian revolt scared the people of the United States, where the ratio of whites to blacks was four to one—much more surmountable than the one white for every eight blacks in Haiti. After a plot to burn down Charleston was uncovered, laws were passed restricting the assembly of blacks without whites present. Between 1794 and 1800, the United States passed anti-slave laws to prevent a revolt. Individual southern states passed even more restrictive laws concerning slave importation. Furthermore, the rapid increase in American free blacks, 82 percent between 1800 and 1810, concerned northerners who refused to accept the notion of white-black coexistence. Southerners feared a slave uprising.

One school of thought holds that freed American slaves founded Liberia. However, an argument can also be made that it was white men, through their founding of the American Colonization Society (ACS) in 1816, who founded Liberia. Their solution to the fear of slave revolt and white-black non-coexistence was to have free blacks deported from the United States. The ASC was an organization of white clergymen, abolitionists, and slave owners formed by Robert Finley, a Presbyterian minister. The group included such notables as President James Monroe, President Thomas Jefferson, President James Madison, President Andrew Jackson, House Speaker Henry Clay, and Supreme Court Chief Justice John Marshall. Many cities and locations in Liberia are named after these individuals.[14]

When Faith Lights the Way

An initial group of eighty-six "Americo-Liberians" arrived in Liberia, which means "land of the free," and established a settlement in Christopolis—now called Monrovia after US President James Monroe—on February 6, 1820. Thousands of freed American slaves and free African Americans arrived during the following years, resulting in the establishment of more settlements. Between 1821 and 1867, the ACS resettled some ten thousand African Americans and several thousand Africans from impounded slave ships. The ACS governed the Commonwealth of Liberia until a declaration of independence from the United States was written, establishing the Republic of Liberia on July 26, 1847. The style of government and constitution was patterned after that of the United States, but in reality a one-party state had been created, ruled by the True Whig Party (TWP). Joseph Jenkins Roberts, who was born and raised in America, was Liberia's first president.

In Liberia's early years, the Americo-Liberian settlers periodically encountered stiff and violent opposition from indigenous Africans because the Americo-Liberian elite monopolized political power and restricted the voting rights of the indigenous population, who were excluded from citizenship in the new Republic until 1904. During this period, the British and French encroached upon Liberia, taking over much of its territory.

The True Whig Party dominated all sectors of Liberia from 1847 until April 12, 1980, when Liberian Master Sergeant Samuel K. Doe, a Krahn (one of Liberia's sixteen indigenous ethnic groups), seized power in a coup d'état. Doe's forces executed President William R. Tolbert and several officials of his government, mostly of Americo-Liberian descent. One hundred and thirty-three years of Americo-Liberian political domination ended with the formation of the People's Redemption Council.

Over time, the new government began promoting members of Doe's Krahn ethnic group, who soon dominated political and military life in Liberia. This raised ethnic tensions and caused frequent hostilities between the politically and militarily dominant Krahns and other ethnic groups in the country. After the October 1985 elections, char-

Appendix

acterized by widespread fraud, Doe solidified his control. The period after the elections saw increased human rights abuses, corruption, and ethnic tensions. The standard of living further deteriorated. On November 12, 1985, former Army Commanding General Thomas Quiwonkpa almost succeeded in toppling Doe's government, but the Armed Forces of Liberia repelled Quiwonkpa's attack and executed him in Monrovia. Doe's Krahn-dominated forces carried out reprisals against Mano and Gio, ethnic groups within Liberia, and civilians suspected of supporting Quiwonkpa. Doe was a staunch US ally and enjoyed considerable American financial support.

On December 24, 1989, a small band of rebels led by Doe's former procurement chief, Charles Taylor, invaded Liberia from Côte d'Ivoire. Taylor and his National Patriotic Front rebels rapidly gained the support of many Liberians and reached the outskirts of Monrovia within six months. From 1989 to 1996, one of Africa's bloodiest civil wars ensued, claiming the lives of more than two hundred thousand Liberians and displacing a million others into refugee camps in neighboring countries. The Economic Community of West African States (ECOWAS) intervened in 1990 and succeeded in preventing Charles Taylor from capturing Monrovia. Prince Johnson—formerly a member of Taylor's National Patriotic Front of Liberia—formed the break-away Independent National Patriotic Front of Liberia. Johnson's forces captured and killed Doe on September 9, 1990.

An Interim Government of National Unity was formed in Gambia under the guidance of ECOWAS in October 1990. However, Taylor refused to work with the interim government and continued fighting. After more than a dozen peace accords and with declining military power, Taylor finally agreed to the formation of a five-man transitional government. A hasty disarmament and demobilization of warring groups were followed by special elections on July 19, 1997. Charles Taylor and his National Patriotic Party won the election by a large majority, primarily because Liberians feared a return to war.

When Faith Lights the Way

For the next six years, the Taylor government failed to improve the lives of Liberians. Unemployment and illiteracy stood above 75 percent, and little investment was made in the country's infrastructure to repair the ravages of war. Pipe-borne water and electricity were generally unavailable to most of the population, especially outside Monrovia. Schools, hospitals, roads, and infrastructure remained derelict. Rather than work to improve the lives of Liberians, Taylor supported the Revolutionary United Front in Sierra Leone. Taylor's misrule led to the resumption of armed rebellion from among Taylor's former adversaries. By 2003, armed groups called "Liberians United for Reconciliation and Democracy" (LURD) and "Movement for Democracy in Liberia" (MODEL) challenged Taylor and his increasingly fragmented supporters on the outskirts of Monrovia.

On June 4, 2003, in Accra, Ghana, ECOWAS facilitated peace talks among the Government of Liberia, civil society, and the LURD and MODEL rebel groups. On the same day, the chief prosecutor of the Special Court for Sierra Leone issued a press statement announcing the opening of a sealed indictment of Liberian President Charles Taylor for "bearing the greatest responsibility" for atrocities in Sierra Leone that had occurred since 1996. In July 2003, the Government of Liberia, LURD, and MODEL signed a cease-fire that all sides failed to respect; bitter fighting reached downtown Monrovia in July and August 2003, creating a massive humanitarian disaster.

Twice in July 2003, President George W. Bush stated that Taylor "must leave Liberia." On August 11, 2003, under increasingly intense US and international pressure, President Taylor resigned office and exiled himself to Nigeria. This move paved the way for the deployment of what became a 3,600-strong peacekeeping mission in Liberia (ECOMIL). On August 18, leaders from the Liberian Government, the rebels, political parties, and civil society signed a comprehensive peace agreement that laid the framework for constructing a two-year National Transitional Government of Liberia, headed by businessman Charles Gyude Bryant. The UN took over security in Liberia in October 2003,

Appendix

incorporating ECOMIL into the United Nations Mission in Liberia (UNMIL), a force that at one point numbered more than 12,000 troops and 1,148 police officers.

The October 2005 presidential and legislative elections and the subsequent presidential runoff were the freest, fairest, and most peaceful elections in Liberia's history. Ellen Johnson Sirleaf defeated international soccer star George Weah 59.4 percent to 40.6 percent to become Africa's first democratically elected female president. She was inaugurated in January 2006. The political situation remained stable after the 2005 elections.

At the 2008 Liberia Poverty Reduction Forum in Berlin, the Johnson-Sirleaf government won substantial donor support for its new poverty-reduction strategy. To maintain stability through the post-conflict period, Liberia's security sector reform efforts led to the disarmament of more than one hundred thousand ex-combatants, the wholesale US-led reconstruction of the Armed Forces of Liberia, and a UN-led effort to overhaul the Liberian National Police. Within UNMIL's mandate was a Peacebuilding Commission focused on promoting the rule of law, security sector reform, and national reconciliation.[15]

In learning the history of this country and how the United States and Liberia were both formed with the same ideals, I wondered how the results could have been so different. Could the conditions that decimated Liberia do the same to the United States? If our two countries are from the same "gene pool," why are so few Americans aware of Liberia and our commonalities? To put it bluntly, why do so few Americans care about Liberia?

Haiti's Political Landscape

Haiti is on the western half of the island of Hispaniola. The Arawak Indians lived there before Christopher Columbus landed at Môle-Saint-Nicolas, on the northwest part of the island, on December 6,

When Faith Lights the Way

1492. Columbus called the island "Española," which was later anglicized to "Hispaniola."

Columbus built a fort on the island and left thirty-nine men there while he returned to Europe to announce his discovery. Upon return in 1493, he found the Arawaks had wiped out the men left at the fort. Within a century, the Arawaks would be nearly wiped out by disease and war with Spain.

Spain claimed ownership of the whole island but settled mainly in the east. The western portion was left uncolonized until 1664, when the French founded Port-de-Paix. Finally, in 1697, the Spanish and French signed a treaty giving France the western third of the island of Hispaniola, calling their colony "Saint-Domingue."

In the eighteenth century, Saint-Domingue's—that is to say, Haiti's—economy flourished. The colony produced and exported sugar, coffee, cotton, indigo, and cocoa. Huge numbers of African slaves were brought to work on plantations. By the end of the eighteenth century, there were about thirty thousand French, about twenty-seven thousand people of mixed race, and nearly half a million black slaves!

After 1789, the goals of the French Revolution, liberty and equality, stirred the imaginations of the oppressed people of Saint-Domingue. On August 14, 1791, the slaves rebelled. The ensuing uprising claimed many lives and had a devastating effect on the economics of the colony. In 1794, the French National Convention abolished slavery by law in France and all its colonies. One of the leaders of the Black Rebels was Toussaint L'Ouverture. When the slave uprising ended in 1794, he and his battle-hardened troops joined the French army. In 1797, L'Ouverture was made commander of the French army in Hispaniola and repelled an invasion by the British, becoming the de facto ruler of the colony.

By 1801, L'Ouverture had taken control of the island and made himself head of a new government, subsequently publishing a constitution. Fearing the French were losing their colony, Napoleon Bonaparte sent an army under General Charles Leclerc to reestablish control of the

Appendix

island. Two of L'Ouverture's trusted staff defected to the French, and, through deception, Leclerc captured L'Ouverture. After L'Overture's capture, one of L'Overture's staff members who had defected to the French was so disgusted by the betrayal that he defected back to the former slaves fighting the French. Jean-Jacques Dessalines, a former slave, continued the struggle. Leclerc's army, interestingly enough, was decimated by fever. On New Year's Day, 1804, the island succeeded in removing itself from the French and became independent. It was renamed "Haiti."

The island was devastated by war, and Dessalines was assassinated in 1806. In 1809, the Spanish captured the eastern part of the island, but President Boyer of Haiti retook the land, which is now the Dominican Republic, in 1822. The two countries separated permanently in 1844. During this period, countries were slow to recognize Haiti as independent. France recognized Haiti as separate from itself in 1825; but in return, the French demanded compensation for the land their plantation owners had lost in Haiti. The Haitians were forced to pay a modern equivalent of twenty-one billion to France as compensation for the loss of slaves. The sum was not repaid until 1893. Britain recognized Haiti in 1833, but the United States didn't until 1862.

Haiti has suffered instability throughout its history. President Boyar was overthrown in 1843. Between 1843 and 1911, there were sixteen rulers, eleven of which were overthrown by revolutions. In the early twentieth century, political instability in Haiti grew worse. In 1915, the United States sent marines to occupy the country and protect American business interests. Not surprisingly, the Haitians resented the occupation, and the US Marines were finally withdrawn in 1934.

Despite the United States's withdrawal and the recognition of Haitian independence, there was no end to political instability in Haiti. In 1946, President Lavaud was removed by a military coup. He was replaced by Dumarsais Estimé, who was also overthrown by the military in 1950. He was then replaced by Paul Malgoire, who was forced to resign in 1956. A series of provisional presidents followed until the people elected François Duvalier—known as Papa Doc—in 1957.

When Faith Lights the Way

Duvalier became a brutal dictator, ruling Haiti with the help of his infamous secret police, the Tontons Macoutes. Under his rule, the press was strictly controlled. In 1961, Duvalier was reelected through a fraudulent election, making himself president for life in 1964. In 1971, he changed the constitution, giving himself the power to name his successor. He died the same year, and his son, Jean-Claude Duvalier (Baby Doc), became president.

Baby Doc proved to be as oppressive as his father. In the late 1970s and early 1980s, many Haitians fled to Florida by boat to escape his rule. By 1984 economic conditions were so bad that the people were again ready to rise up. Violent demonstrations took place.[16]

In Memoriam

Ma Nowai: I had the privilege of being mothered by Ma Nowai during my 2013 and 2014 trips to Gbarnga, Liberia, and again in 2016 in Monrovia. Ma Nowai passed in April 2018. She was a wonderfully kind person who will be missed.

Samuel Dixon, Jr., age sixty, died doing what he loved: working for the welfare of the world's poor and rejected in the name of Jesus Christ. His life ended before he could be rescued from the ruins of a hotel toppled by a powerful earthquake that struck Haiti. Reverend Dixon and two others from the United Methodist General Board of Global Ministries had gone to the Hotel Montana to meet colleagues from other agencies and plan improved health services in the western hemisphere's poorest country.[17] The world lost a great man. Power From the SON has never been able to establish any relationship with UMCOR since Sam's death. I have lost a man I greatly admired.

Jack Barlow was a gentle soul who made everyone feel at ease. Jack suffered various illnesses and maladies for nineteen years. His passing in 2017 meant I lost my last strong connection to my childhood and college years.

Endnotes

1. (Ganta United Methodist Hospital, 2015)
2. Haiti Project Underway!! (1985, June 7). *The United Methodist Reporter.* Dallas, Texas, USA: Newspaper Division, United Methodist Communications Council.
3. (Auch, 2016)
4. (Barzey, 2105)
5. (BHATIA, 2011)
6. (Matthew 14:29, 2007)
7. (Jesse N. Mongrue, 2011)
8. (2014 Ebola Outbreak in West Africa - Case Counts, 2016)
9. (CHAL At-A-Glance, 2016)
10. (Milestones, 2014)
11. (Sirleaf, 2011)
12. (Vincent, Summer 2015)
13. (U. S. Department of State, 2012)
14. (Jesse N. Mongrue, 2011)
15. (U. S. Department of State, 2012)
16. (Lambert, 2012)
17. (Bloom, 2010, January 22)

Acknowledgments

I love to discuss Power From the SON's (PFS) efforts to electrify schools and hospitals in some of the most challenging places on earth. Hopefully, the discussions have encouraged others to follow their calling. So many people have told me, "You should write a book about this!" Their encouragement led me on another quest, one that lasted three years.

Writing about all the things that led me to step out of my comfortable life bubble was difficult for someone who has spent their adult life as an engineer and businessman. Putting this story on paper was more difficult than changing careers to provide state of the art electric systems in the most impoverished parts of the world.

The finished product of *When Faith Lights the Way* was only accomplished with the help of many people.

My wife, Linda, had to endure so many interruptions where I spewed ideas and words asking for her suggestions. I thank her for her patience and valuable contribution. She was the one who suggested the theme of stepping out of my boat or comfort zone. She suggested I call the book, "What Am I Doing Out of the Boat?" I love that title.

The encouragement of friends, Bob and Susan Bingham, Rev. Jeremy Bassett, Dr. James Hallmark, Dr. John Innis, Major Touhidul (Touhid) Islam, Dr. William Lawrence, Captain Andy Miller, Dr. David Mosser, Dr. Don and Joyce Pike, Dr. Sara Alpern Tarlow, Dr. Peter Tarlow, and Bishop Bennie Dee Warner that offered improvements was most appreciated.

The first efforts as an author were made readable by Lindsey Barlow and Jonathan Baker.

It is not easy to find someone to believe in a rough story and turn it into a printed book. Finding the right person was a similar journey to the unexplainable events that permitted us to electrify the hospital. After many rejections, Jessica Ward, previously with the Fedd Agency and a sorority sister of my daughter Kylie, passed the story to The Fedd Agency. Their agency understood the message and having a team with their capabilities has been a fabulous experience. They were indispensable.

Giving electricity to UMC Ganta was a success. A wonderful initial project for Power From the SON. Without the selfless efforts of everyone who took part in the Ganta project, electrification efforts would have disappeared, and this story would not have been written.

Many who were part of the Ganta team, along with new servants, have completed additional projects that provide electricity to schools, orphanages, and seminaries in Africa and Central America.

David Cunningham, Frank Daniel, Miguel Galaviz, Betty Gudgell, Earl Harcrow, Martin and Didi Jahn, Preston Kissman, Bradley Norris, Chris Olson, Hassan Shaw, Terry Thornhill, Donald Turner, Albert Travell, Tom Wightman, Gary Wilson, Tom Ware, and Victoria Warren have been boots on the ground and more for additional projects.

Randall Rose and Larry Bothe of J.P. Morgan Chase have provided advice and counsel.

Hesta Stuart Christian Trust provided financial support.

Former Bishops John Innis and Bennie Dee Warner have provided counsel.

First United Methodist Church of Arlington, especially the Lamplighters Class has provided funds, materials, and counsel.

Rotary International and particularly the Rotary Club of Arlington partnered with PFS on lighting projects in Honduras.

Individual donors gave material and funds.

Power From the SON is looking forward to the future. A&M United Methodist Church and The Bush School of Texas A&M University have been added to the list of wonderful people who are willing to act to give the gift of electricity, to heal, educate, and light the darkness.